BLACK AMERICA SERIES

BUCKINGHAM COUNTY

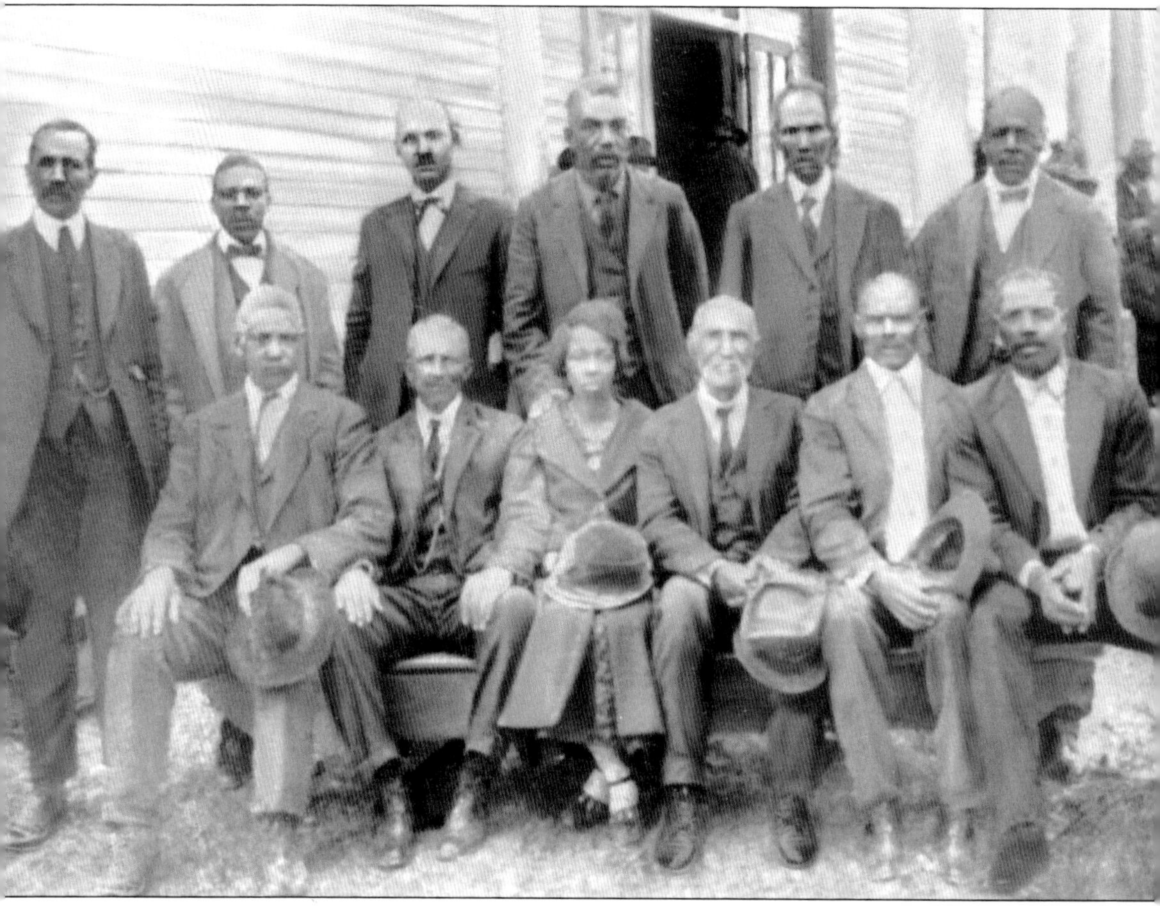

Buckingham County educators and civic and religious leaders are shown here attending the Buckingham County Training School commemoration in 1924. Those identified are (first row) educator Mary Frances Redwood, third from left; Wilson Ellis, fourth from left; and Charles Allen, far right; (second row) Rev. Solomon West, far left; John Jones, second from left; and Edward Payne, fourth from left.

On the Cover: The Virginia Seminary and College class of 1908 from Lynchburg, Virginia, is pictured here. In the first row, second from left, is Buckingham County native and educator Mary Frances Redwood. On the far right in the first row is Buckingham County native and religious leader Junius Caesar Austin.

BLACK AMERICA SERIES

BUCKINGHAM COUNTY

E. Renée Ingram and Charles W. White Sr.

ARCADIA PUBLISHING

ISBN 978-0-7385-1842-8

Published by Arcadia Publishing
Charleston, South Carolina

Printed in the United States of America

Library of Congress Catalog Card Number: 2005924318

For all general information contact Arcadia Publishing at:
Telephone 843-853-2070
Fax 843-853-0044
E-mail sales@arcadiapublishing.com
For customer service and orders:
Toll-Free 1-888-313-2665

Visit us on the Internet at www.arcadiapublishing.com

I dedicate this book to my mother, Edith Marie Stanton Ingram, and in memory of my Buckingham County ancestors. —E. Renée Ingram

I dedicate this book to my wife, Margaret, who has given me nearly 50 years of love and devotion. —Charles W. White Sr.

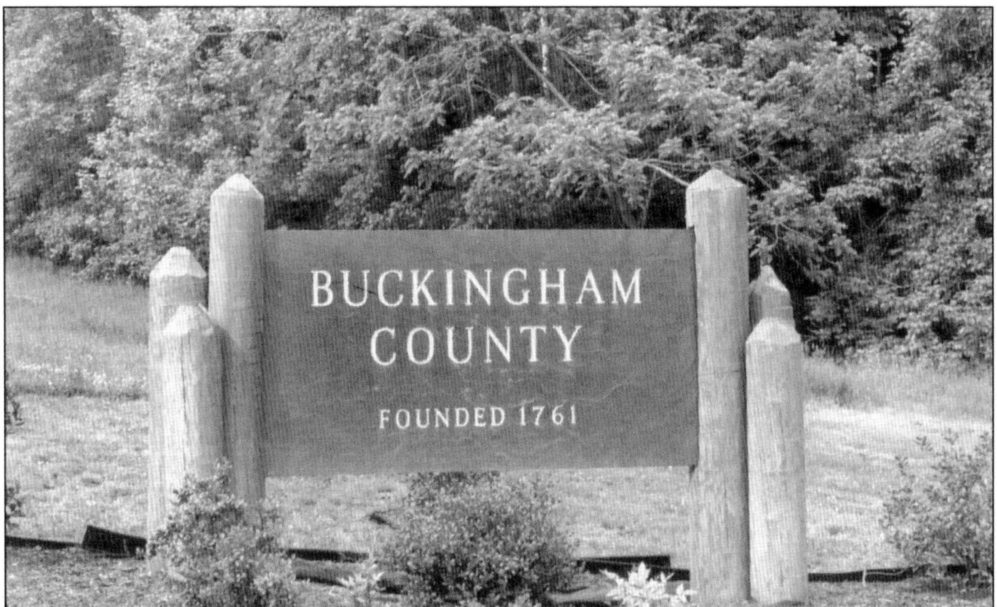

This slate Buckingham County marker is located on U.S. Highway 15 near the James River at the county line of Buckingham and Fluvanna.

CONTENTS

Acknowledgments 6

Introduction 7

1. Portraits of Our Ancestors: Our Families 9

2. Our Pioneers and Trailblazers 37

3. Our Faith: Near and Far 45

4. Reflections on Our Education 65

5. A Glimpse of Our Military Service 85

6. Civic and Social Organizations 95

7. 20th-Century Life in Our County 105

8. Our Arts and Entertainment 115

9. Buckingham Today 121

10. Our Place in History 125

About the Authors 128

ACKNOWLEDGMENTS

We wish to express our sincere appreciation to the many Buckingham County families and descendants for submitting their precious photographs for this pictorial history publication. We wish to personally thank Ancella R. Bickley, historian; Randall K. Burkett, curator of African American Collections, Woodruff Library, Emory University; Lucious Edwards, archivist, Special Collections and Archives, Johnson Memorial Library, Virginia State University; John A. Fleckner, archivist, National Museum of American History, Smithsonian Institution; Selicia N. Gregory, archivist, Archives and Special Collections, L. Douglas Wilder Library, Virginia Union University; Ed Hicks, West Virginia archives photographer, West Virginia State Archives; William V. Jones, assistant manager, Maryland Department, Enoch Pratt Free Library; Sally Kousser, reference librarian, Pasadena Public Library; Dale L. Neighbors, picture collection coordinator, Special Collections Branch, Library of Virginia; Michael Plunkett, director of Special Collections, Alderman Library, University of Virginia; Karen A. Robertson, director of Library Services, Soper Library, Morgan State University; and Donna M. Wells, prints and photographs librarian, Moorland-Spingarn Research Center, Howard University.

INTRODUCTION

Truth comes to us from the past, then like gold washed down from the mountains.

—Carter G. Woodson (1875–1950)

Buckingham County, located in the heart of central Virginia, was established in 1761. It is approximately 60 miles west of the state capitol, Richmond, and 45 miles south of the city of Charlottesville. The county's gently rolling hills are bounded by the James River on the northwest and the Appomattox River on the south.

The county is made up of six magisterial districts: Curdsville, Francisco, James River, Marshall, Maysville, and Slate River. The northern part of Buckingham County was one of the first developed parts of the county, largely because of its proximity to the James River and its rich natural resources and deposits, including slate, iron ore, coal, and gold. Buckingham County was the main source of gold within the United States from 1830 until the California gold rush in 1849. During that time, there were several mines located in the Arvonia, New Canton, and Dillwyn areas. Today, the Buckingham Virginia Slate Corporation is still in operation, providing one of the hardest slates in the world, and the Kyanite Mining Corporation on Willis Mountain is still the world's largest and oldest producer of heat-resistant and ceramic raw materials.

Since Buckingham County's formation, African Americans have contributed to the rich history of this county. The English were the first Europeans to settle in Buckingham, by way of Jamestown in the early 17th century. The African American population increased significantly in the last half of the 18th century. In the early 19th century and continuing through the antebellum period, the county consisted of many African Americans who were free property holders and business owners.

Many African Americans from the county, both free and enslaved, were conscripted during the Civil War and were assigned as laborers to the James River and the Kanawha Canal Company, the Niter and Mining Bureau, and High Bridge, which was located in Prince Edward County, Virginia.

Buckingham native Francis (Frank) Moss, born free about 1825, was a lawmaker who was elected as the county delegate to the Virginia Constitutional Convention during the Reconstruction period. In 1869, Moss was elected to the Virginia State Senate, where he represented Buckingham and Appomattox Counties. He was an opponent of the sharecrop system and insisted that former slaves were entitled to a portion of the land they had worked as slaves; thus he became known as Francis "Forty-Acres-and-a-Mule" Moss.

Caesar Perkins, born into slavery, was elected to the Virginia House of Delegates in 1869 and served one term; he was reelected in 1887 to serve a second term. The Honorable Caesar Perkins was a leader in the welfare of African Americans for over 45 years.

Buckingham County's history boasts the birthplace of Carter Godwin Woodson, noted African American educator and "the father of black history." He received a doctorate in history from Harvard University in 1912, becoming only the second African American to earn such a degree from this institution. In 1926, he organized the first Negro History Week, now celebrated each February as Black History Month, to encourage the study of African American history. Dr. Woodson authored numerous scholarly books on the positive contributions of African Americans in the development of this country. One of Dr. Woodson's best-known books is *The Mis-Education of the Negro*, originally published in 1933 and still relevant today.

In Buckingham County, some African Americans, free and enslaved, were able to obtain basic literary skills in the early 19th century. However, the first documentation of public education was recorded during the Reconstruction period, when an appropriation from the Freedmen's Bureau was granted to build a school for freedmen at Maysville (Buckingham Court House) and named the Lincoln School.

Another school, located in the James River District of the county, was built and known as the Alexander Hill School on land donated by Cornelius Palmer, who was a free property holder during the antebellum period. The New York Freemen's Union Commission as well as the Freedmen's Bureau financially supported this school. The teacher appointed to the school was Edward S. Lomax Sr., who became the first African American teacher in Buckingham County.

The county was also the site of two historic Julius Rosenwald–funded schools during the early 20th century: the Buckingham County Training School and the Liberty School. The Rosenwald-funded schools varied in size from small, one-teacher schools to large, 11-teacher facilities that offered instruction from first grade through high school.

Religion has always been woven into the fabric of the African American community. Buckingham County's oldest African American church is Alexander Hill Baptist Church, which was established after emancipation in 1865. Other churches established in the late 1860s included Baptist Union Baptist Church, Fork Union Baptist Church, Salem Baptist Church, and Warminster Baptist Church, which are still in existence today. Subsequently other Baptist churches were established as an outgrowth of many early churches, including Chestnut Grove, Clear View, Jerusalem, Mourner's Valley, New Hope, Ridgeway, Spreading Oak, Union Branch, Union Hill, and Upper and Lower Liberty (First and Second Liberty) Baptist Churches.

Agriculture was an important element in the county's economy. African American farmers planted and harvested large crops such as corn, tobacco, and wheat for commercial use. Today, most of the farms have disappeared, and government, the largest area employer, has replaced the agricultural industry. Many African Americans who reside in the county are entrepreneurs, government officials, professionals, and business, community, and religious leaders.

This publication is a compendium of the African American experience in Buckingham County that contains over 200 images dating from the mid-19th century to the present. It is impossible to depict a comprehensive pictorial history reflecting each individual that has contributed to the rich legacy of this county; however, we hope that this publication will inspire and encourage each reader to further explore the contributions of African Americans in Buckingham County.

One

PORTRAITS OF OUR ANCESTORS

Our Families

In every conceivable manner, the family is link to our past, bridge to our future.

—Alex Haley (1921–1992)

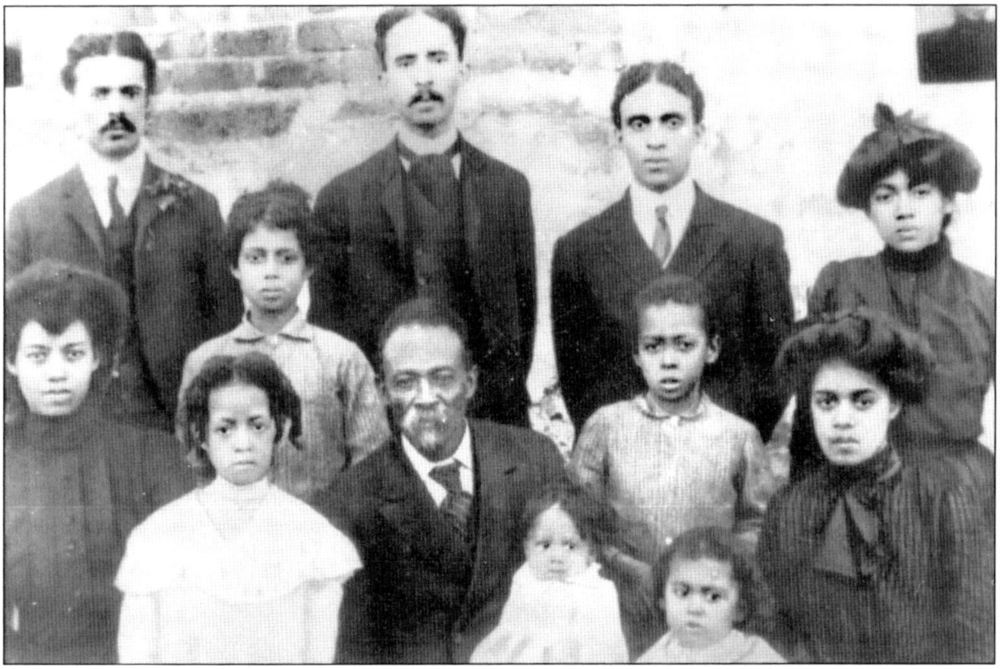

Mrs. Josephine A. Lomax and her husband, Edward S. Lomax, were among the first African American teachers in Buckingham County and also conducted training institutes for African American teachers. Shown in this family photograph are Edward S. Lomax Sr. and his children. The three eldest sons, in the back row, were also pioneers. They are, from left to right, Roger W. Lomax, who became a prominent physician in Pocahontas and Lynchburg, Virginia; Eugene W. Lomax, who became a physician and is credited with the founding of the Lomax Hospital in Bluefield, West Virginia; and Edward S. Lomax Jr., who was the first known African American college athlete from Buckingham. Edward Jr. played football at Virginia State Normal Institute (Virginia State University). (Courtesy Joyce Gooden.)

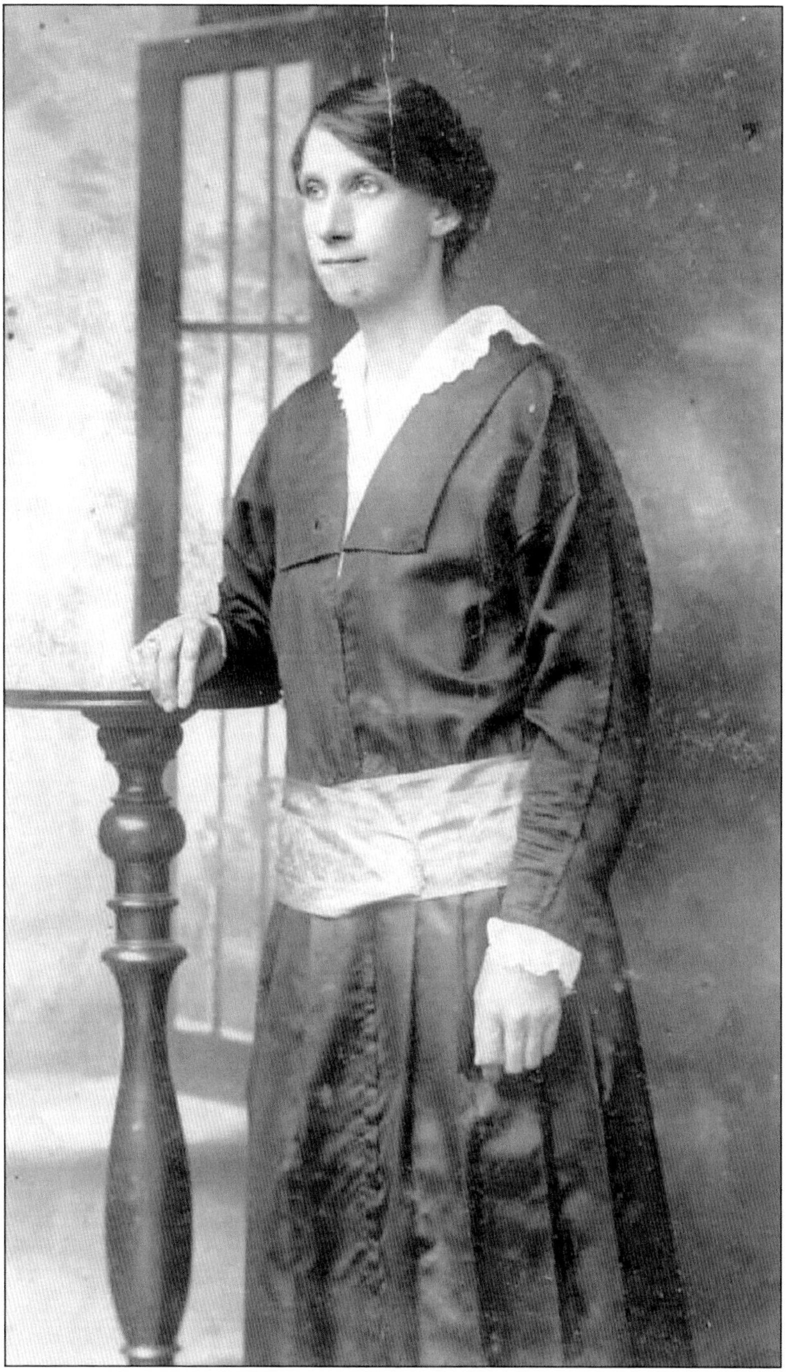

Frances (Hemmings) Dean, who died sometime after 1865, was the daughter of Betsy Hemmings. The Buckingham Hemmings are descended from Betsy Hemmings, a daughter of Mary Hemings and a niece of Sally Hemings. Betsy was born a slave at Monticello in 1783 but spent most of her adult life as a nurse at Millbrook Plantation in the Curdsville District of Buckingham County, where she died in 1857, still in bondage. (Courtesy Deborah M. Daniels and Edna Bolling Jacques, Hemmings descendants.)

Harriett Dean Hemmings (1842–1920) was the daughter of Frances (Hemmings) Dean and Peyton Dean. (Courtesy Deborah M. Daniels and Edna Bolling Jacques.)

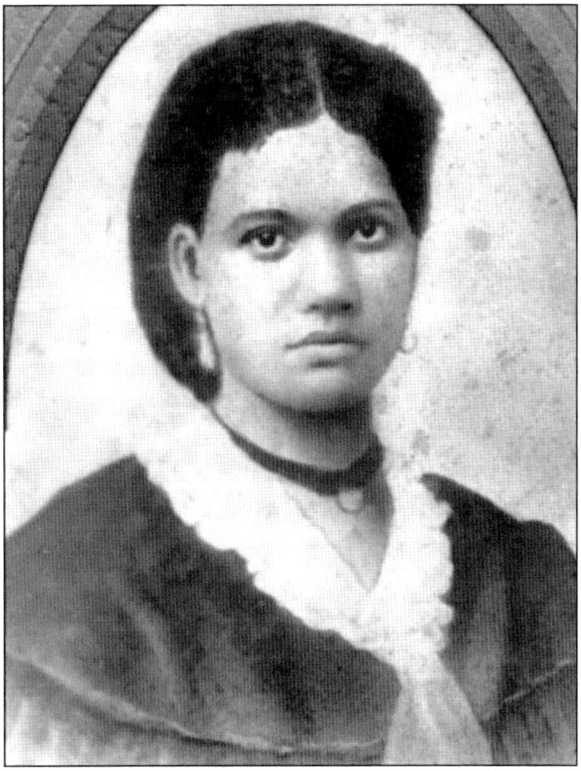

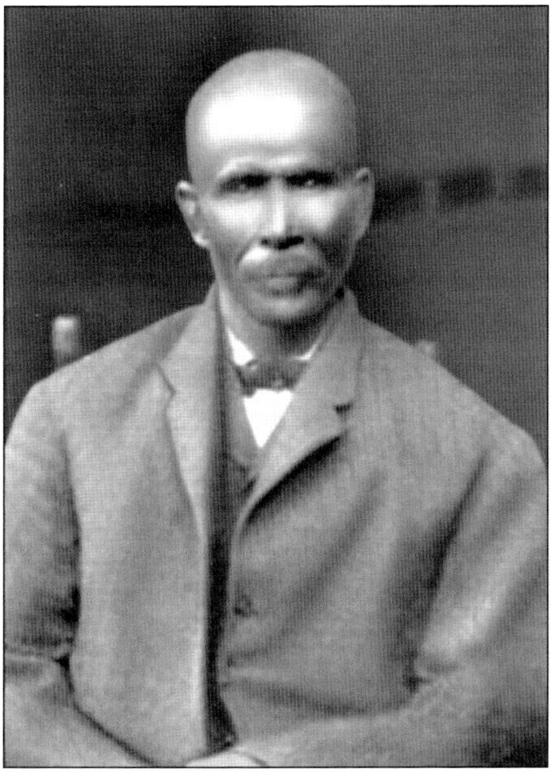

Fossett J. Hemmings (1843–1916) was the son of Joseph Hemmings and grandson of Betsy Hemmings. Fossett J. Hemmings married Harriet Dean Hemmings. Their descendants have owned the family homestead, which was once part of the Millbrook Plantation in Buckingham County, for over 125 years. (Courtesy Deborah M. Daniels and Edna Bolling Jacques.)

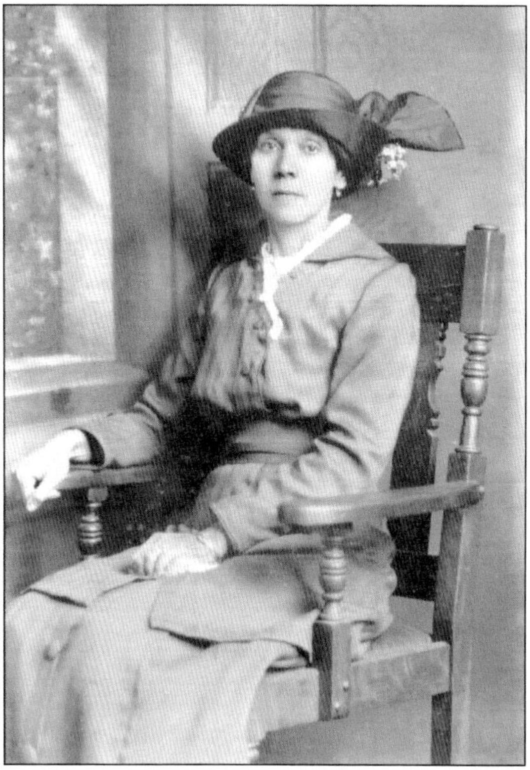

Elizabeth (Bettie) Dean Bolling (1859–1933) was the daughter of Frances (Hemmings) Dean and Peyton Dean. (Courtesy Deborah M. Daniels and Edna Bolling Jacques.)

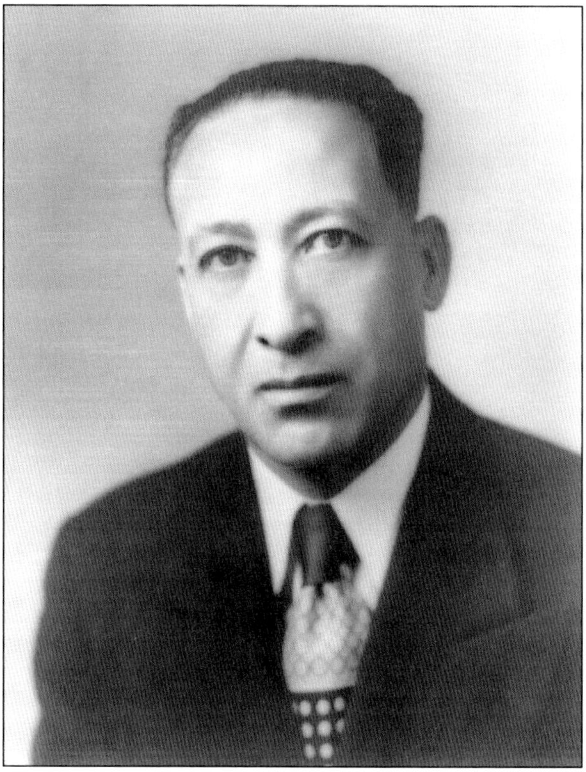

James Sherman Bolling (1897–1983), son of Elizabeth Dean Bolling and Lewis Robert Bolling, was a graduate of Howard University's College of Dentistry and practiced in Washington, D.C. James Sherman Bolling was the grandson of Delegate Samuel P. Bolling and nephew of educator Eliza Wayles Bolling. (Courtesy Deborah M. Daniels and Edna Bolling Jacques.)

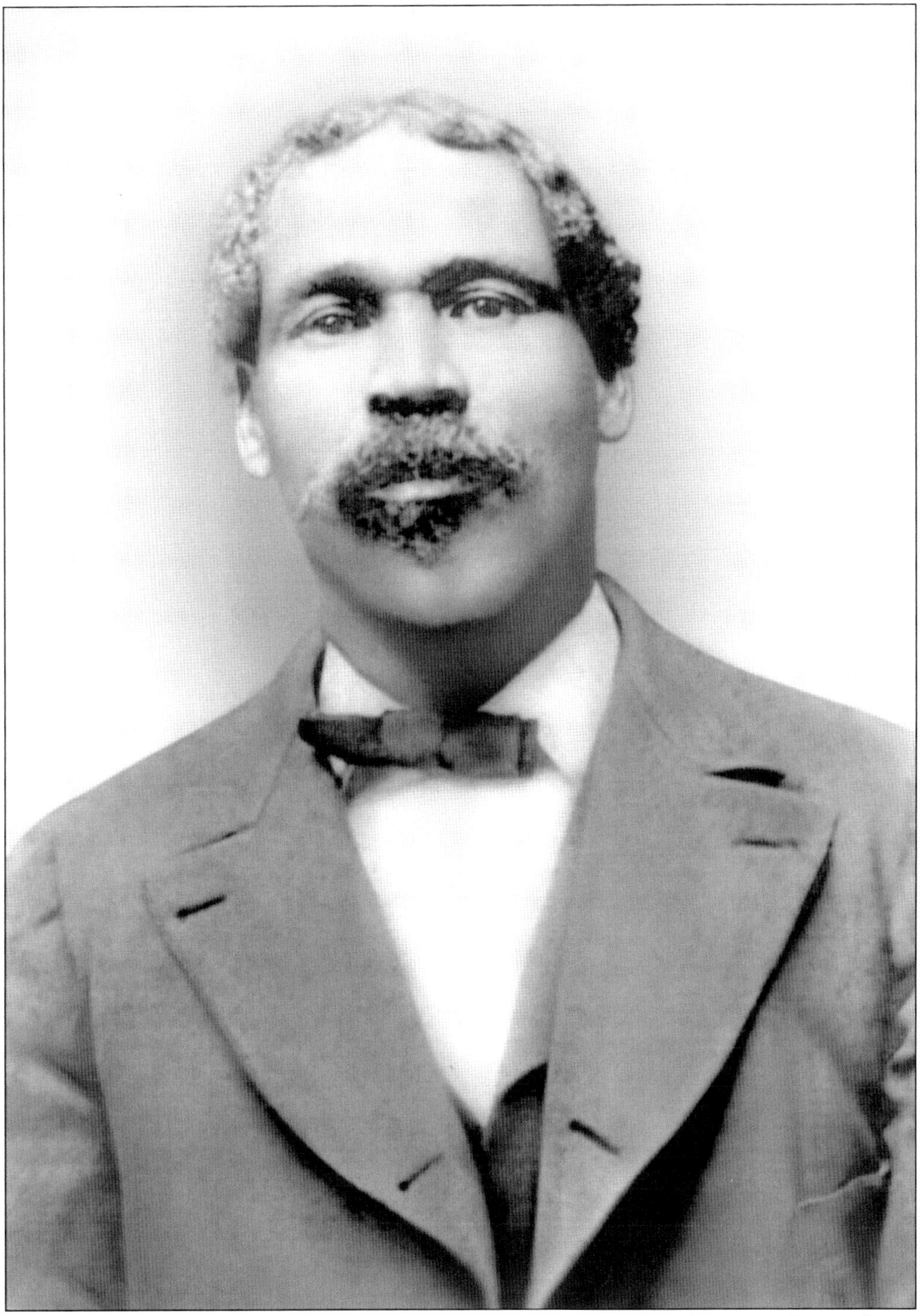

Thomas Washington was born free in Buckingham County. He was a farmer and a significant property holder, owning more than 50 acres of land in 1860. He served in the 38th Regiment of the U.S. Colored Troops in the Civil War. (Courtesy Otto K. Washington.)

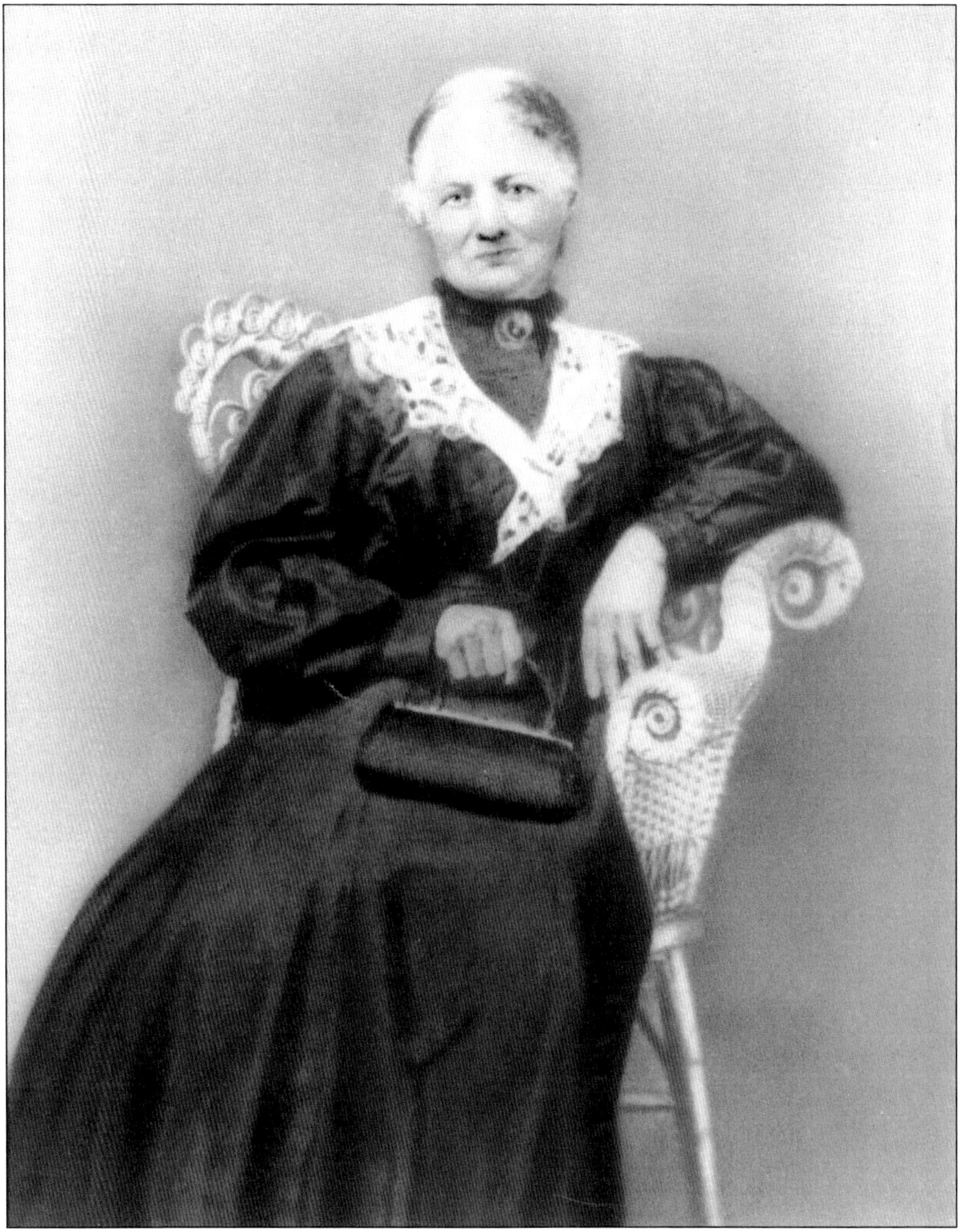

Eliza Riddle Woodson was born into slavery about 1843 in Buckingham County. Eliza was the mother of Carter Godwin Woodson. This is a reproduction of a tintype photograph. (Courtesy Belva Clark Collection.)

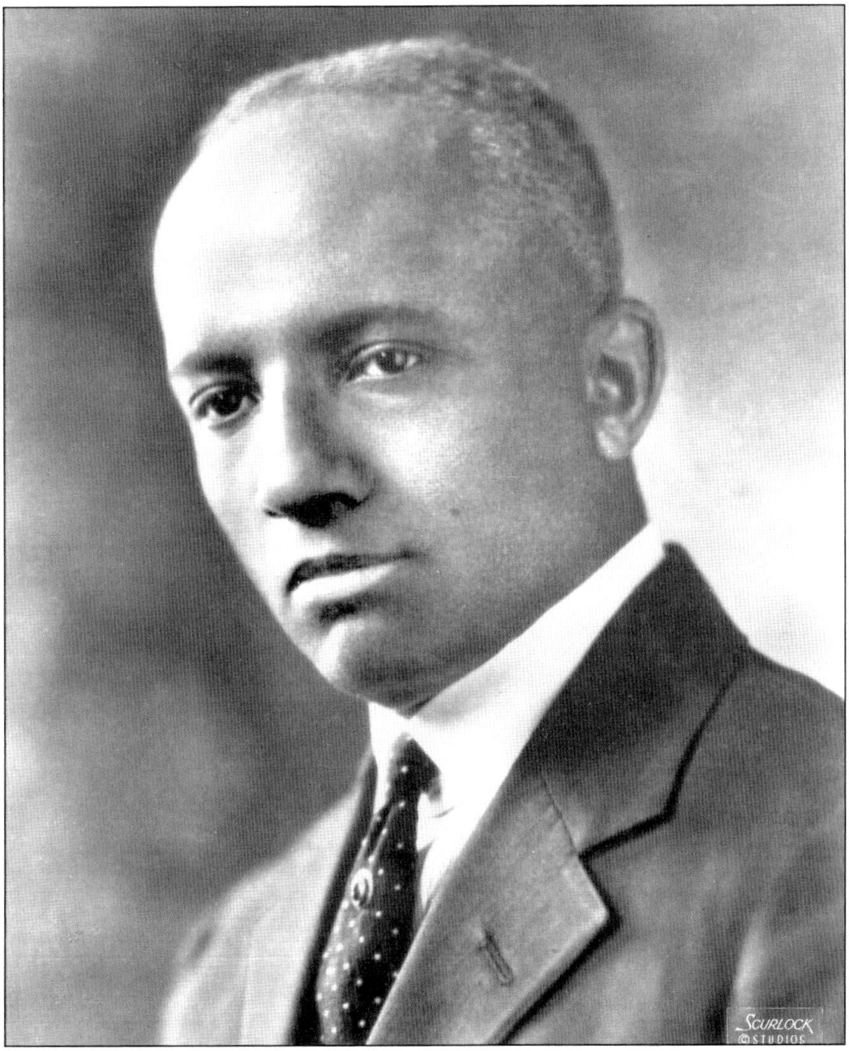

This photograph of Carter Godwin Woodson at 25 years of age was taken by noted African American photographer Addison Scurlock. Woodson, known as "the father of black history," was born on December 19, 1875, in New Canton, in the Marshall District of Buckingham County. Woodson was the son of former slaves James Henry and Eliza Riddle Woodson. When he could, he attended the local Buckingham school and eventually went to Berea College in Kentucky. Ultimately he obtained a bachelor of arts degree from the University of Chicago in 1907. In 1908, he attended Sorbonne University in Paris, where he became fluent in French. He received a doctorate in history from Harvard University in 1912, becoming only the second African American to earn such a degree from Harvard. Woodson taught briefly and held educational administrative positions in the Philippines, at Howard University (where he was dean of the School of Liberal Arts), and at West Virginia State College. Woodson was the founder of the Associated Publishers, Inc., founder and editor of *The Negro History Bulletin*, and the author of more than 30 books. Woodson's best-known book is probably *The Mis-Education of the Negro*, originally published in 1933 and still relevant today. He died on April 3, 1950, in Washington, D.C. (Courtesy Scurlock Studio Records, Archives Center, National Museum of American History, Behring Center, Smithsonian Institution.)

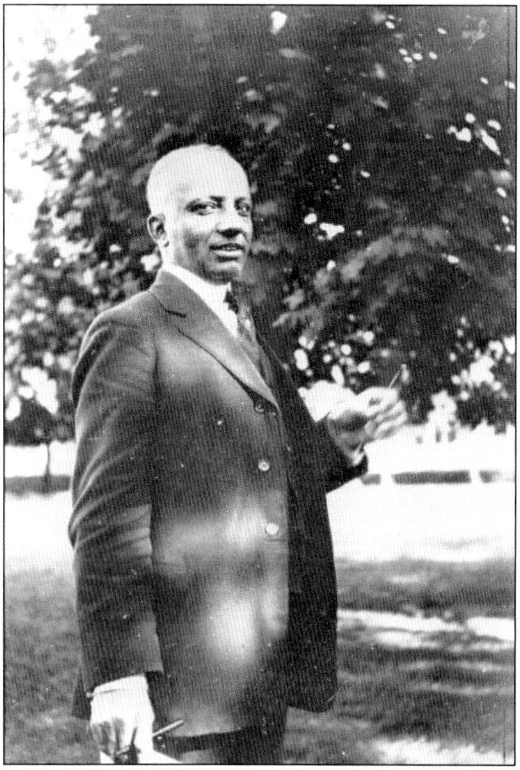

Dr. Carter Godwin Woodson is standing on the campus of the historically black college West Virginia State College (now West Virginia State University) in Institute, West Virginia. This photograph was taken *c.* 1930. (Courtesy Miriam Hamblin.)

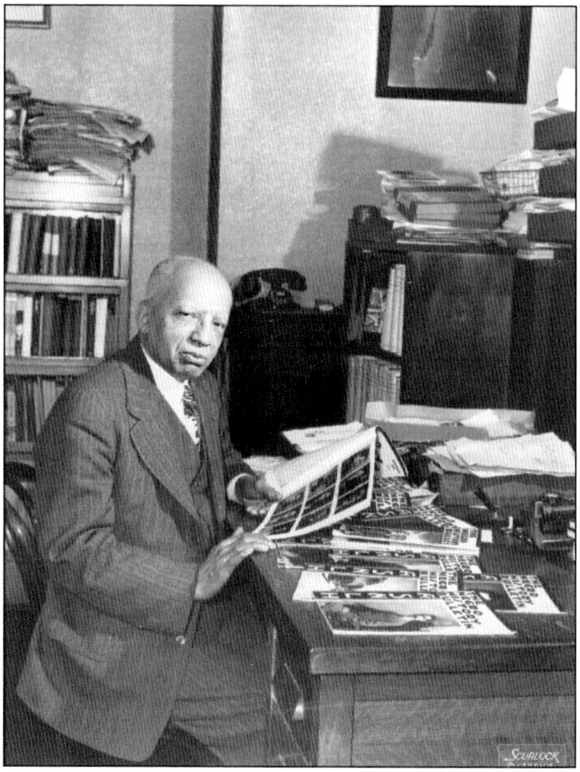

This photograph of Carter Godwin Woodson was taken in 1948 by noted African American photographer Addison Scurlock. Dr. Woodson is seated at his desk with *The Negro History Bulletin.* (Courtesy Scurlock Studio Records, Archives Center, National Museum of American History, Behring Center, Smithsonian Institution.)

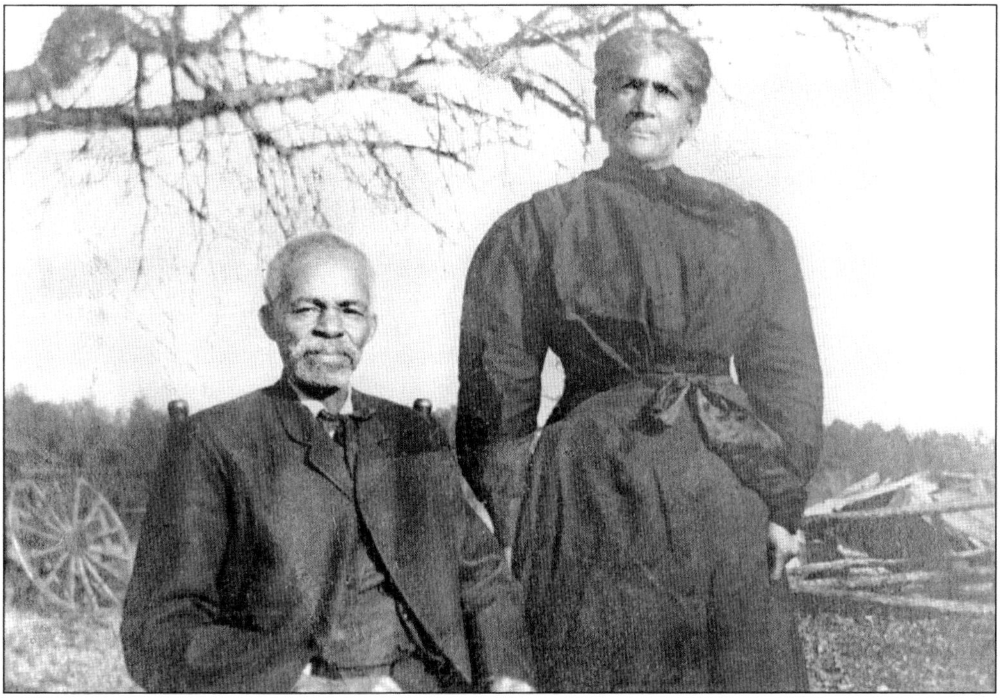

This is a photograph of Herod and Lucia (Rain) Page of the Curdsville District of Buckingham County. The photograph was taken sometime from the mid- to late 19th century in Buckingham County and developed in New York. (Courtesy Paige Washington.)

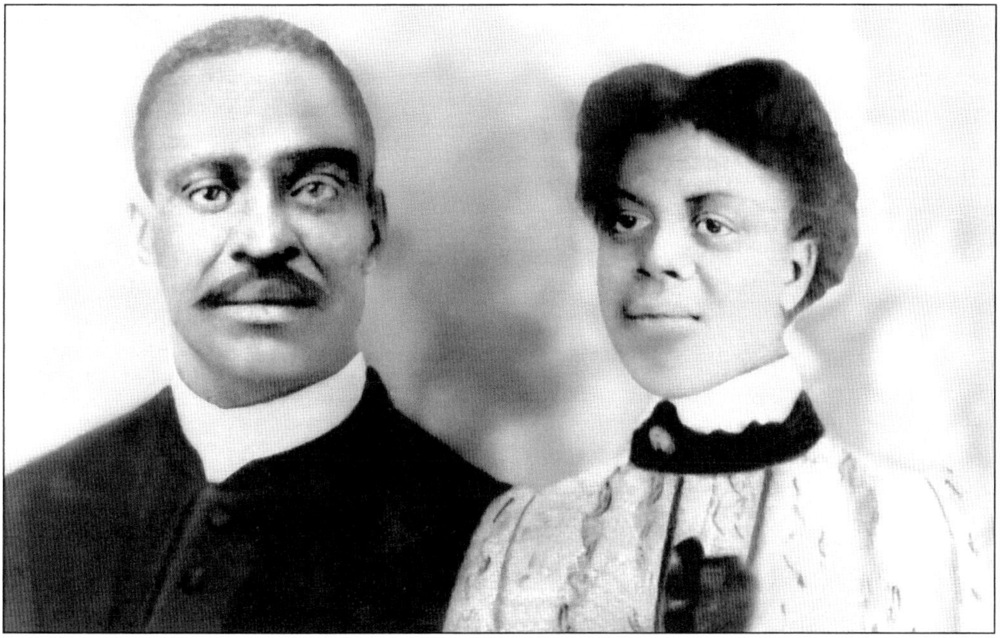

This is a photograph of Thomas and Beatrice Richardson of New Canton, in the Marshall District of Buckingham County. Mrs. Richardson was a local midwife known throughout the community. The Richardsons sold two acres of their property for the establishment of the Liberty School in the 1920s. (Courtesy Charles and Susan Dwan.)

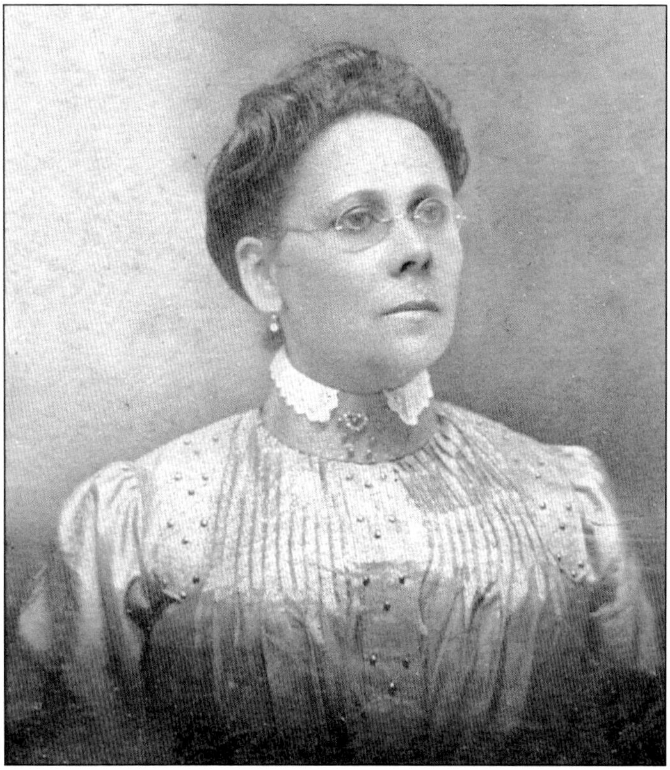

Paralee L. (Gough) Sampson, from Buckingham County, was the mother of Jacob Milton Sampson, LL.B., who is pictured below. (Courtesy Milton Brooks.)

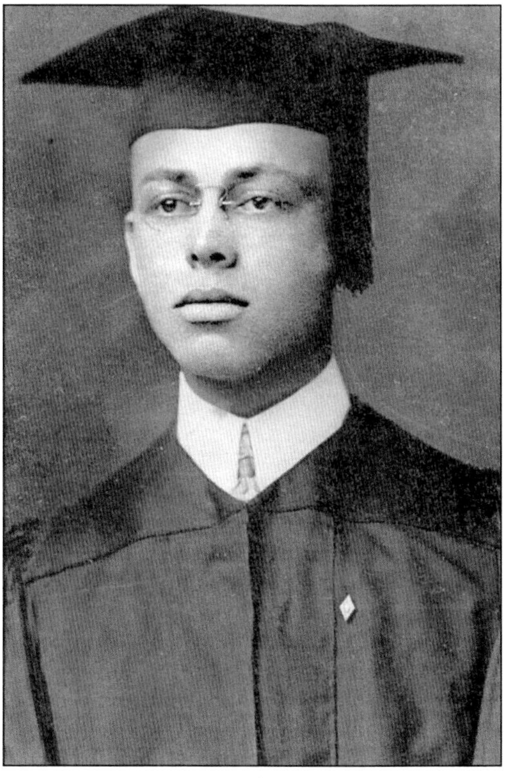

Jacob Milton Sampson, LL.B., was born August 4, 1890, in Buckingham County and was the son of James Henry and Paralee L. (Gough) Sampson. J. Milton Sampson attended Wayland Academy of Virginia Union University from 1905 to 1908 and received an bachelor's degree from Virginia Union University in 1912. He taught English, French, and German at Virginia Union until 1921. He attended Columbia University Post-Graduate School of Philosophy. Sampson also received a bachelor of law degree from Chicago Kent College of Law in 1925. J. Milton Sampson was a World War I veteran and served in France. He was director of research for the Chicago Urban League from 1921 to 1923 and was named supervisor of the National Youth Administration by President Roosevelt in 1935. He also worked for the Housing Authority in Richmond. He was a member of the Alpha Phi Alpha Fraternity and the historic Ebenezer Baptist Church in Richmond until his death on June 21, 1987. (Courtesy Milton Brooks.)

Mr. and Mrs. Cary Austin of Buckingham County, pictured here, were the parents of Junius Caesar Austin, D.D. (Courtesy Dorothy Austin Bowling.)

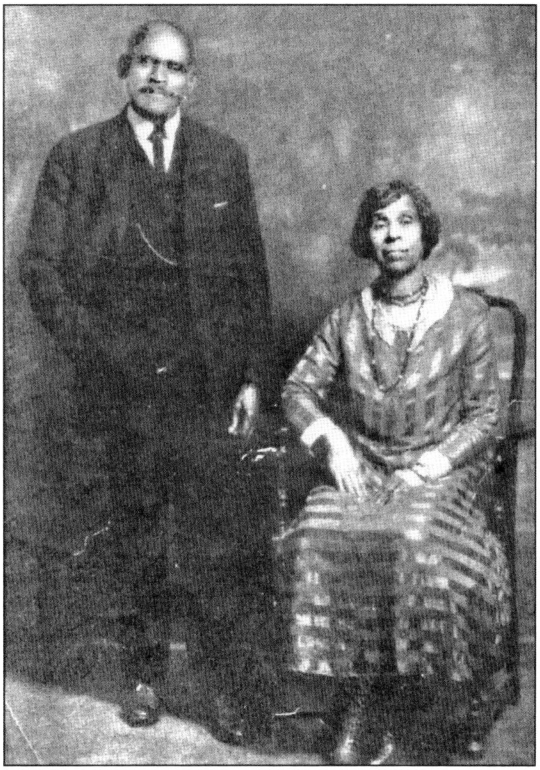

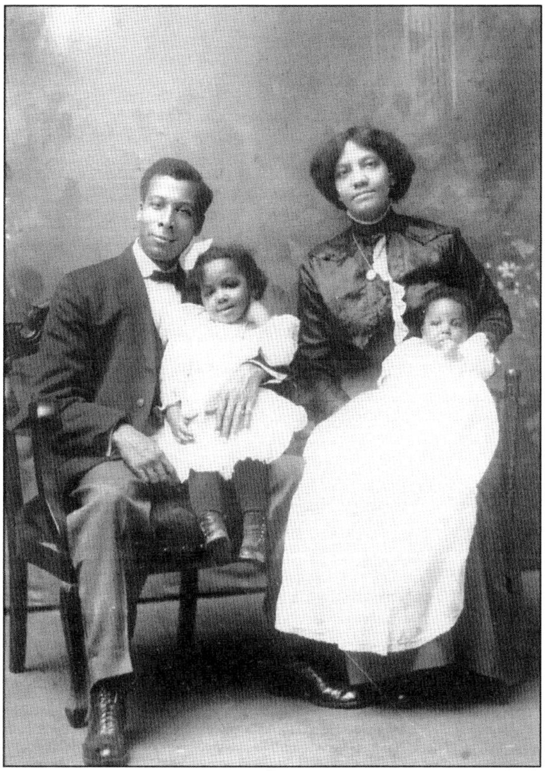

Shown here are Rev. Junius Caesar Austin, D.D.; his wife, Inez (Klosking) Austin; their daughter, Dorothea Inez Austin; and son, Junius C. Austin Jr. Junius Caesar Austin was born in 1887 in New Canton. He was awarded a bachelor of art degee in 1905 and a bachelor of divinity degree in 1908 from Virginia Seminary and College, as well as a doctorate of divinity degree in 1910 from the same institution. He also earned a master of theology degree from Temple University in Philadelphia, Pennsylvania. Reverend Austin first served at Main Street Baptist Church in Clifton Forge, Virginia; Reverend Austin served his longest pastorate at Pilgrim Baptist Church in Chicago, Illinois, from 1926 until his death in 1968. (Courtesy Randall K. Burkett Collection.)

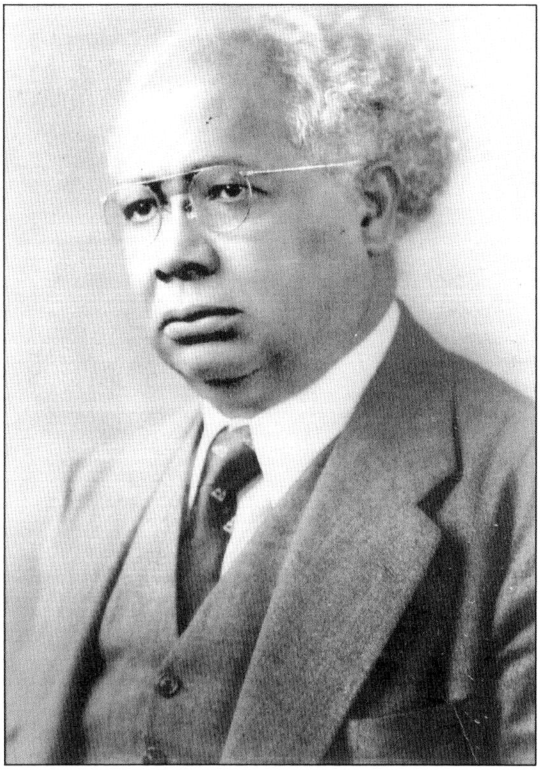

Madison Crencha "M. C." Allen, D.D., was born on June 24, 1880, in Buckingham County. M. C. Allen was the fourth of nine children of former slaves Cary and Cornelia (Winston) Allen. Allen received a bachelor of arts degree from Virginia Seminary and College in 1918. During World War I, he answered his country's call to service and became one of the few African American chaplains in the U.S. Army. Reverend Allen was the editor of *The Expected* magazine and was instrumental in the early beginnings of the black power movement. In 1946, Dr. Allen became the president of Virginia Seminary and College. Under his leadership, the college established the Department of Black History. (Courtesy Charles W. White Sr.)

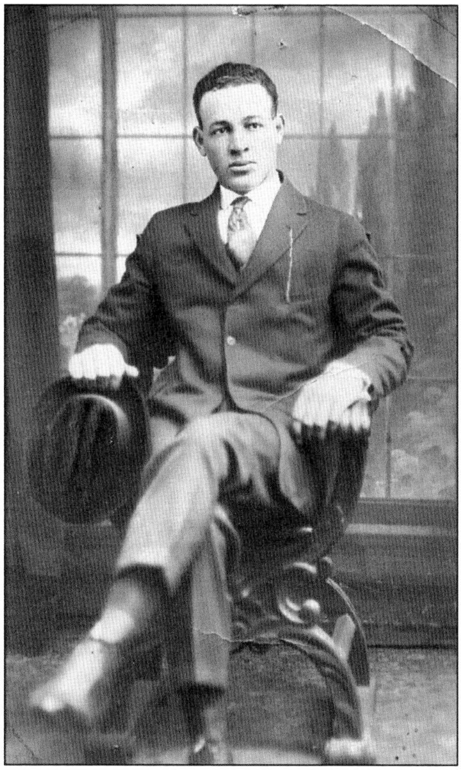

Thomas Hemoline "T. H." Allen was born on December 8, 1898, to Cary E. and Cornelia (Winston) Allen and was the younger brother of Madison Crencha Allen. T. H. Allen served as president of the county's chapter of the National Association for the Advancement of Colored People (NAACP) for over 35 years. He was also instrumental in the integration of public schools in Buckingham County. (Courtesy Charles W. White Sr.)

Born on May 4, 1877, in the Marshall District of Buckingham County, Rev. William Waverly Fleming was the eldest of nine children of Rev. Elijah and Mary Ellen (Cox) Fleming. Reverend Fleming became the pastor of Mount Olivet Baptist Temple in Newark, New Jersey, in 1915. He served as pastor for 40 years. Reverend Fleming also served on the Board of Trustees of Virginia Seminary and College in Lynchburg, Virginia. (Courtesy Edith M. Stanton Ingram.)

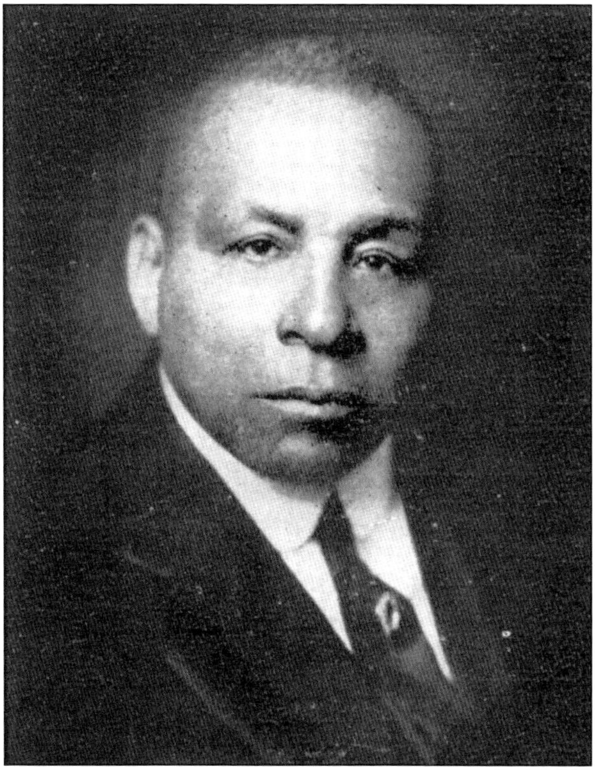

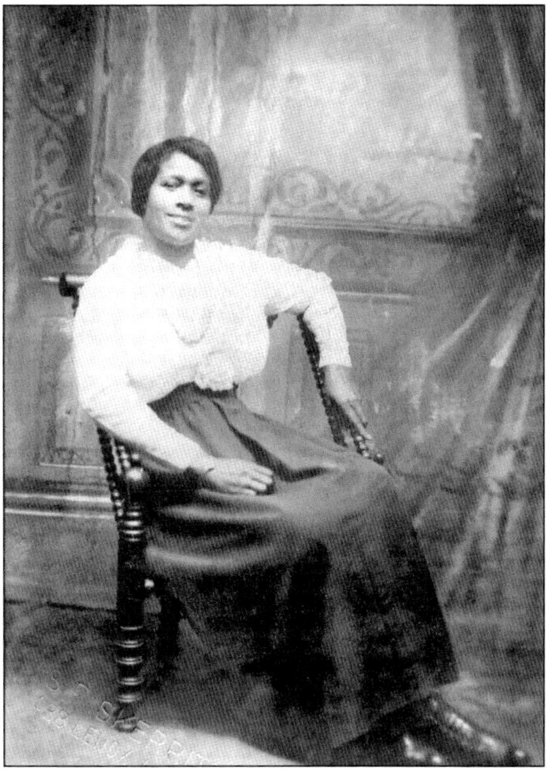

Znada Leslie (Fleming) Stanton, born on November 15, 1881, was the eldest daughter of Rev. Elijah and Mary Ellen (Cox) Fleming and sister of Rev. William W. Fleming, D.D. Her parents were among the founders of the New Hope Baptist Church, which was established in 1881 in Gold Hill in the Marshall District of Buckingham County. Znada, along with her brother, William Waverly, and mother, Mary Ellen (Cox) Fleming, are interred in the New Hope Baptist Cemetery. (Courtesy Edith M. Stanton Ingram.)

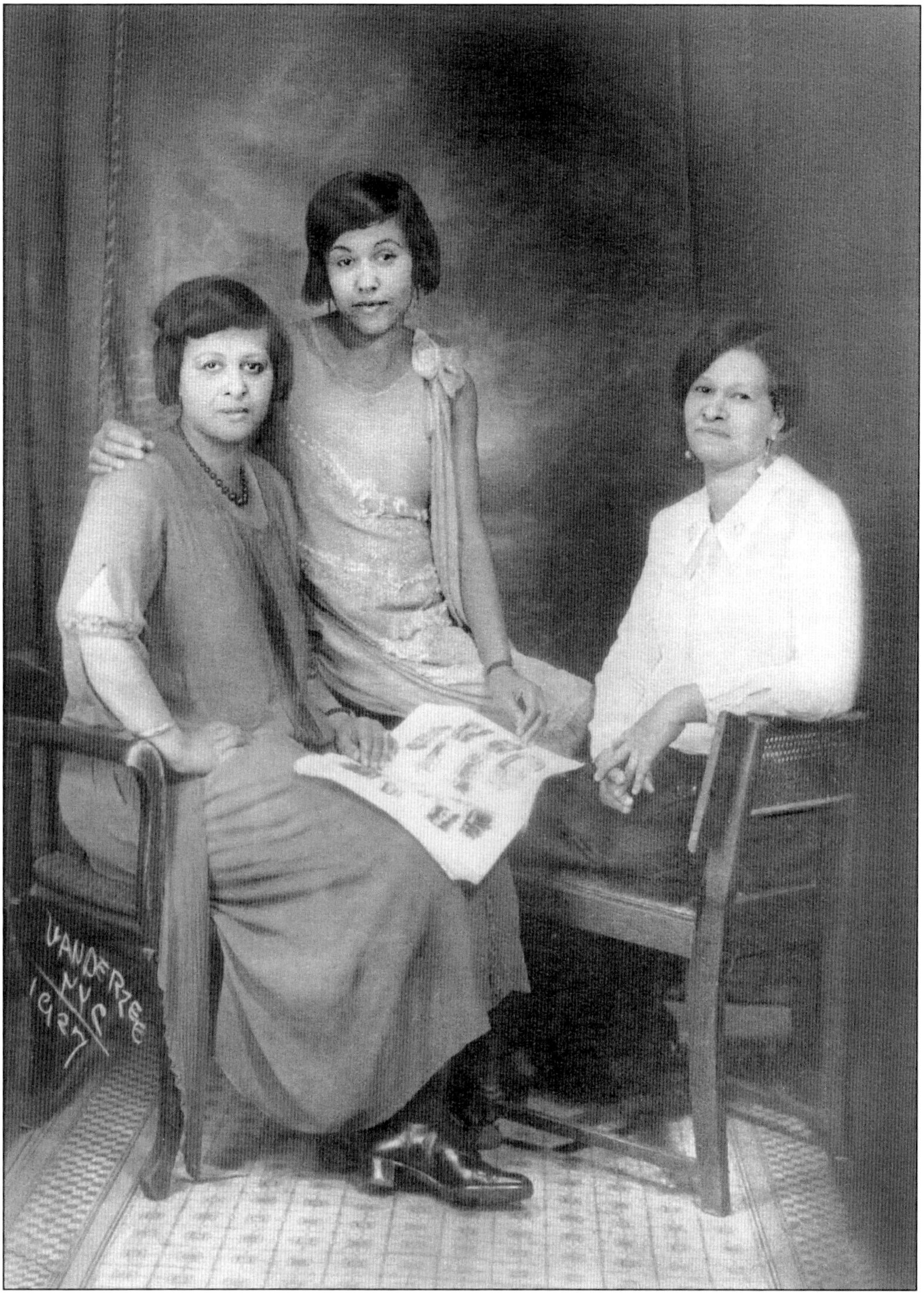

The Booker sisters of Buckingham County, Virginia, pictured from left to right, are Ophelia (Booker) Taylor, Leona (Booker) Gibson, and Edna (Booker) Anderson, daughters of Archer Cary and Sallie (Stanton) Booker. This photograph was taken in 1927 by noted African American Harlem Renaissance photographer James VanDerZee. (Courtesy E. Renée Ingram.)

Evangeline Lomax Bransford was born about 1870 in the James River District of Buckingham County. She was the daughter of Washington and Mary B. Lomax. This photograph was taken in the early 20th century. (Courtesy Charles W. White Sr.)

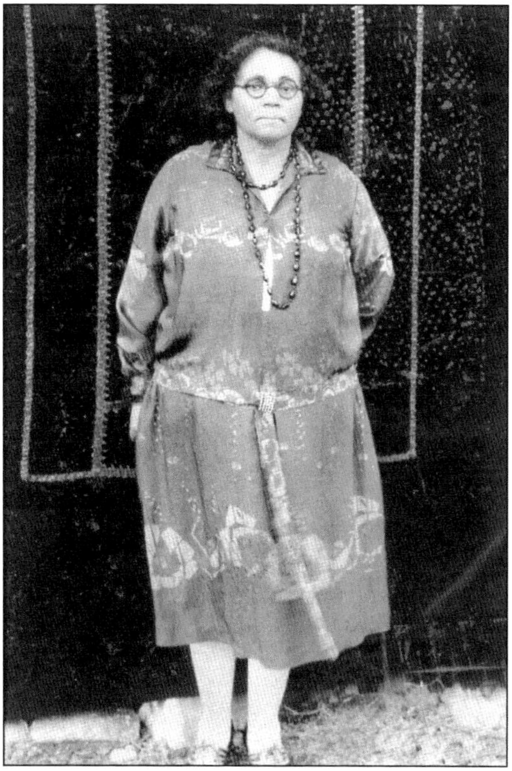

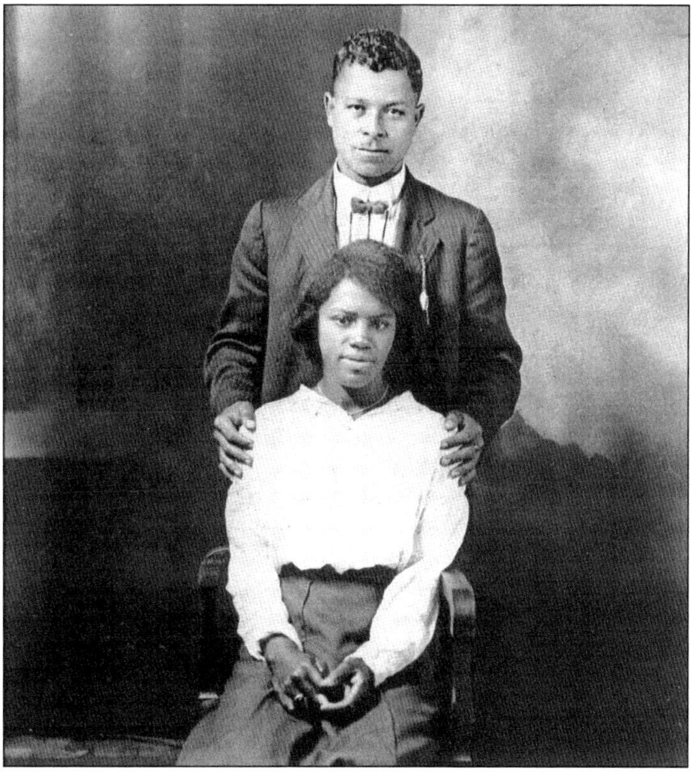

This 1947 photograph shows Jimmy and Maria (Morris) Austin from Warminster, in the James River District of Buckingham County. (Courtesy Dorothy Austin Bowling.)

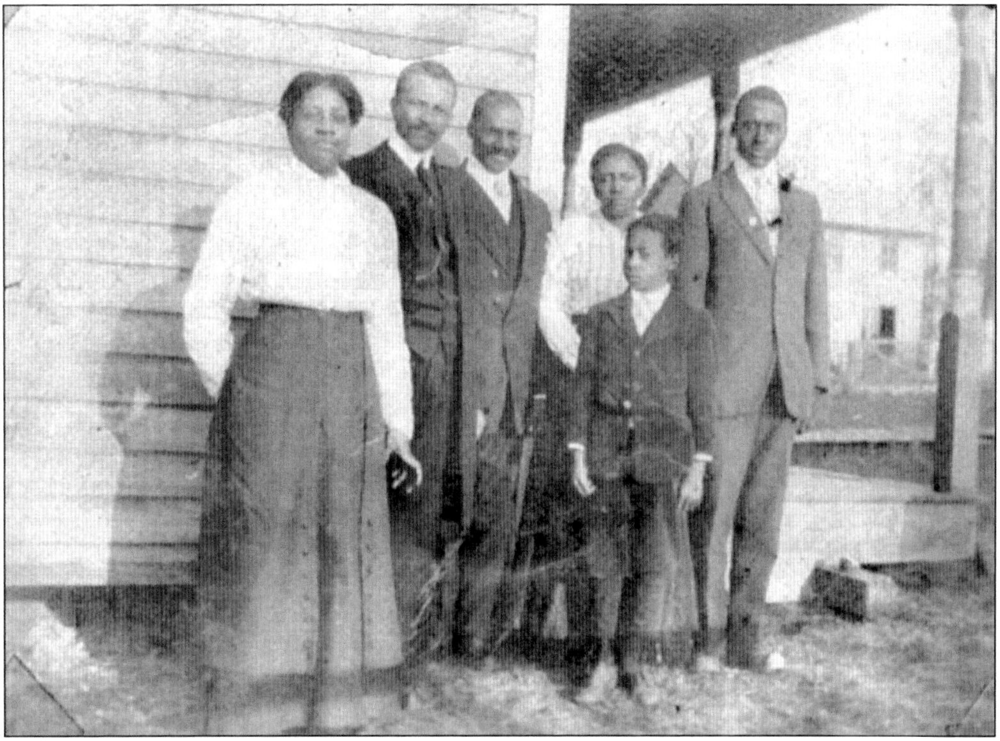

The Washington family is pictured here in front of their home in Buckingham County *c.* 1930. (Courtesy Otto K. Washington.)

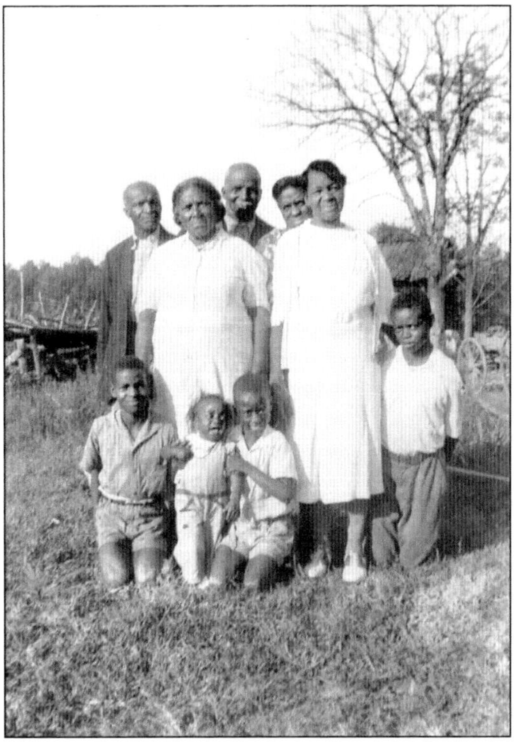

Pictured here is the Laury family in 1930. (Courtesy Joyce Gooden.)

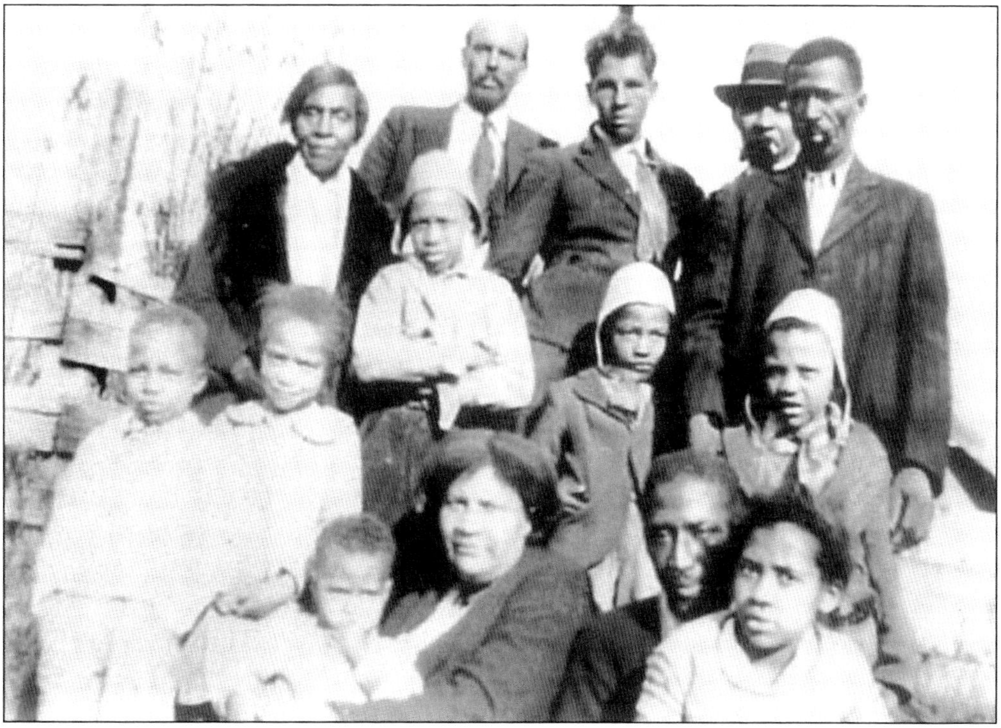

Pictured here is the West family in the 1930s. (Courtesy of Morris M. King.)

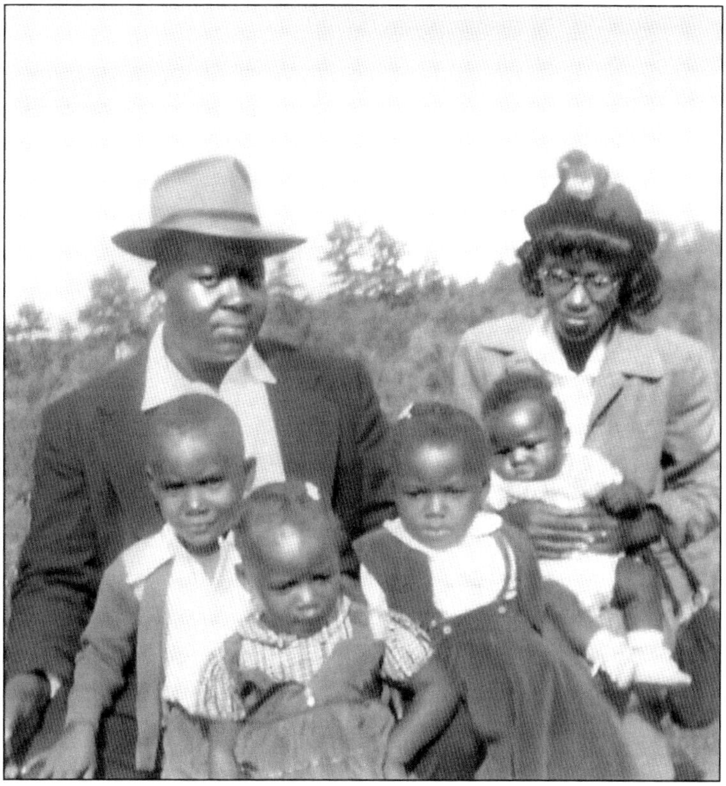

The James and Irene Cottrell family is pictured here in 1947. Their children (first row) are, from left to right, Edward, Thelma, Estelle, and Aubrey. (Courtesy Irene Cottrell Collection.)

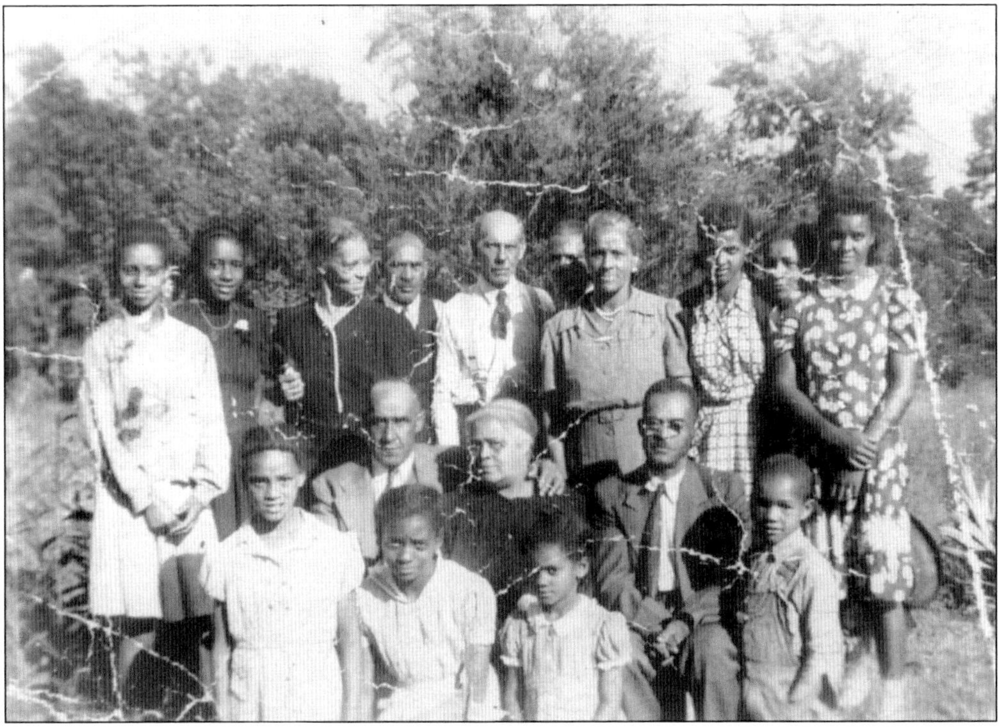

This photograph was taken of the John Hudgins family, *c.* 1940. (Courtesy the Hudgins family.)

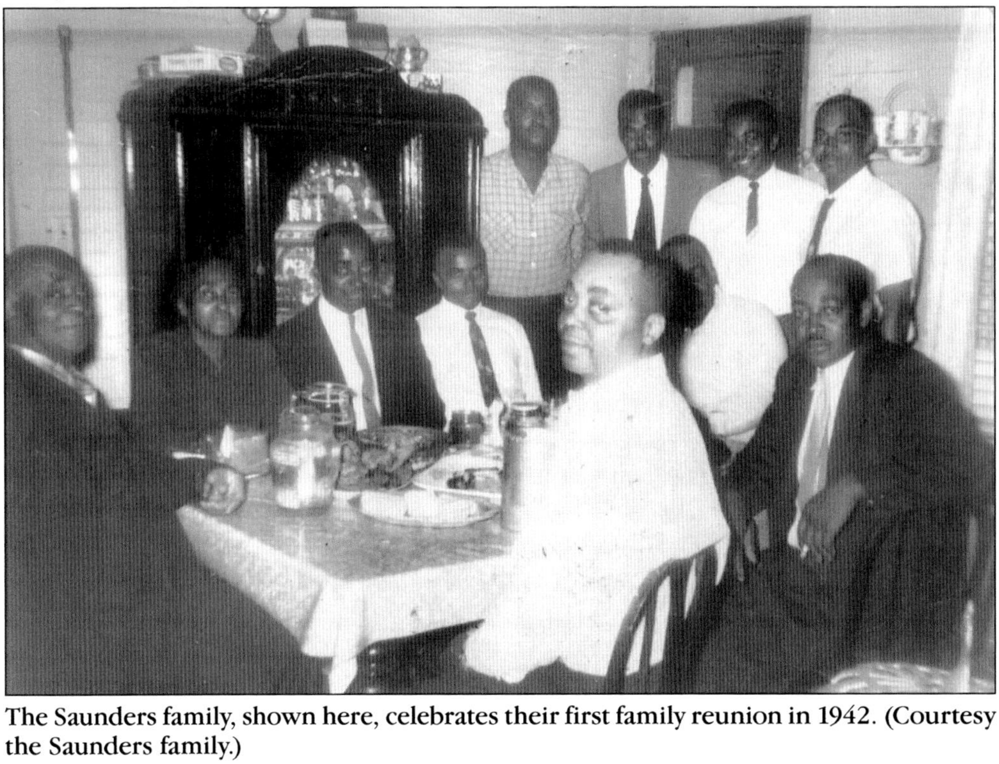

The Saunders family, shown here, celebrates their first family reunion in 1942. (Courtesy the Saunders family.)

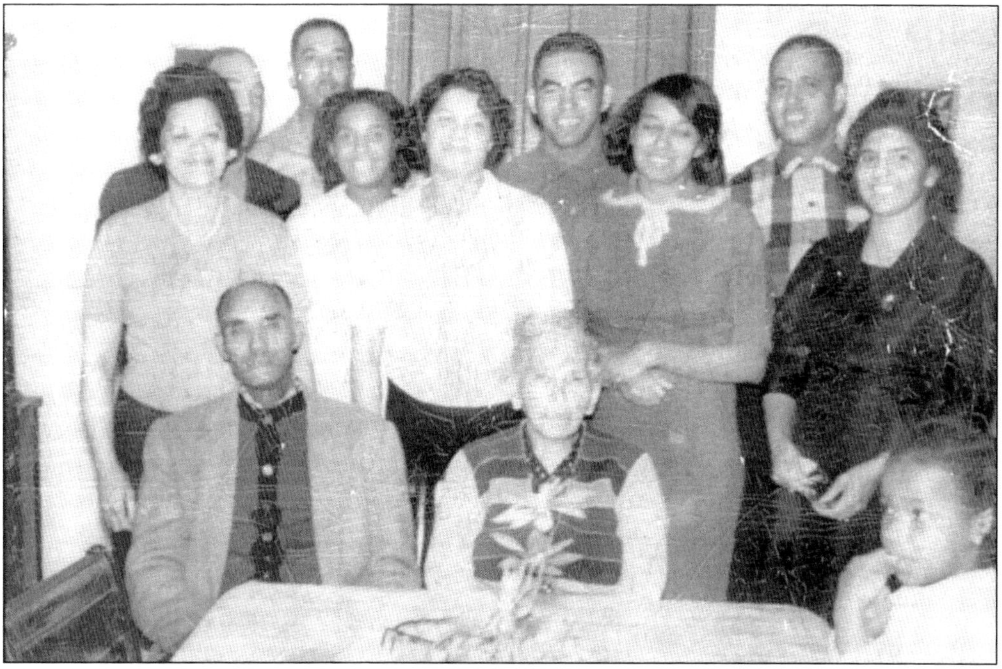

The Shelton family is shown here from left to right: (first row) Edward L. Shelton, Willie Leatha Shelton (his wife), and Belinda M. Jones (their granddaughter); (second row) Martha, Mary, Leatha, Lillie, and Pauline (the Sheltons' daughters); (third row) James, Mack, John, and Haywood (the Sheltons' sons). (Courtesy Mary S. Jones.)

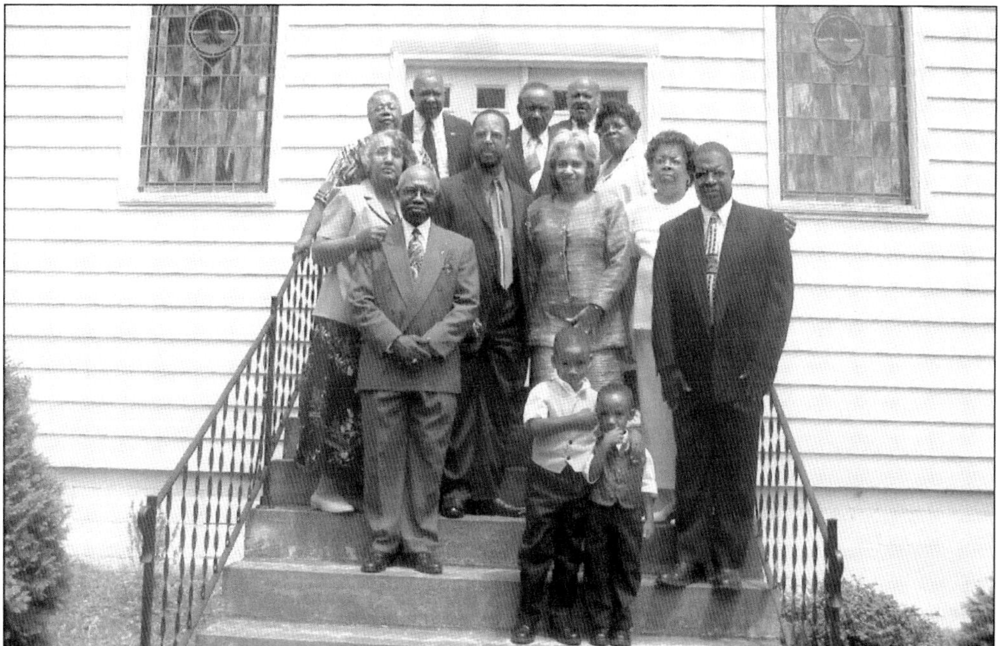

Members of the Mollie "Cotton" Perkins family are standing in front of the Oak Hill Baptist Church in Buckingham County during their family reunion celebration in 2003. (Courtesy Perkins Family Reunion Committee.)

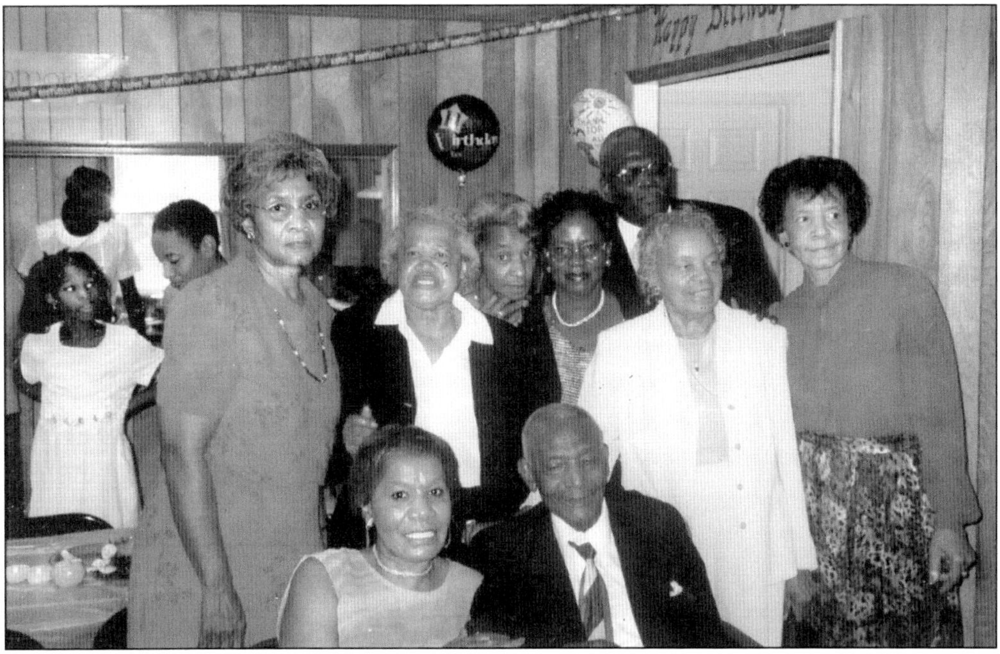

Members of the Bolling family are pictured here celebrating the 100th birthday of George W. Bolling, who is seated in the front. (Courtesy Arlene Bolling Woodson.)

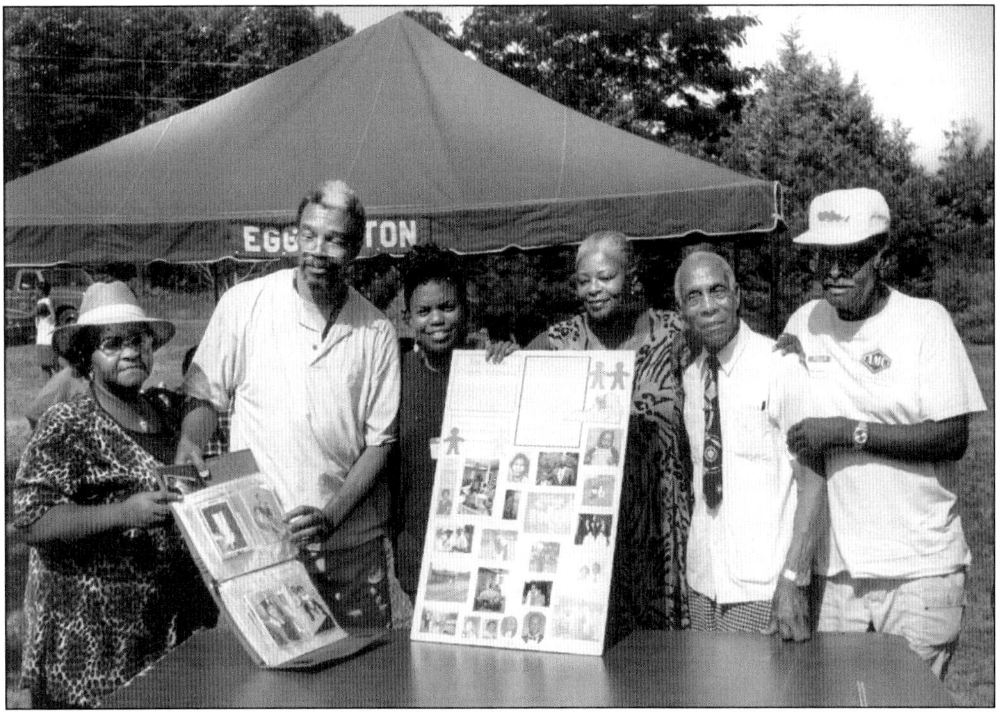

This is a photograph of the Saunders family taken at their family reunion in Buckingham County. Members of the family are standing with their ancestry documentation. (Courtesy the Saunders family.)

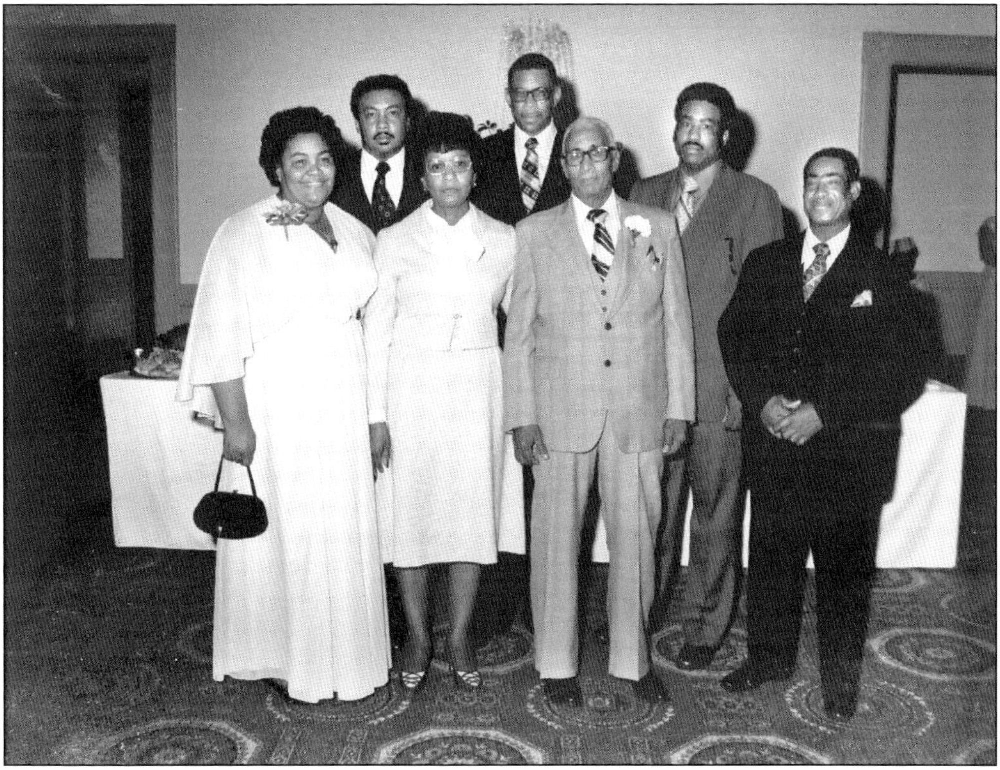

Pictured here is the Scruggs family. (Courtesy the Scruggs family collection.)

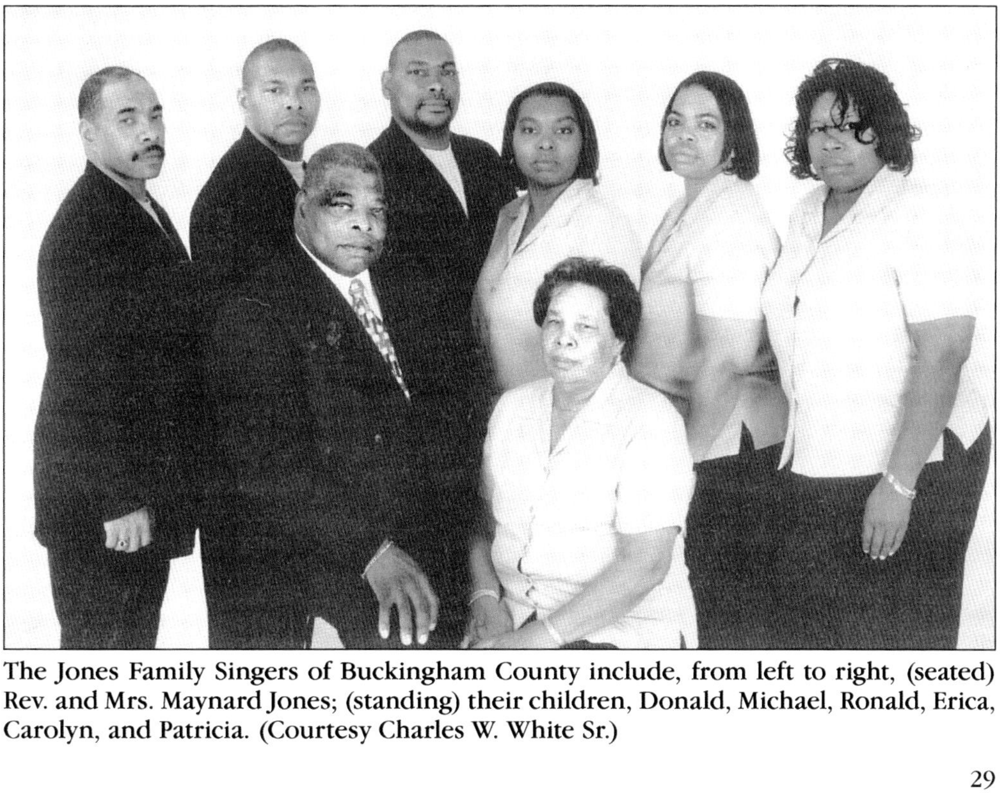

The Jones Family Singers of Buckingham County include, from left to right, (seated) Rev. and Mrs. Maynard Jones; (standing) their children, Donald, Michael, Ronald, Erica, Carolyn, and Patricia. (Courtesy Charles W. White Sr.)

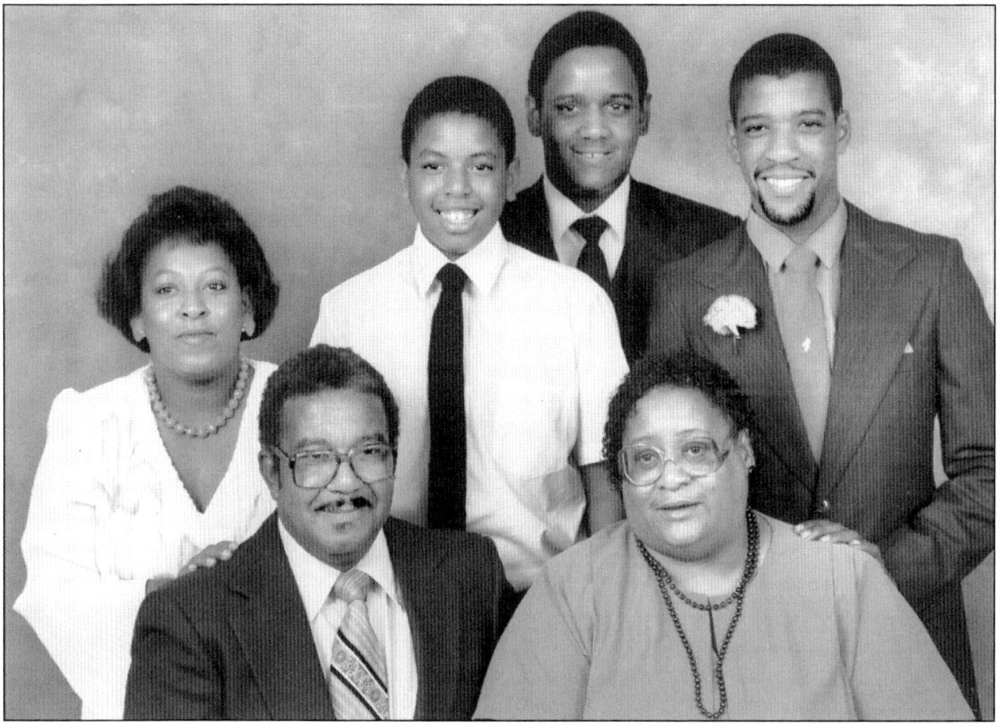

This is a photograph of the Bernard and Edith James family. (Courtesy Arlene Bolling Woodson.)

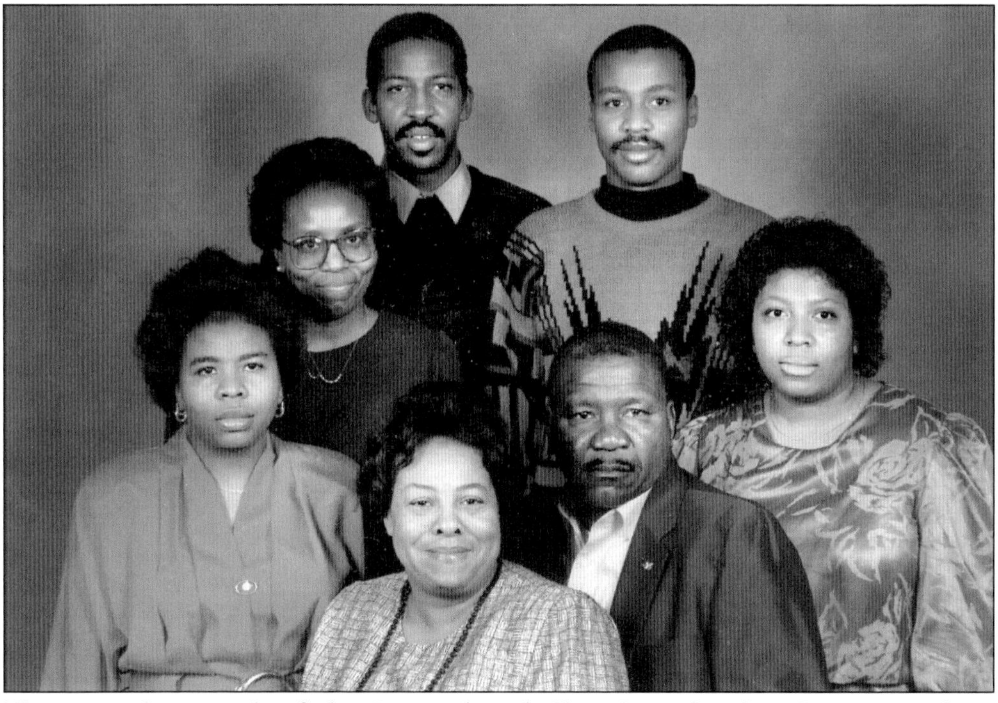

This is a photograph of the Bernard and Cleo Opie family. (Courtesy Arlene Bolling Woodson.)

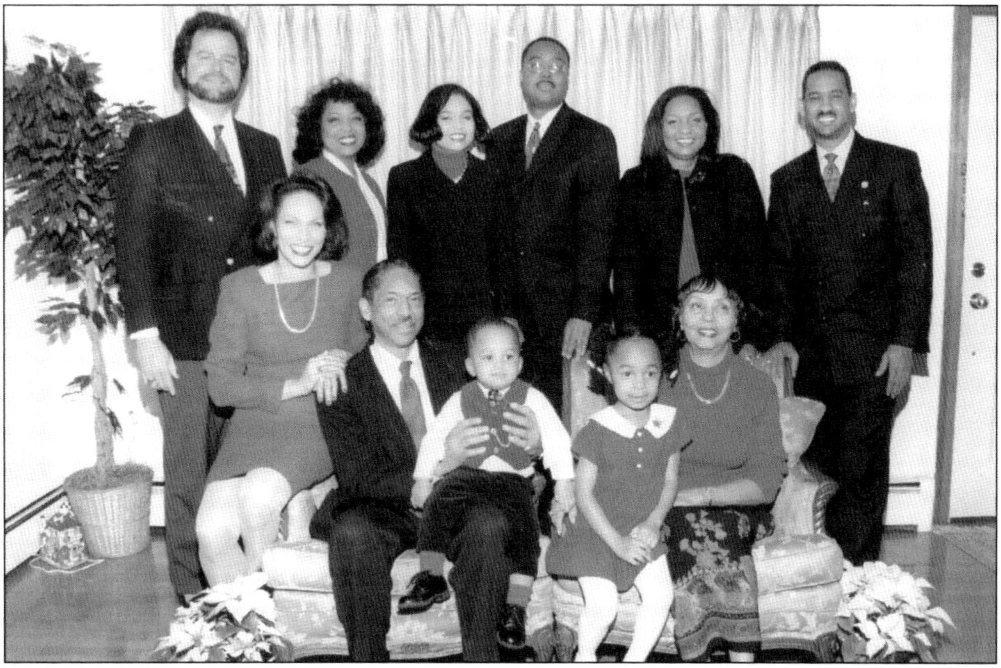

Rev. Robert R. and Lular (Moore) Parson are shown here with their family during the holiday season. From left to right are (seated) Melody Z. Day, Rev. Robert R. Parson, Marc I. Davis, Charissa J. Davis, and Lular (Moore) Parson; (standing) Philip E. Day, Dr. Monica L. Parson, Merisa V. Davis, Marc R. Davis, Martika A. Parson, and R. Mark Parson. (Courtesy Lular Moore Parson.)

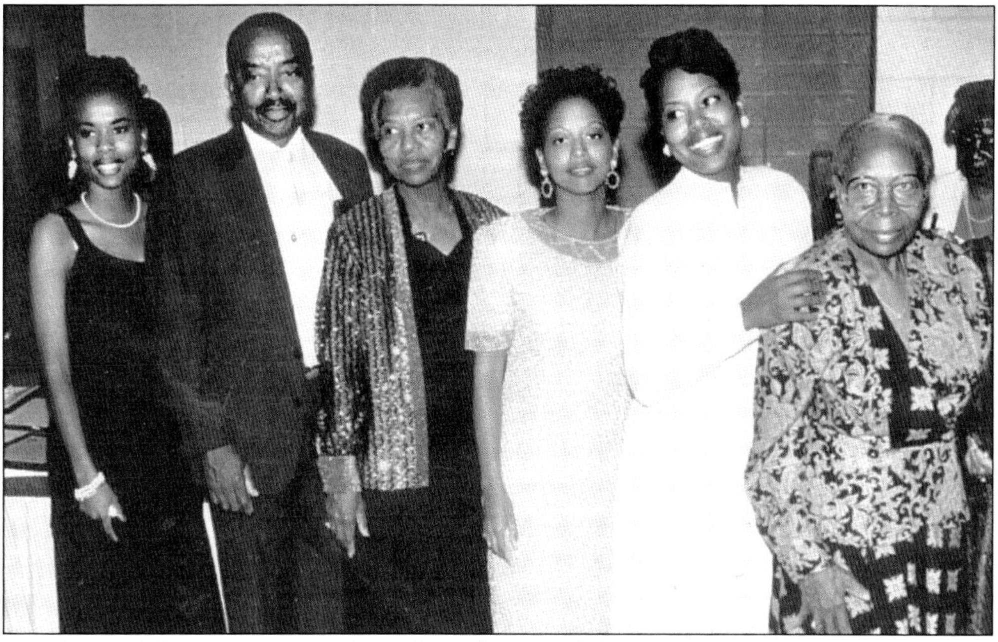

Members of the Norman-Candie-Wilson family celebrate their 25th family reunion in 1994. Pictured from left to right are Danlyn M. Wilson, Alfred D. Wilson, Evelyn H. Wilson, Alfreda Wilson, Jahala A. Wilson, and Rose S. Sheppard. (Courtesy Evelyn Wilson.)

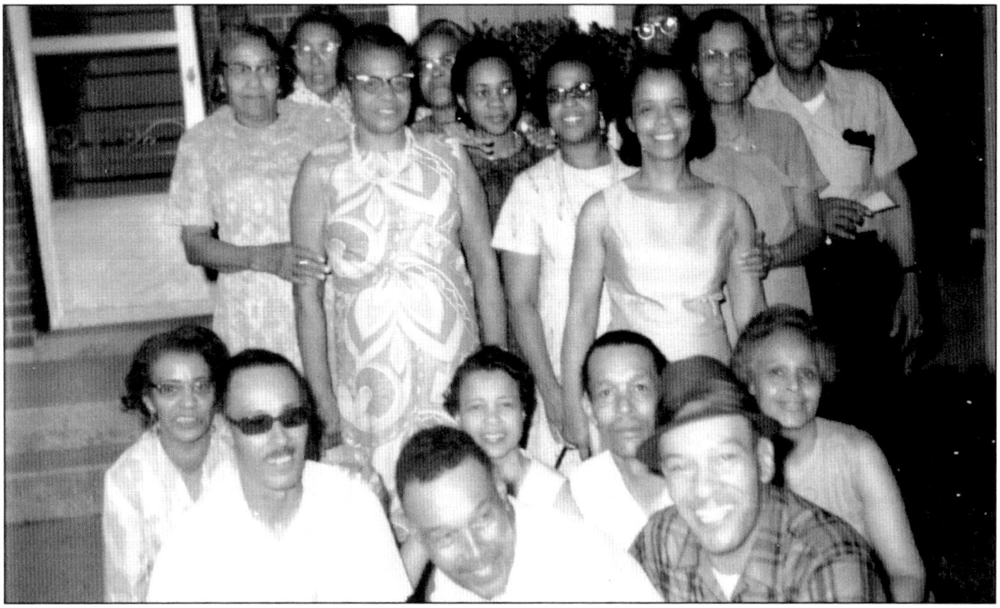

The Znada and Sidney Trent Stanton Jr. family is shown at a 1968 reunion at Lucian Willis Stanton's Alexandria, Virginia, home. From left to right are (first row) Lois Stanton Swingler, Lucian Stanton, Godfrey Stanton, Edith Stanton Ingram, Marshall Stanton, James Woodson, and Louise Stanton Mitchell; (second row) Effie Stanton Woodson, Nannie Stanton Burke, Ophelia Stanton Brown, Sarah Anderson Stanton, Pauline White Stanton, Florence White, Viola White Stanton, Sallie Stanton Webb, and Richard Stanton. (Courtesy of Edith M. Stanton Ingram.)

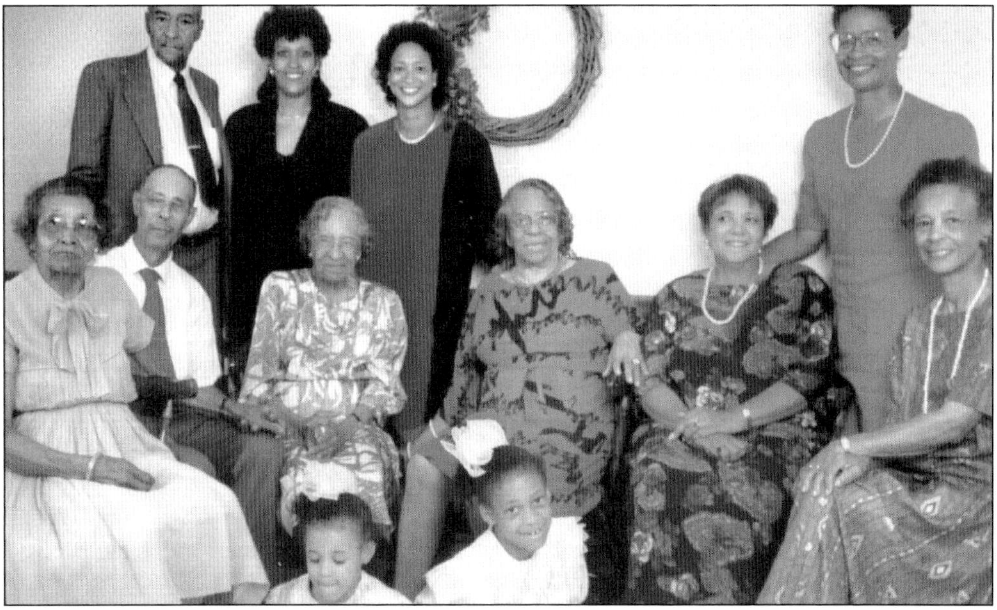

Descendants of Znada and Sidney Trent Stanton Jr. are shown here during the 1993 Historic Stanton Family Cemetery dedication in Dillwyn. From left to right are (first row) Zelexis and Znada Morse; (second row) Nannie Stanton Burke, Willis Lucian Stanton, Sallie Stanton Webb, Ophelia Stanton Brown, Juanita Jean Swingler Turner, and Edith Stanton Ingram; (third row) James Woodson, Cernata Stanton Morse, E. Renée Ingram, and Joyce Ingram McGlaston. (Courtesy E. Renée Ingram.)

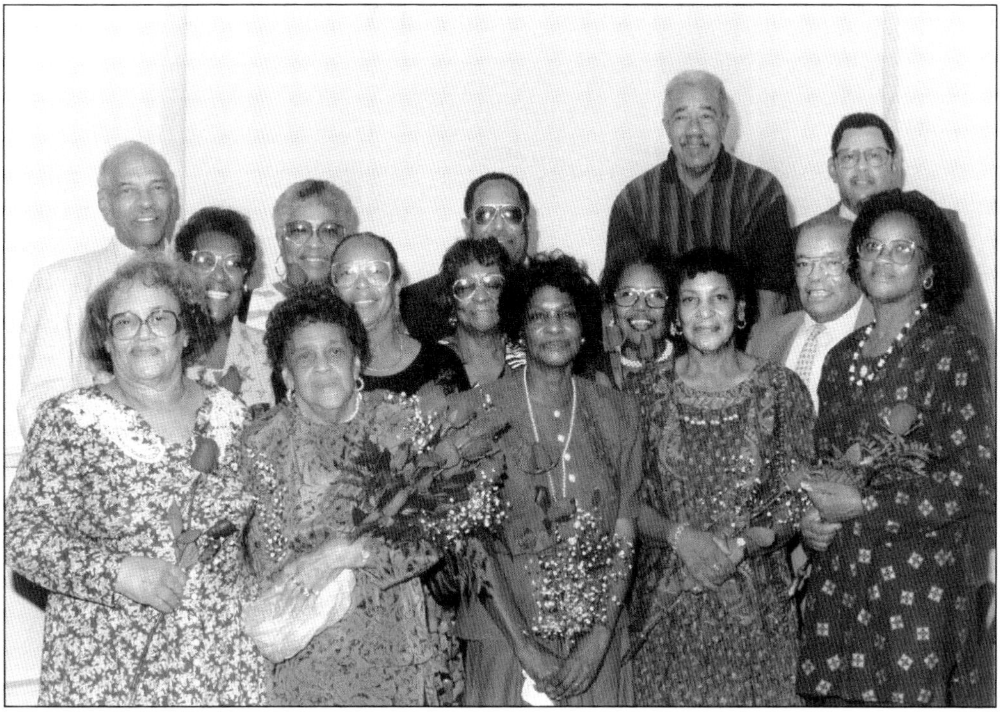

Pictured here are the elder family members at the Seay-Gray family reunion. This photograph was taken in 1989 in Hampton, Virginia. (Courtesy Catherine Seay Redcross.)

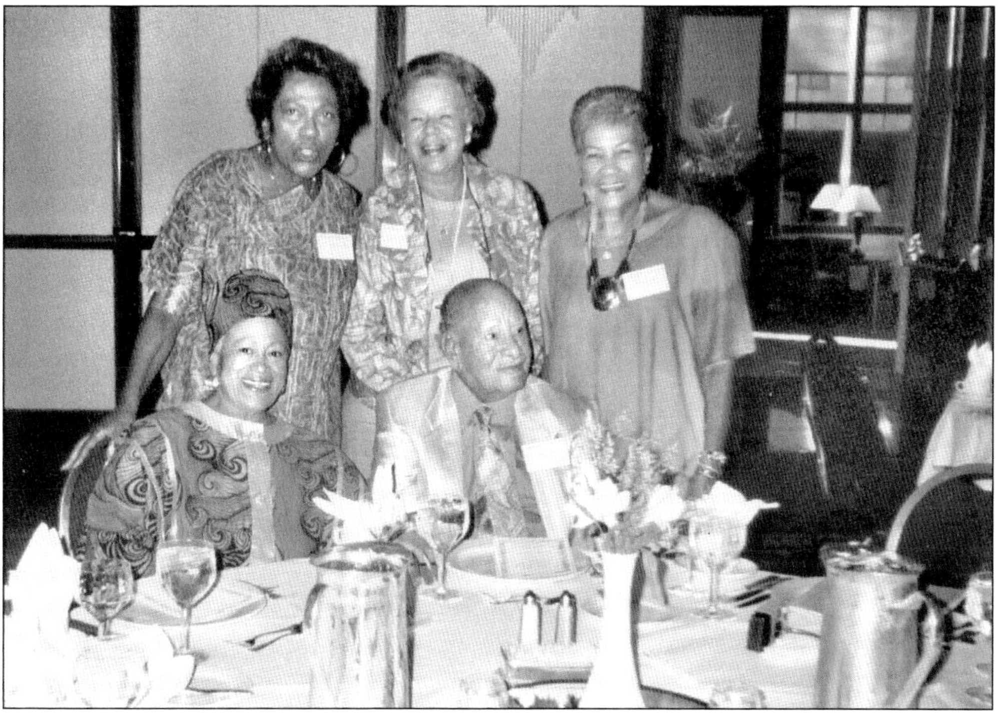

Members of the Washington family are pictured here at their family reunion dinner, which was held in Cincinnati, Ohio, in 2000. (Courtesy Otto K. Washington.)

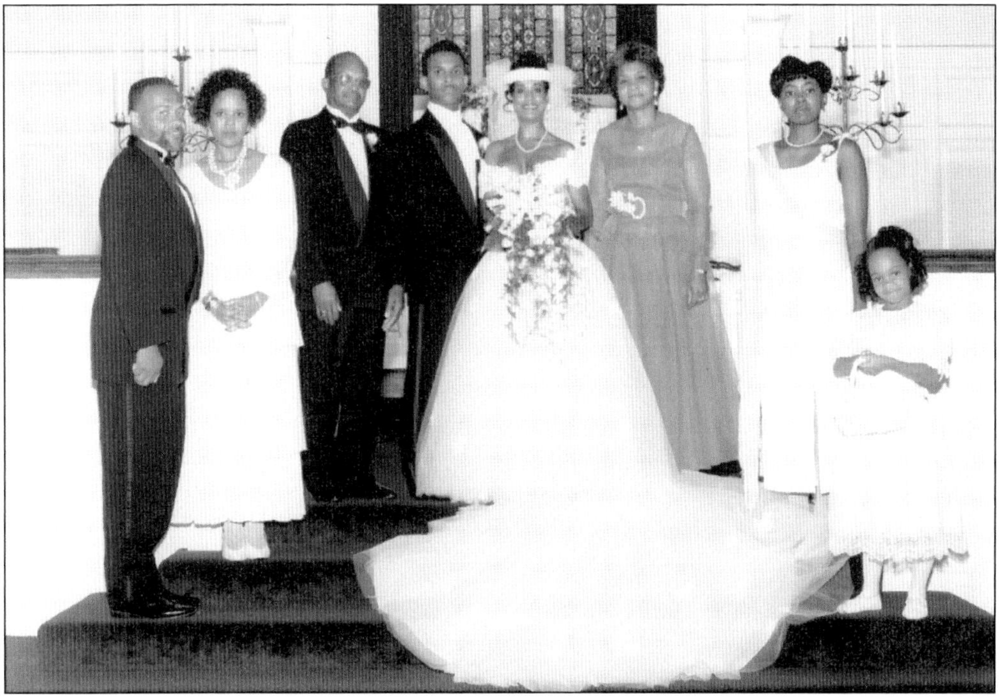

The Thomas and Tracey (Fellows) Woodson wedding party is shown here on their special day in San Bernadino, California. The bridegroom, Thomas Woodson, standing fourth from left, is also a member of the Bolling family of New Canton, Marshall District of Buckingham County. (Courtesy James Woodson family.)

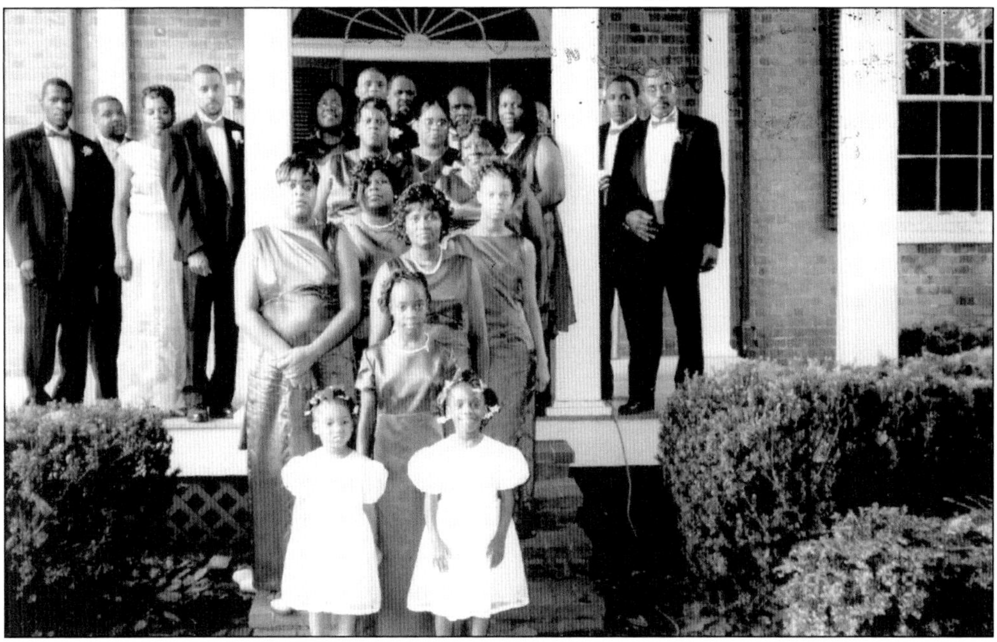

Delano and Jean Scruggs renewed their wedding vows on their 25th anniversary. Members of the wedding anniversary party shown here participated in the celebration. (Courtesy Arlene Bolling Woodson.)

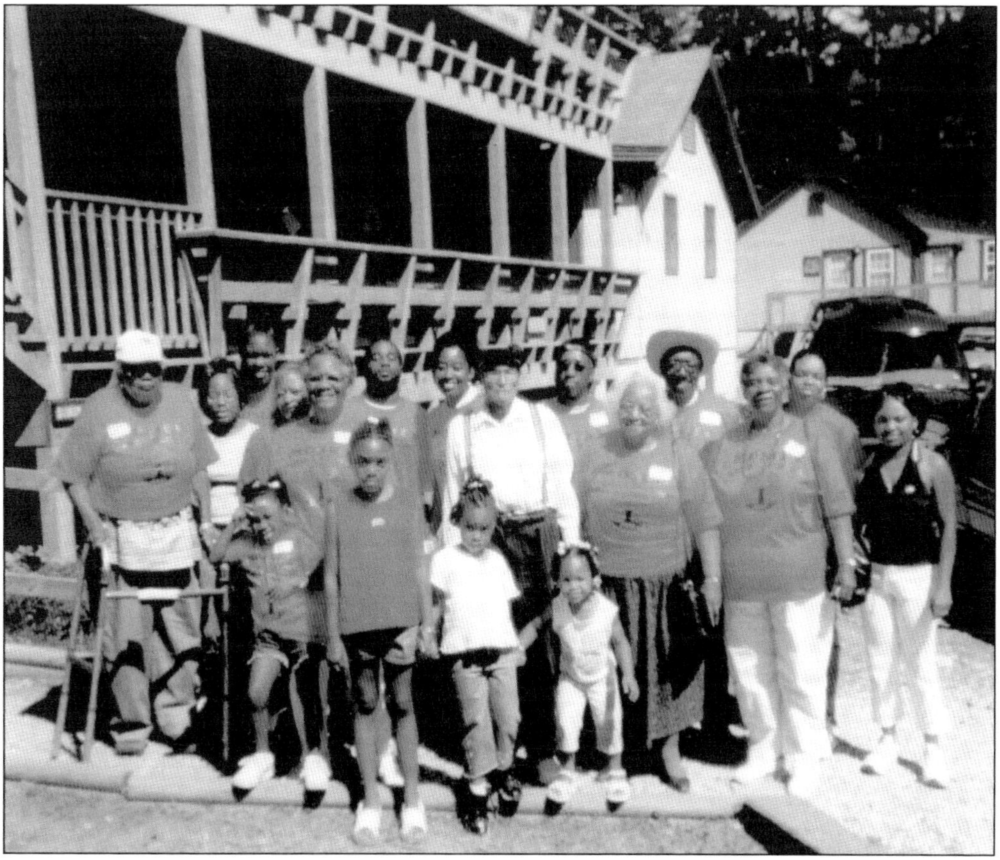

Members of the Mosley family, gathered for this photograph in 2002 during their family reunion in Buckingham County. (Courtesy Charles W. White Sr.)

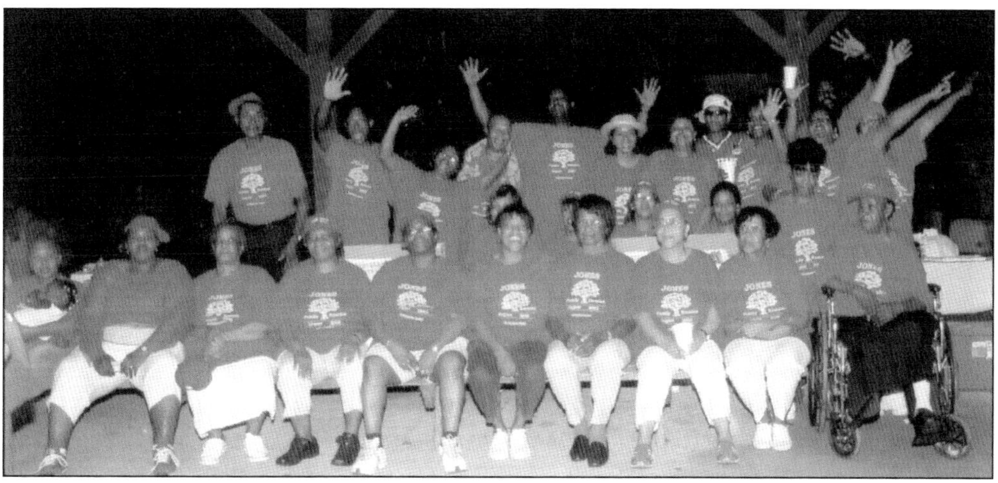

Members of the Jones family are pictured here during their family reunion celebration that was held in 2005 in Buckingham County. (Courtesy Charles W. White Sr.)

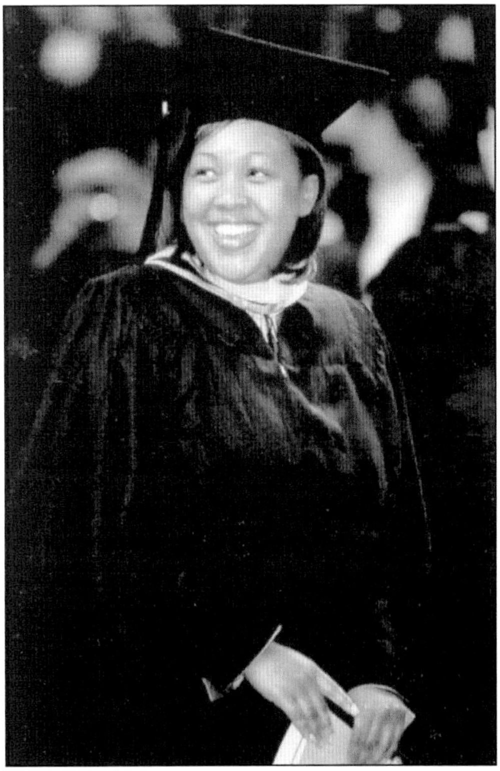

Pictured here is LaToya T. Chambers on her graduation day from Virginia Commonwealth University in Richmond, Virginia. LaToya T. Chambers is the daughter of Eugene and Marjorie Chambers of New Canton in the Marshall District of Buckingham County. (Courtesy Marjorie Chambers.)

Pictured here is Marjorie Chambers on her graduation day. (Courtesy Marjorie Chambers.)

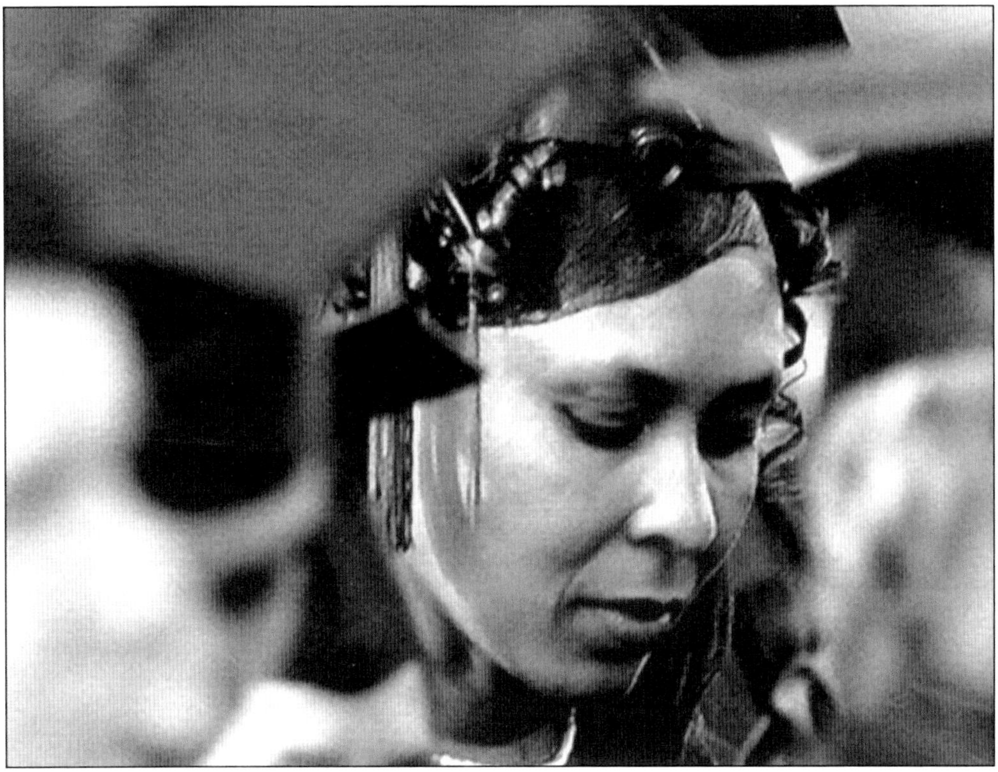

Two

Our Pioneers and Trailblazers

Every people should be originators of their own destiny.

—Martin R. Delany (1812–1885)

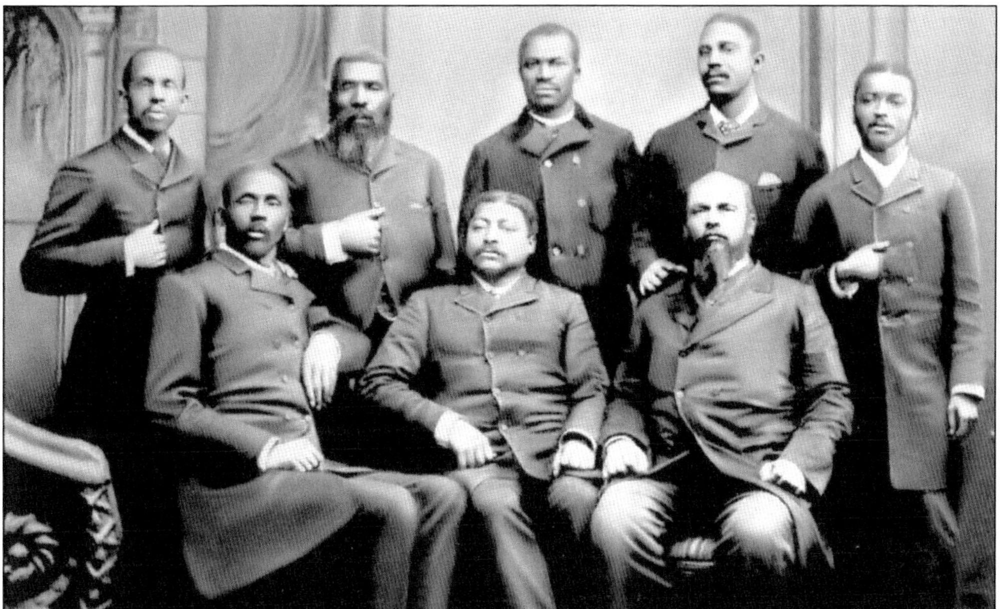

This is a photograph of the members of the Virginia General Assembly 1887–1888. From left to right are (front row) Alfred W. Harris (Dinwiddie), William W. Evans (Petersburg), and Caesar Perkins (Buckingham); (back row) John H. Robinson (Elizabeth City), Goodman Brown (Surry), Nathaniel M. Griggs (Prince Edward), William H. Ash (Nottoway), and Briton Baskerville Jr. (Mecklenburg). (Courtesy Moorland-Spingarn Research Center, Howard University.)

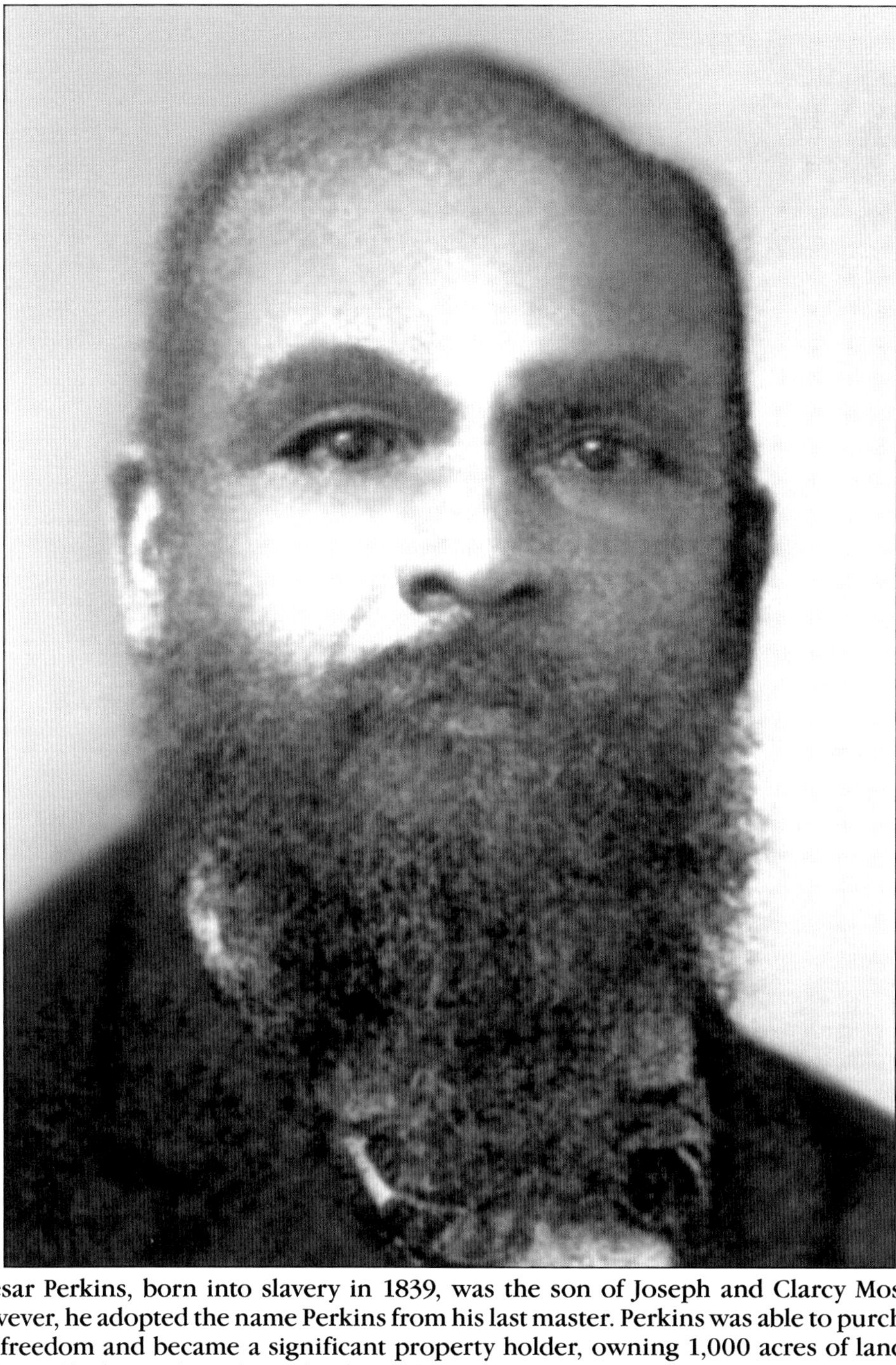

Caesar Perkins, born into slavery in 1839, was the son of Joseph and Clarcy Mosely; however, he adopted the name Perkins from his last master. Perkins was able to purchase his freedom and became a significant property holder, owning 1,000 acres of land by 1860. Self-educated, Perkins displayed his commitment to education when he built a school near the Buckingham Court House. Caesar Perkins was a highly respected minister and served at the Jerusalem Baptist Church. In 1869, he was elected to the Virginia House of Delegates, served one term (1869–1871), and was reelected for a second term in 1887. Perkins was also an active member of the Colored Knights of Pythias. (Courtesy Moorland-Spingarn Research Center, Howard University.)

Morton Deane, born free in Buckingham County in December 1852, was the son of Gabriel and Rachel Deane. The family moved to Richmond, Virginia, during Morton's childhood, and he attended the first African American schools in the state capitol. Morton was an ironworker with the Tredegar Ironworks and clerk of the Second Baptist Church in Richmond for many years. In 1895, Morton Deane became one of five African Americans who won a seat on the eight-man Richmond City Council. (Courtesy the Library of Virginia.)

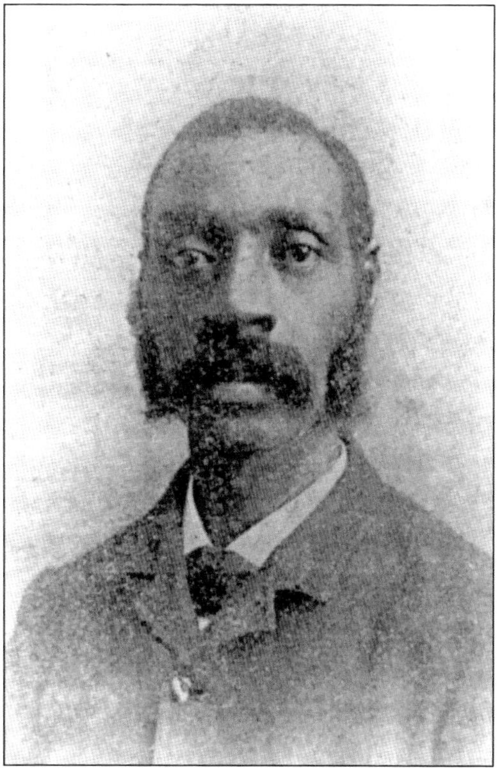

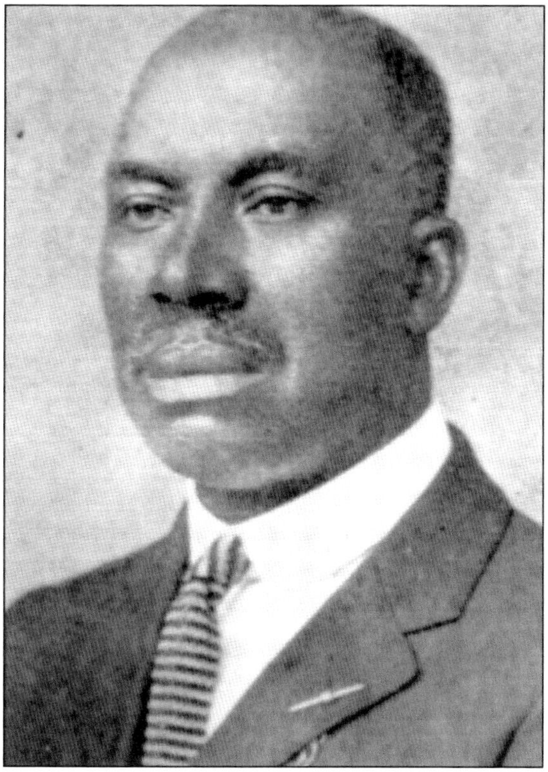

Quinn Shelton was born about 1861 in Manteo in the James River District of Buckingham County to Allen and Nellie (Cox) Shelton. Shelton left Buckingham in the late 19th century to earn a living in Richmond, Virginia. He became the first vice president and director of the Second Street Savings Bank and a director of the Consolidated Bank and Trust in Richmond, Virginia. He also served as a director at the Sixth Mount Zion Baptist Church in Richmond. (Courtesy William Shelton.)

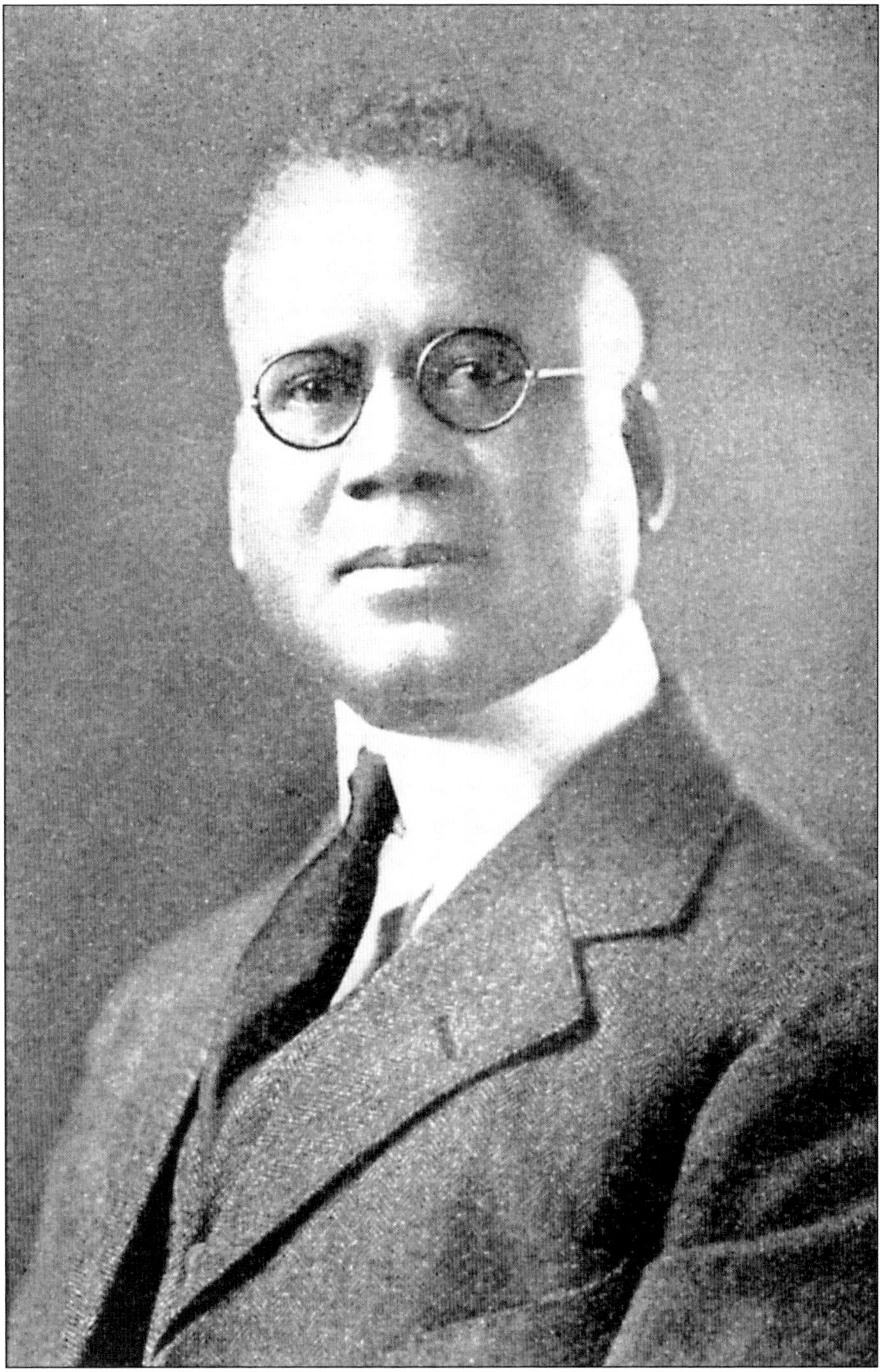

Constantine Clinton "C. C." Barnett, born on November 30, 1869, in New Canton, was the son of Nelson and Betty (Woodson) Barnett and the first cousin of Carter Godwin Woodson. In 1912, he founded Barnett Hospital and Nurses Training School, which became known as the largest and best-equipped hospital of its kind in Huntington, West Virginia. Dr. Barnett became the superintendent of the State Hospital for Colored Women in Lakin, West Virginia. (Courtesy West Virginia State Archives.)

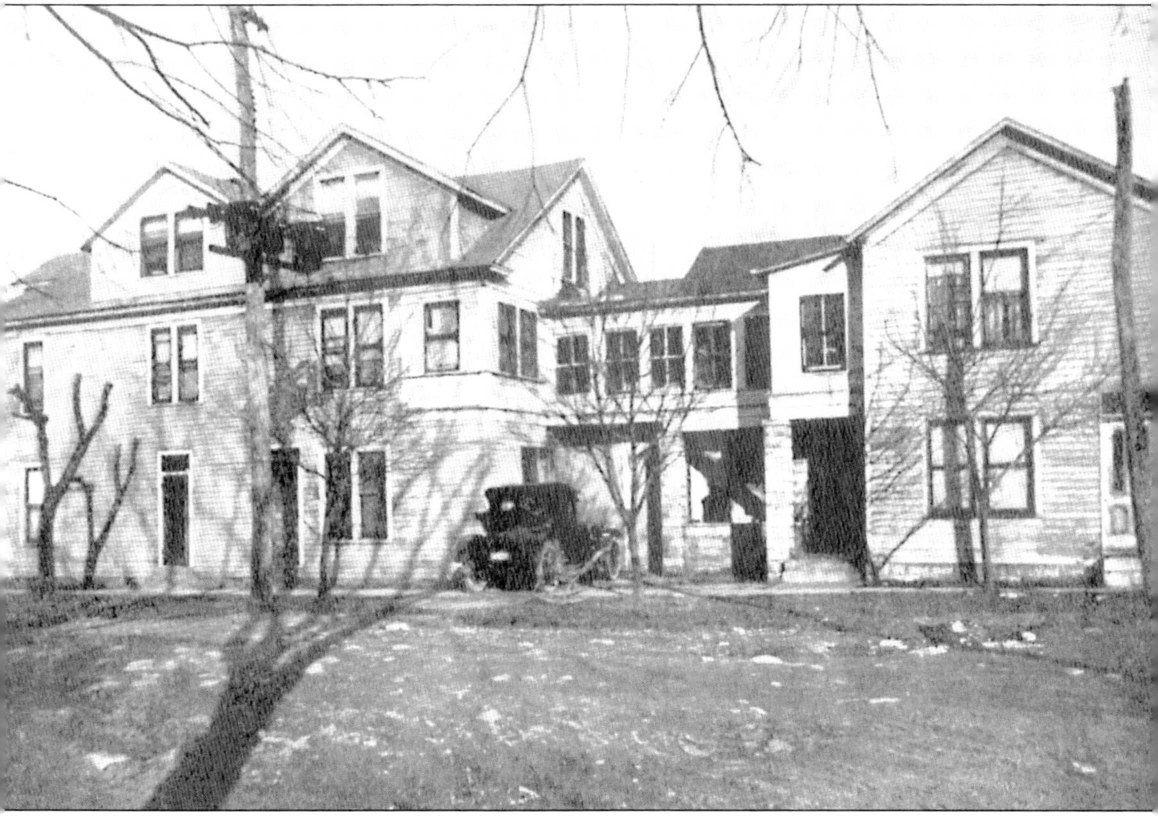

The Barnett Hospital and Nurses Training School, which was located in Huntington, West Virginia, was established in 1912. The institution had 30 beds and was the official city hospital for African Americans for many decades. The photographs shown here appear to have originated from the publication entitled *History of the American Negro—West Virginia Edition* in 1923. (Courtesy West Virginia State Archives.)

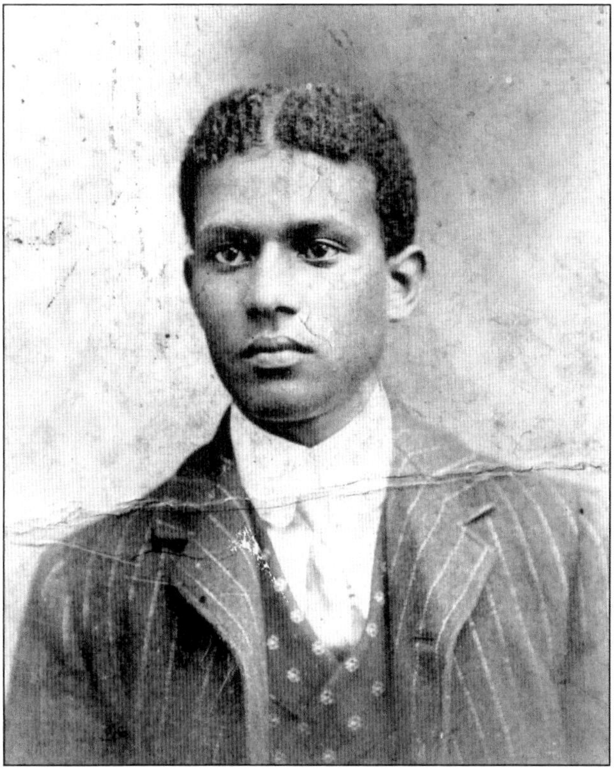

John Wilbur Chambers, born in 1879 near Buckingham Court House, was the son of Wilbur and Matilda Chambers. Chambers graduated from Howard University's School of Pharmacy in 1905 and subsequently moved to Lynchburg, where he practiced his profession for several years. Dr. Chambers had an opportunity to operate his own business, known as the Chamber's Drugstore, which lasted nearly 60 years in Richmond, near Virginia Union University. (Courtesy Charles W. White Sr.)

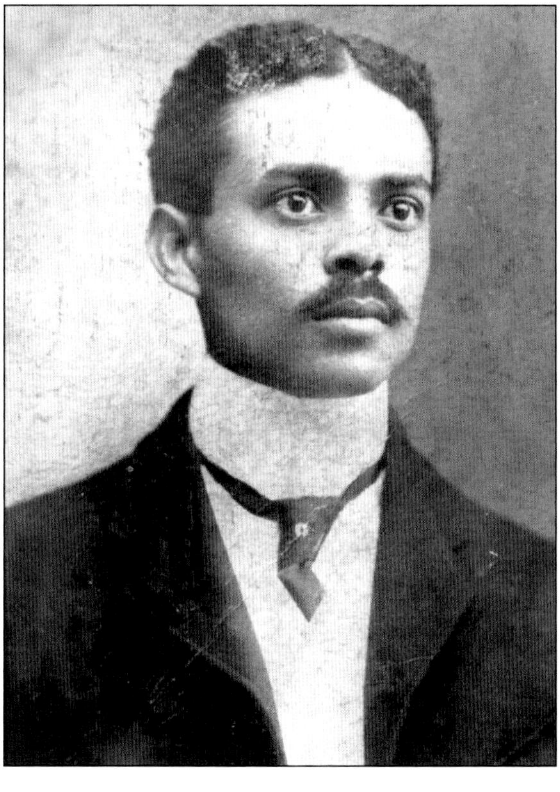

Roger William Lomax, born on May 24, 1881, was a county educator like his parents, Edward S. and Josephine A. Lomax. After two years of teaching, he decided to continue his education and graduated from Leonard Medical School at Shaw University in Raleigh, North Carolina, in 1907. After graduation, Dr. Lomax established a medical practice in Pocahontas and Lynchburg, Virginia. (Courtesy Joyce Gooden.)

Willard W. Allen, born May 3, 1888, in Buckingham County, was the son of George and Elizabeth Allen. Allen served as president of the Southern Life Insurance Company in Baltimore, Maryland, from 1925 until he retired in 1959. He served on the Board of Trustees of Virginia Union University in Richmond from 1950 to 1960. Allen also served on the Board of Trustees of Morgan State College (Morgan State University) for more than 20 years and received honorary doctor of law degrees from Allen University in Columbia, South Carolina, and Wilberforce University in Wilberforce, Ohio. Dr. Allen was also the regional vice president of the National Negro Business League and a director of the NAACP. Allen was the grand master of the Prince Hall Masons of Maryland and Jurisdictions, Inc., for 38 years and was unequivocally the "dean" of grand masters in the United States. (Courtesy Prince Hall Grand Lodge of the State of Maryland and Jurisdictions, Inc.)

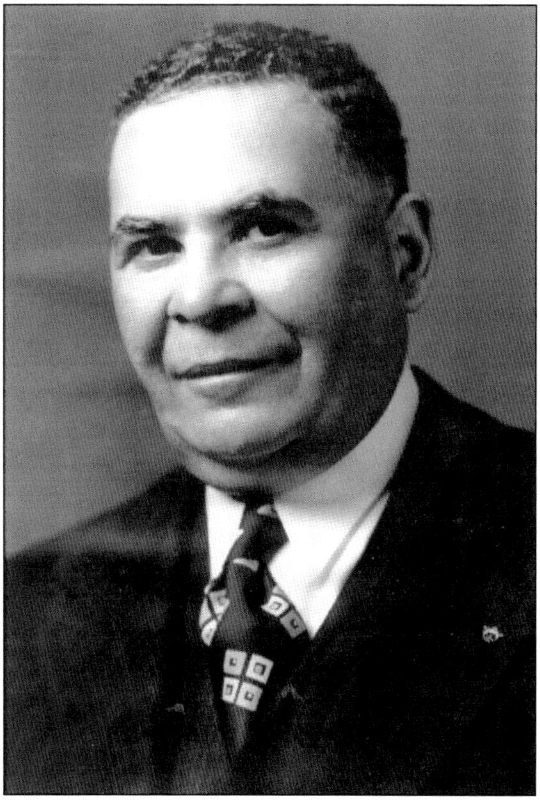

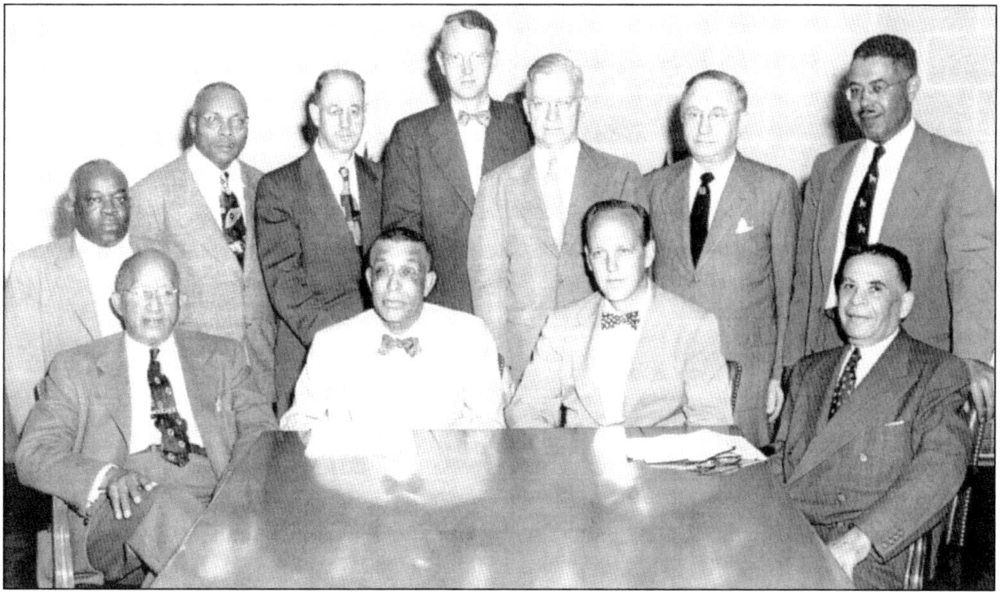

The Board of Trustees of Morgan State College (Morgan State University), shown here in the 1950s, includes member of the board Dr. Willard W. Allen, seated in the far right corner of this photograph. (Courtesy Morganiana Collection, Prints and Photographs Collection, Beulah M. Davis Special Collections Department, Soper Library, Morgan State University.)

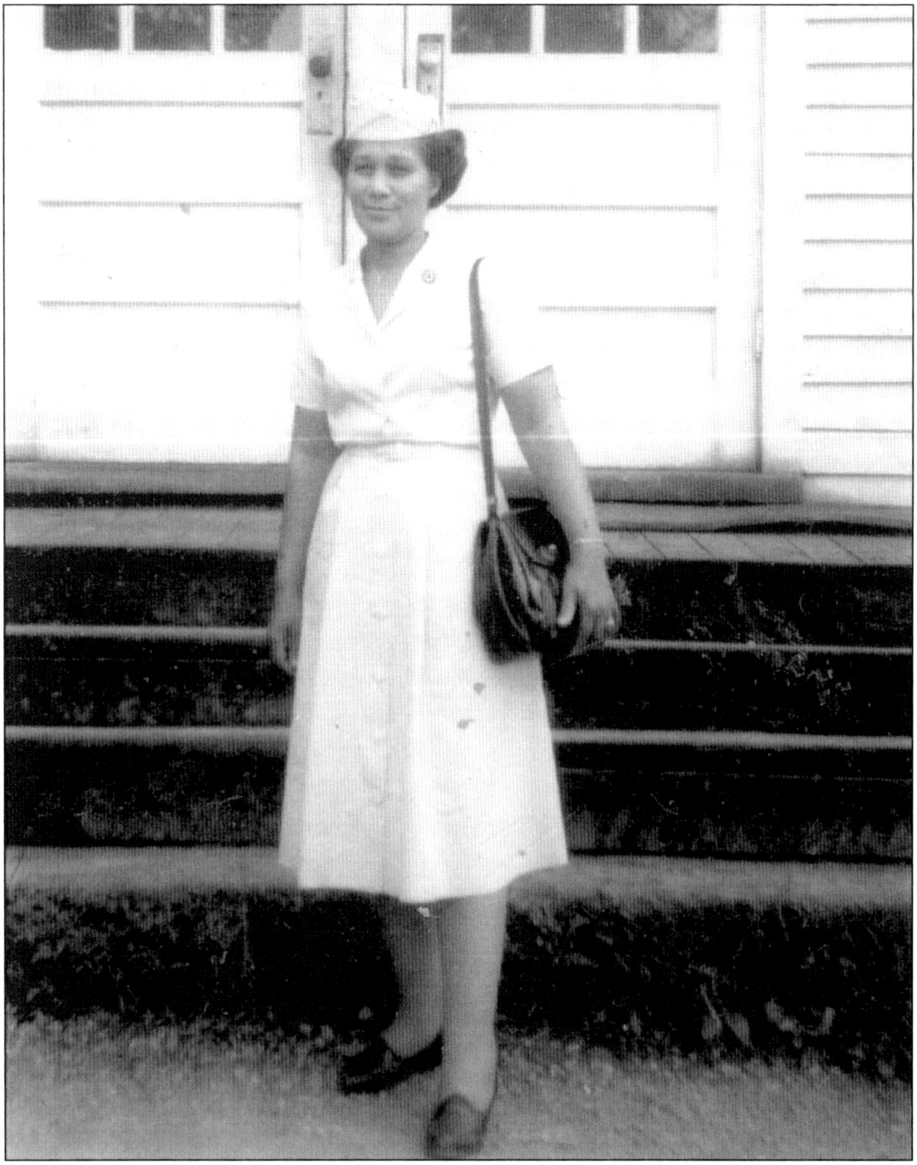

Odessa Moss Branch, born March 21, 1921, was the daughter of James A. and Susie B. (Loveless) Moss of the Maysville District of the county. She became the first African American public health nurse in Buckingham County on November 16, 1948, and retired in 1977. She graduated from the St. Philip School of Nursing (now the Virginia Commonwealth University School of Nursing) in Richmond in 1943. She initially worked at the Harlem Hospital in New York and then returned to Richmond to accept a 12-month fellowship in public health nursing at the Medical College of Virginia. She stayed in Richmond as public health nurse from 1945 to 1946 and worked in the area of polio during the epidemic. She has been a Red Cross nurse since 1943 and a member of the American Nurses Association, Virginia Nurses Association, Medical College of Virginia Alumni Association, St. Philip School of Nursing Alumni Association, life member of Virginia Governmental Employees Association, and charter member of Club XXV. (Courtesy Charles W. White Sr.)

Three

OUR FAITH
Near and Far

Faith is the first factor in a life devoted to service. Without it, nothing is possible. With it, nothing is impossible.

—Mary McLeod Bethune (1875–1955)

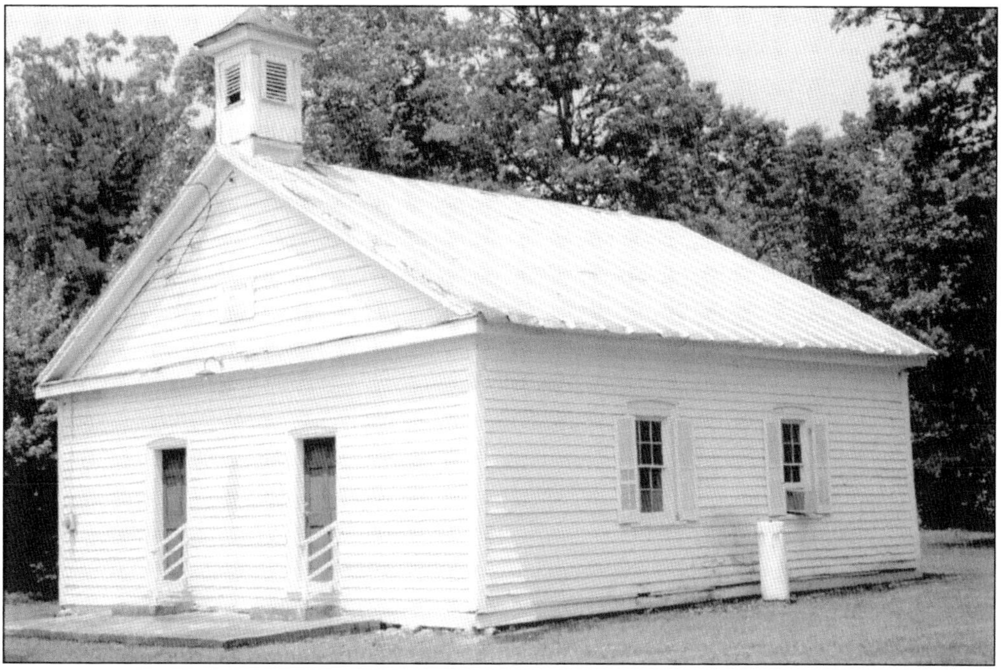

The Alexander Hill Baptist Church, pictured here, is Buckingham County's oldest African American church. In the summer of 1865, Rev. Gabriel Palmer organized the Alexander Hill Baptist Church with approximately 500 followers. The first structure was a brush arbor, and by 1867, the congregation relocated to a log building for worship. The church is located in the James River District of Buckingham County. (Courtesy E. Renée Ingram.)

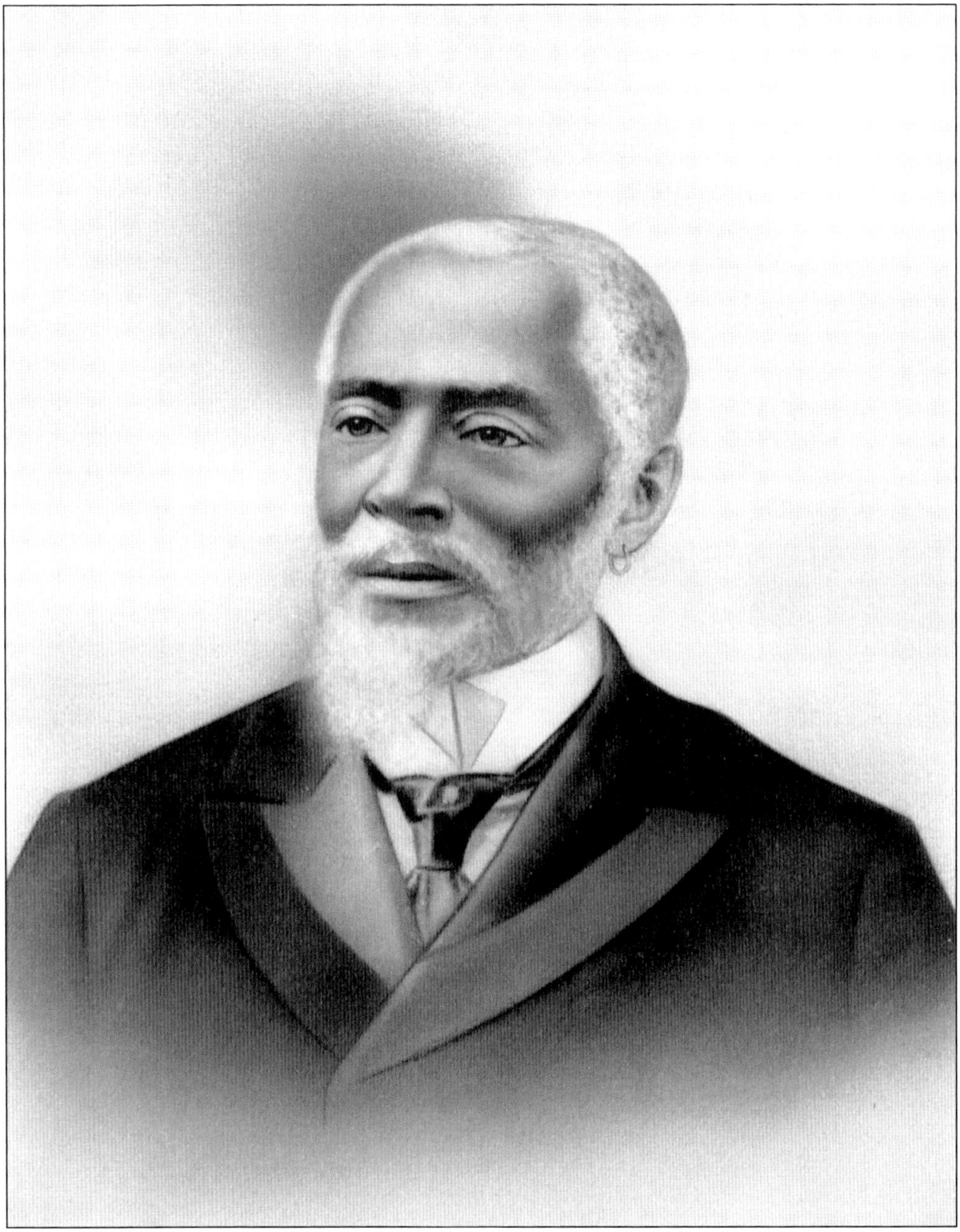

Rev. Watson Jennison was born into slavery about 1837 in the Marshall District of Buckingham County. Reverend Jennison became the second pastor of Baptist Union Baptist Church and served the congregation for 42 years. "Reverend Watt," as he was known, taught himself to read and write in a very extraordinary way. As a slave, he unloaded packet boats along the James River and Kanawha Canal and learn to read the advertisements on the fertilizer bags and other cargo. Because of his basic education, Dr. Carter G. Woodson wrote, "Reverend Jennison became a useful minister in Buckingham County." (Courtesy E. Renée Ingram.)

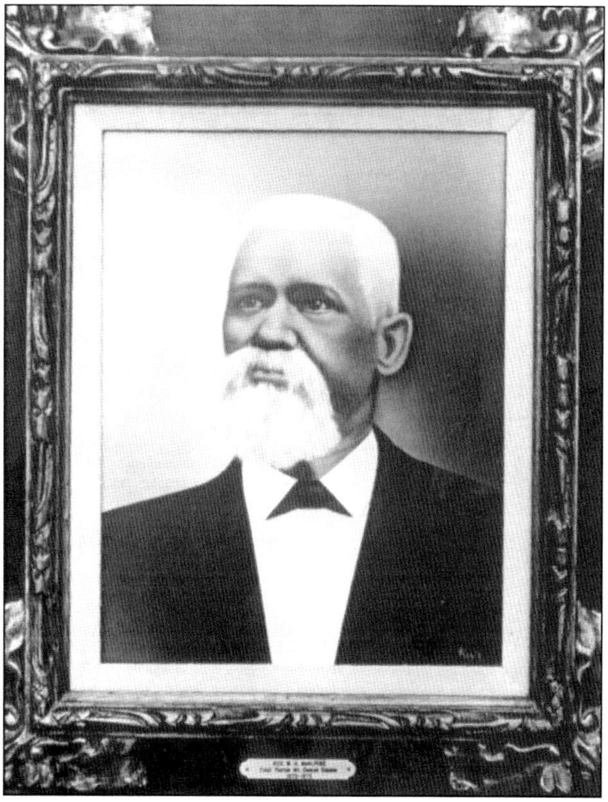

Rev. William H. McAlpine was born into slavery in Buckingham County in June 1847. In 1850, he, his mother, and his brother were carried to Alabama and sold by a slave trader to a Presbyterian minister named Dr. Robert McAlpine, whom he stayed with until the end of the Civil War. William H. McAlpine attended Talladega College. In 1869, he was licensed to preach and was ordained two years later. Reverend McAlpine became the first president of the National Baptist Convention and served two terms. He was the founder and second president of Alabama Baptist Normal and Theological School (Selma University). McAlpine was also the editor of an Alabama newspaper entitled *Baptist Pioneer.* (Courtesy *Jet Magazine*, Johnson Publishing Company.)

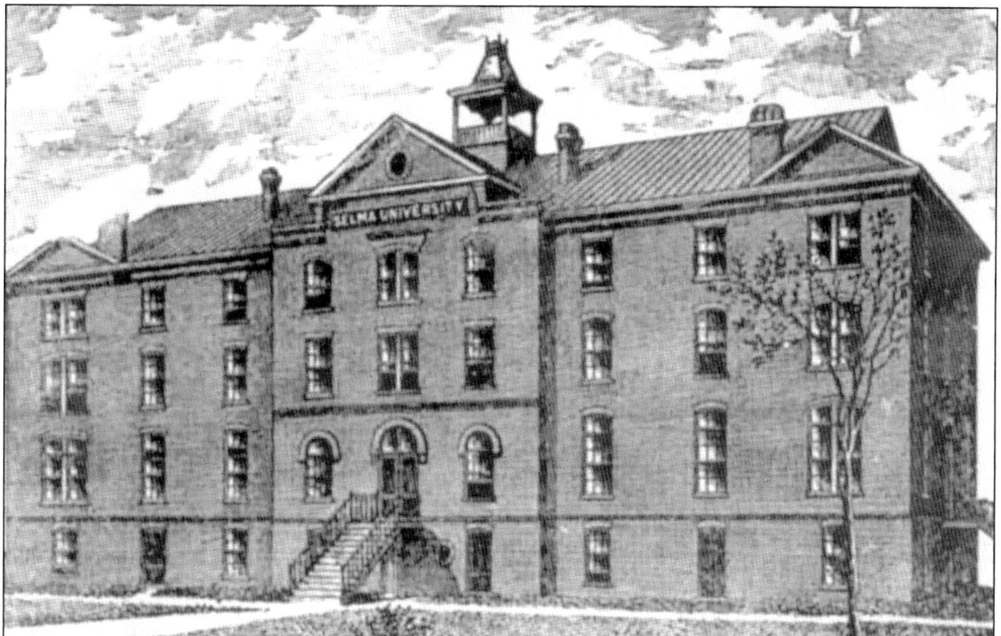

This is an illustration of Alabama Baptist Normal and Theological School (Selma University), *c.* 1890. (Courtesy *The Cyclopedia of the Colored Baptists of Alabama: Their Leaders and Their Work*, Birmingham: Alabama Publishing Company, 1895.)

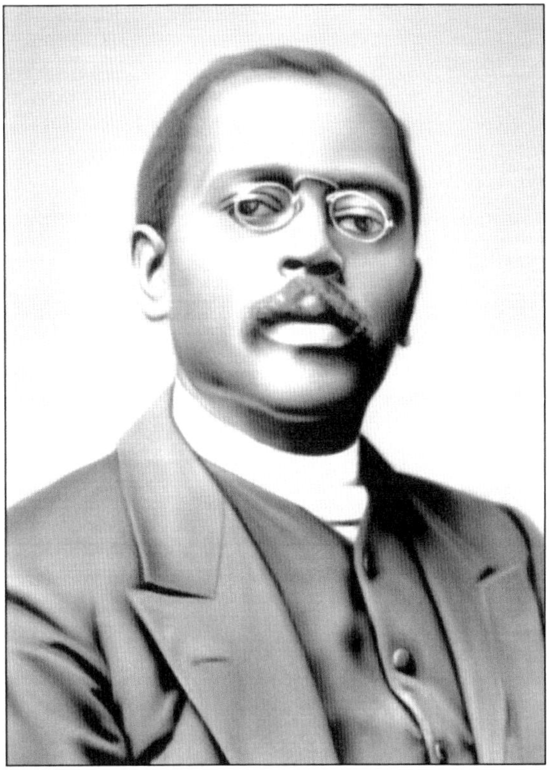

Rev. Richard Spiller, D.D., born in June 1851 in Buckingham County, was the son of William and Delphia Spiller. Reverend Spiller was pastor of the First Baptist Church in Hampton, Virginia, and a leading organizer of the Virginia Baptist State Convention. He was founder and principal of Spiller Academy (Tidewater Institute), *c.* 1891. On June 23, 1894, he wrote: "I attribute my success largely to the training I received at the Richmond Institute, combined with the early training of my parents." (Courtesy Moorland-Spingarn Research Center, Howard University.)

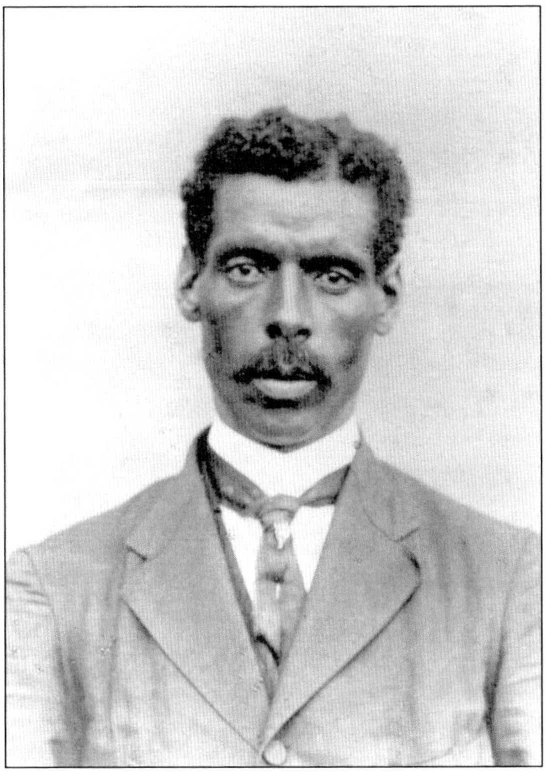

Alexander Trent, born about 1874, became the third pastor at Baptist Union Baptist Church following Rev. Watson Jennison. He served as pastor for 25 years, from 1912 until his death in 1937. (Courtesy E. Renée Ingram.)

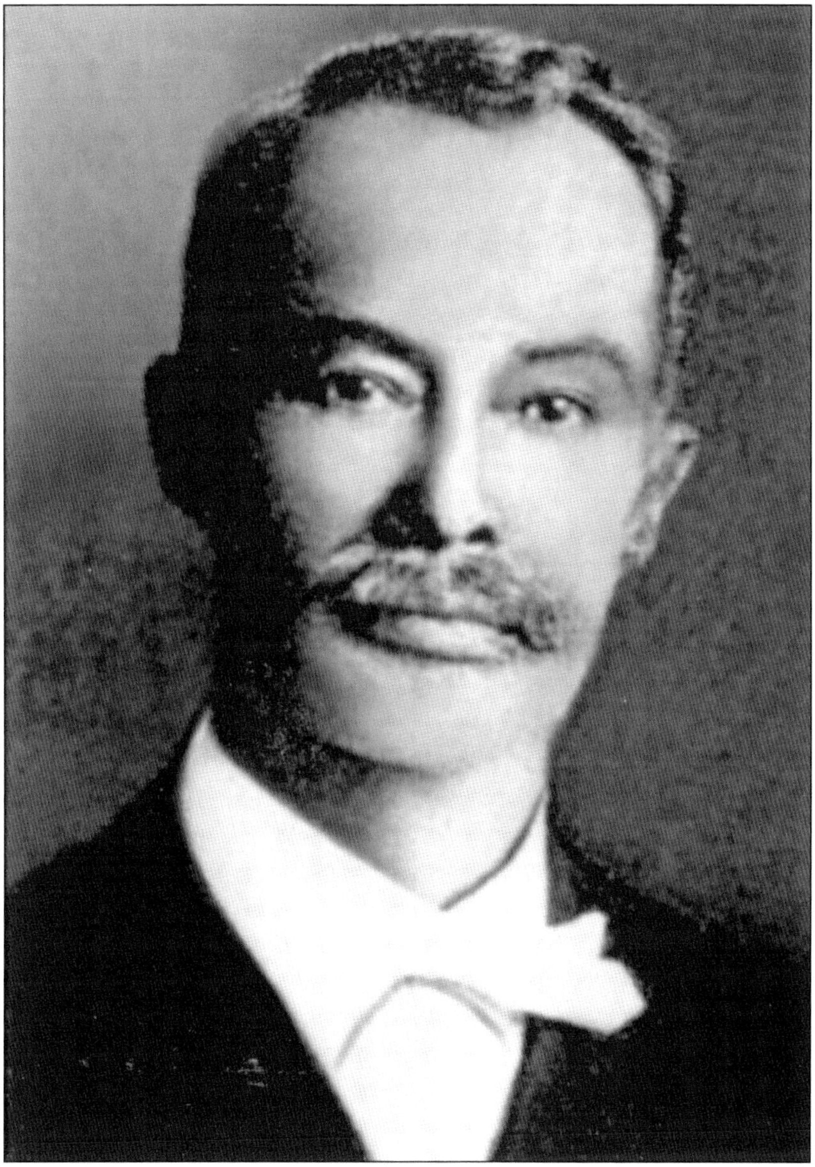

Rev. James M. Riddle, D.D., born on May 15, 1860, into slavery in Buckingham County, was the son of Henry and Susan Riddle. His early childhood was embroiled with many severe whippings for refusing to call the little children of his owner "Master" and "Miss." At the end of the Civil War, James Riddle was able to obtain an education, and at the age of 18, he began his career as a public school teacher. By the age of 22, he was elected justice of the peace, and within two years, he became a licensed preacher. In the early 20th century, his religious work took him to Rendville, Ohio, where he was involved with the Ministerial Institute and Western Union Baptist Association and became its critic. He also served as president of the Ohio Baptist State Convention for 13 years. Reverend Riddle was one of the editors of the *Columbus Standard* newspaper. By 1915, Reverend Riddle had relocated to Pasadena, California, and served as pastor of the Friendship Baptist Church until 1917. During his pastorate, the church became affiliated with the Northern Baptist Convention. (Courtesy Friendship Baptist Church, Pasadena, California.)

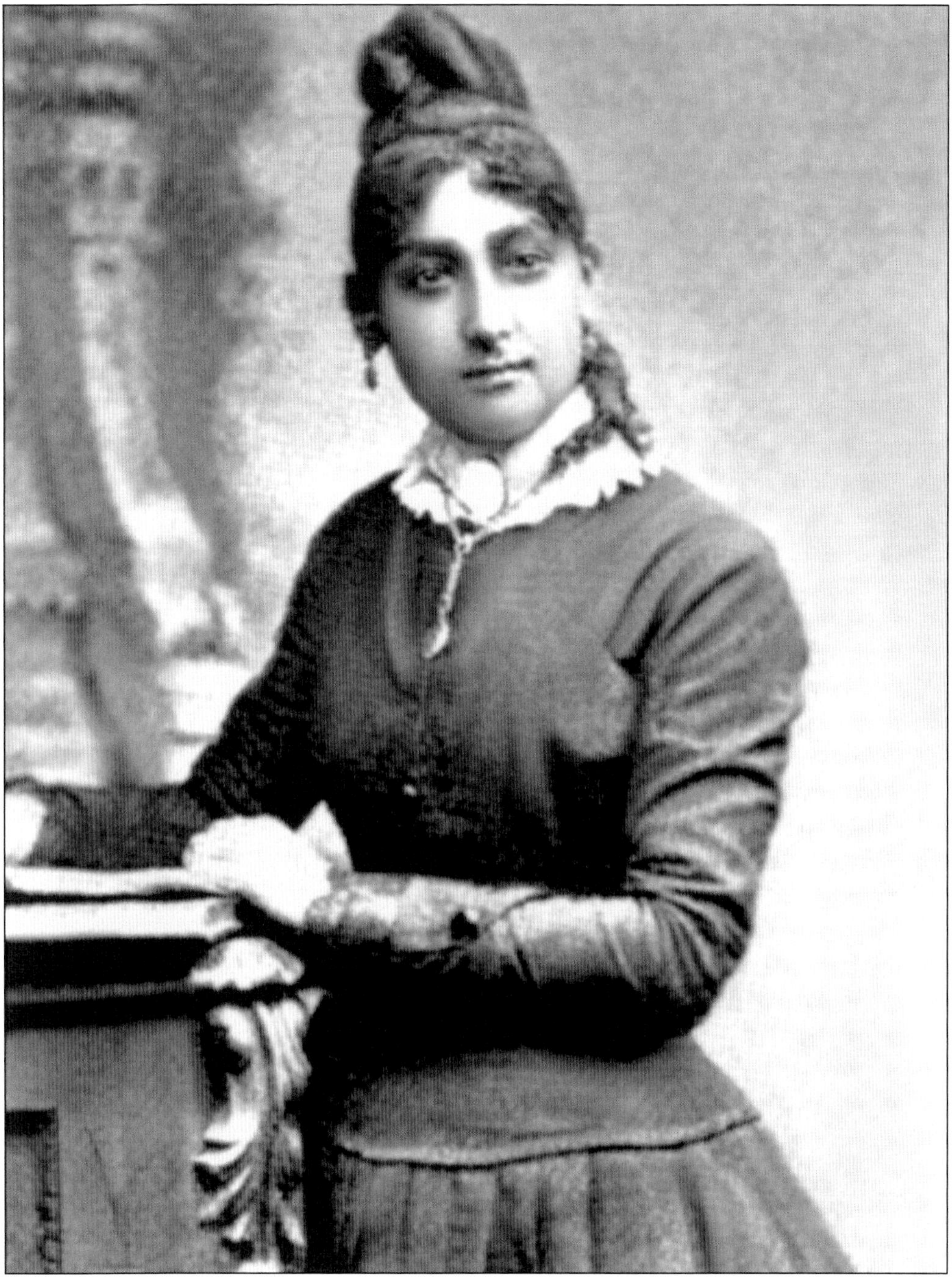

Harriette (Hattie) Estelle (Harris) Presley was born in 1862, the daughter of Emily Mills. She attended Richmond Institute (Richmond Theological Seminary). On May 29, 1883, she married Rev. James H. Presley, and on December 1, 1883, they set sail to Africa, where they began their missionary work. Tragically, Estelle Presley became ill and subsequently died in Africa. In the publication *Women of Distinction: Remarkable in Work*, she was described as follows: "In her death the mission has lost a vigorous and energetic worker." (Courtesy Moorland-Spingarn Research Center, Howard University.)

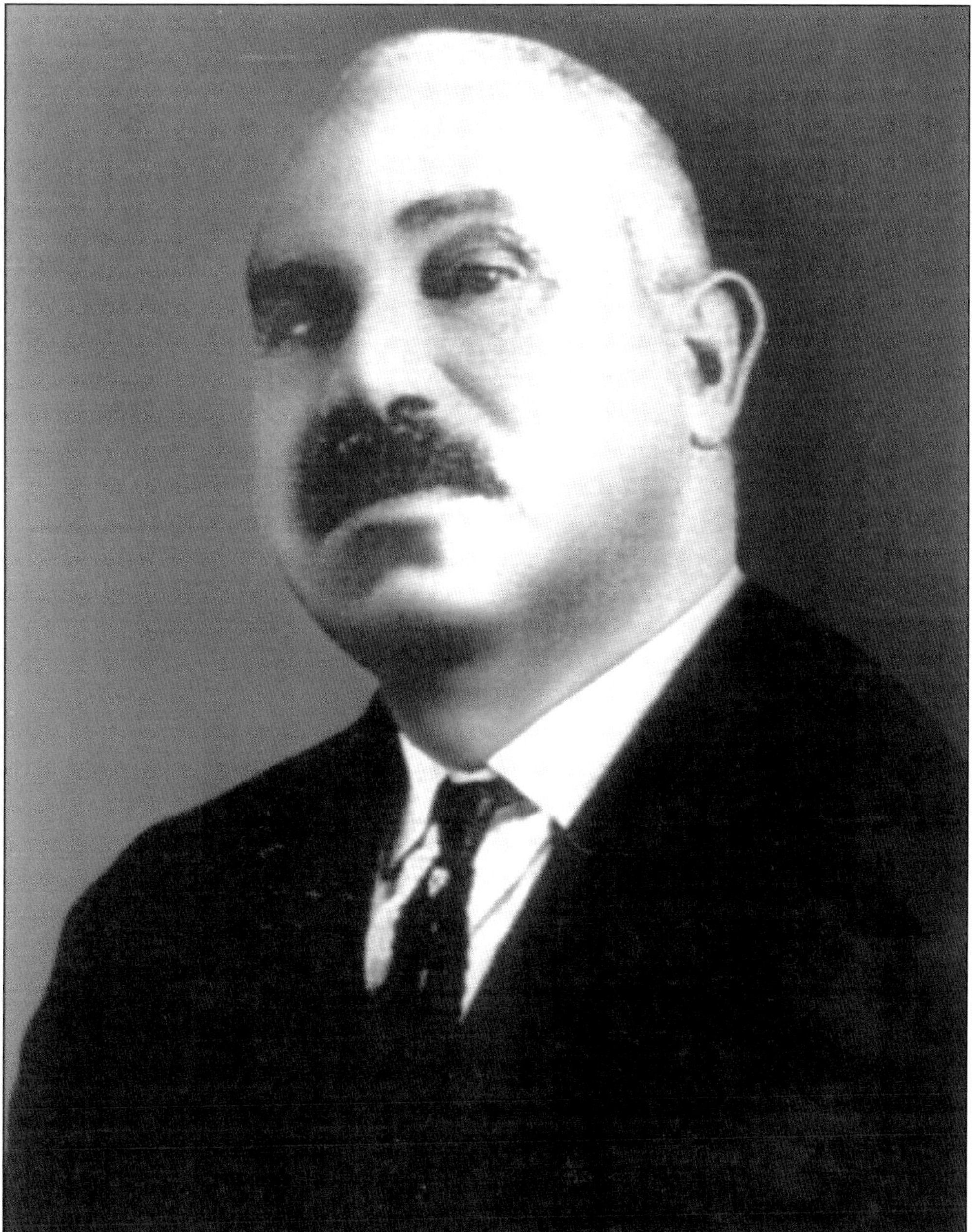

Rev. Stephen J. Ellis, born in 1871 in the Curdsville District of Buckingham County, led the effort to build a black high school in Buckingham County. He called together local ministers and community leaders concerned about the lack of secondary educational opportunities in the county. As a result of Reverend Ellis's community activism, Buckingham County Training School opened in 1924. (Courtesy of Charles W. White Sr.)

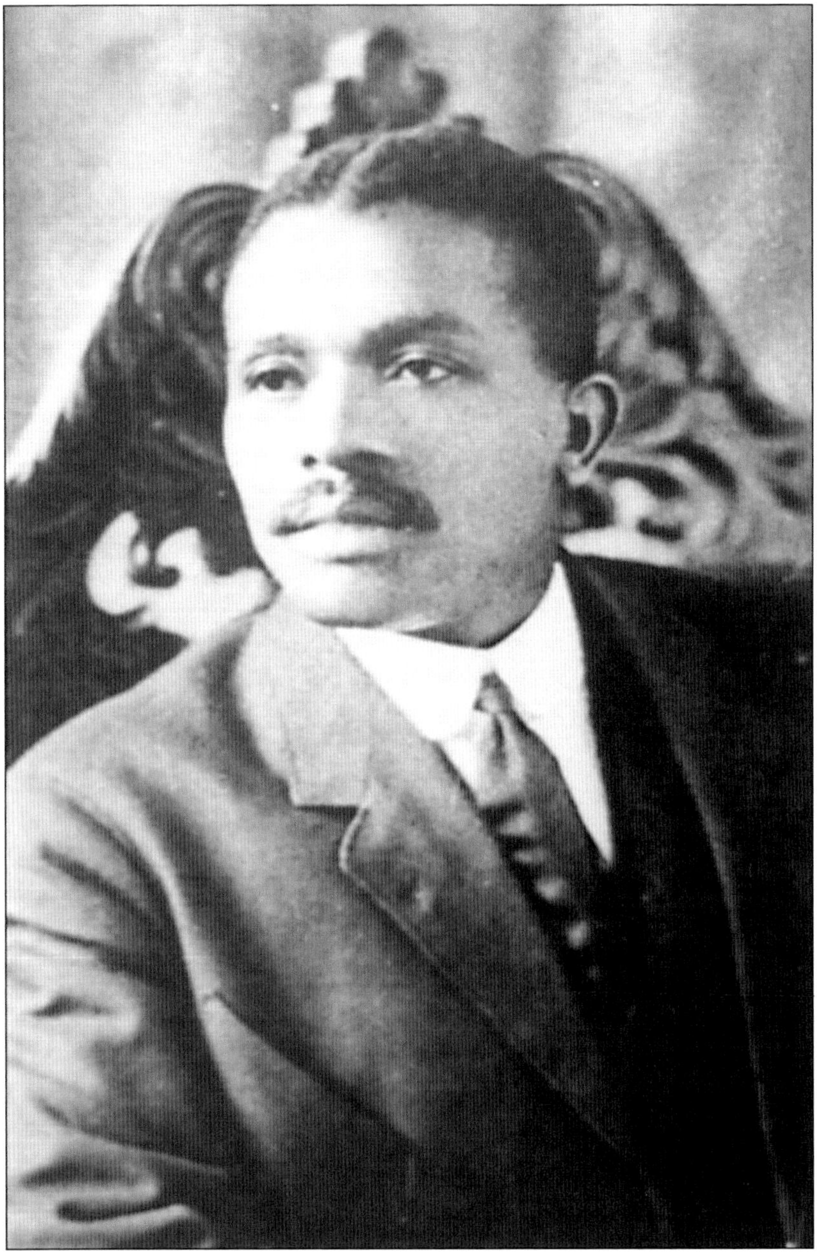

Rev. Oscar Conklin Jones, D.D., was born in Arvonia, in the Marshall District, on January 1, 1876. He was the son of Oscar and Louvenia (Young) Jones. Jones began his early education in Arvonia and continued his education at the West Virginia Colored Institute (West Virginia State University) and Virginia Union University, where he graduated in 1900 with a bachelor of divinity degree. Reverend Jones first served at Mount Zion Baptist Church in Fairmont, West Virginia, and moved to Georgia, where he served at Friendship Baptist Church in Toccoa and Flagg Chapel Baptist Church in Milledgeville. His alma mater, Virginia Union University, conferred upon him an honorary degree of Doctor of Divinity. Dr. Jones returned to Virginia, where he served at Mount Hermon Baptist Church in Portsmouth from 1911 to 1959. (Courtesy Willard A. Stanback.)

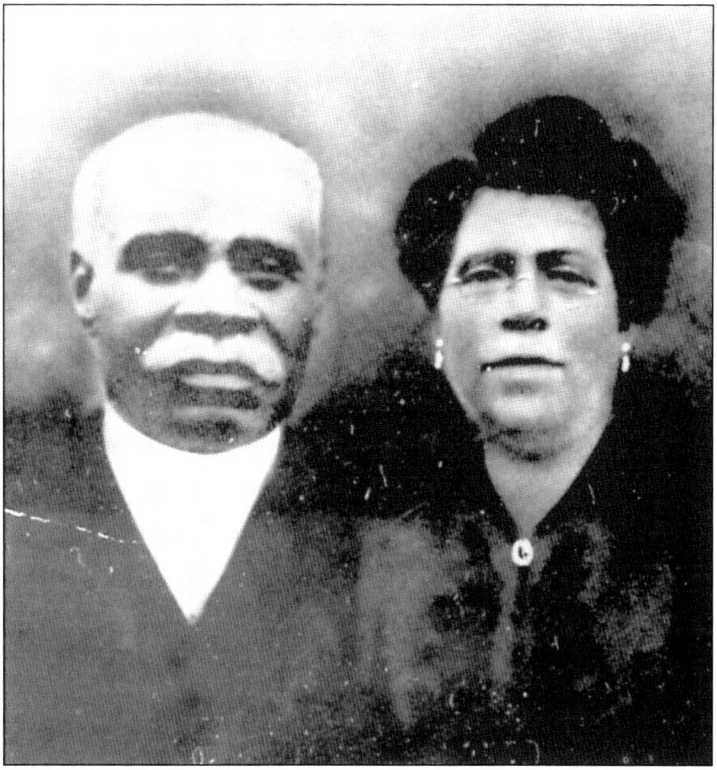

This is a portrait of the Rev. Robert and Mrs. Emma Daniel. Reverend Daniel was the founder and first pastor of St. Joy Baptist Church, located in the James River District of Buckingham County. The St. Joy Baptist Church was established in 1871. (Courtesy Charles W. White Sr.)

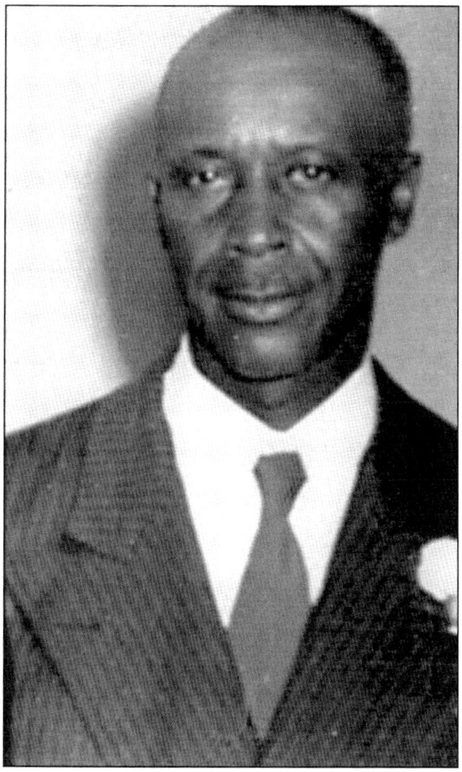

The Reverend John E. "J. E." Tyree served at Chief Cornerstone Baptist Church in the town of Dillwyn for 33 years and served as a revivalist at many churches in Buckingham County. (Courtesy Eliza T. Spencer.)

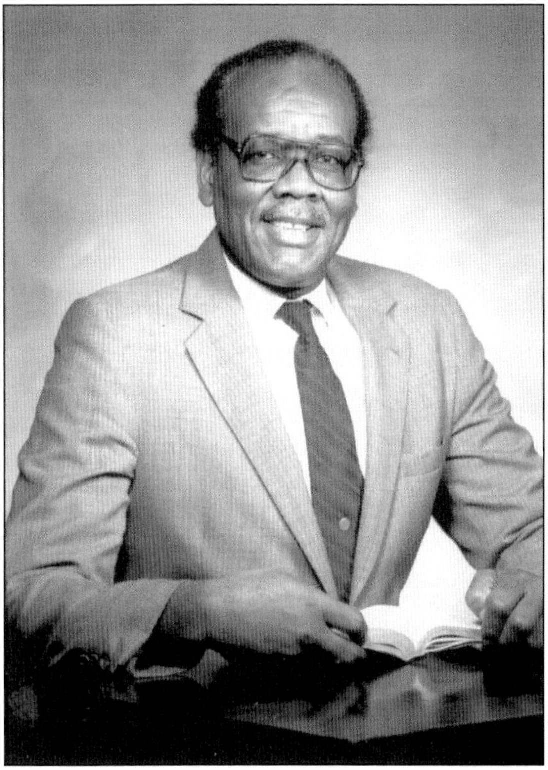

The Reverend Johnnie W. Steed serves at the Jerusalem Baptist Church and has served other county churches as well, including New Hope Baptist Church, First Liberty Baptist Church, and Ridgeway Baptist Church. (Courtesy Rev. Johnnie W. Steed.)

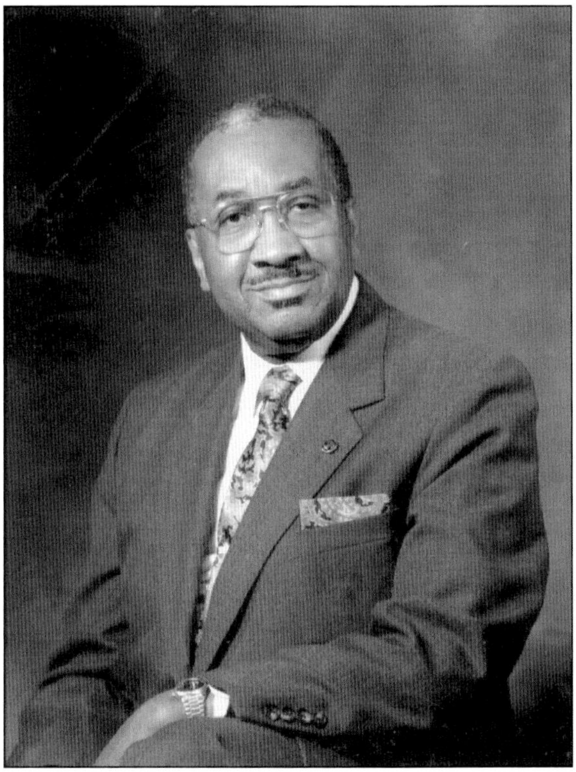

The Reverend Dr. Donald Winston Johnson has served as pastor at Mount Nebo Baptist Church for the past 10 years. Mount Nebo Baptist Church, which was established in 1872, is located in Willis Mountain in the Curdsville District of Buckingham County. (Courtesy Rev. Dr. Donald Winston Johnson.)

Rev. Denzel H. Washington was born October 5, 1909, in the Curdsville District of Buckingham County. He was the son of William and Virginia Washington. Reverend Washington served at the Church of God in Christ. The late Reverend Washington is the father of Academy Award–winning actor Denzel Washington. (Courtesy of Charles W. White Sr.)

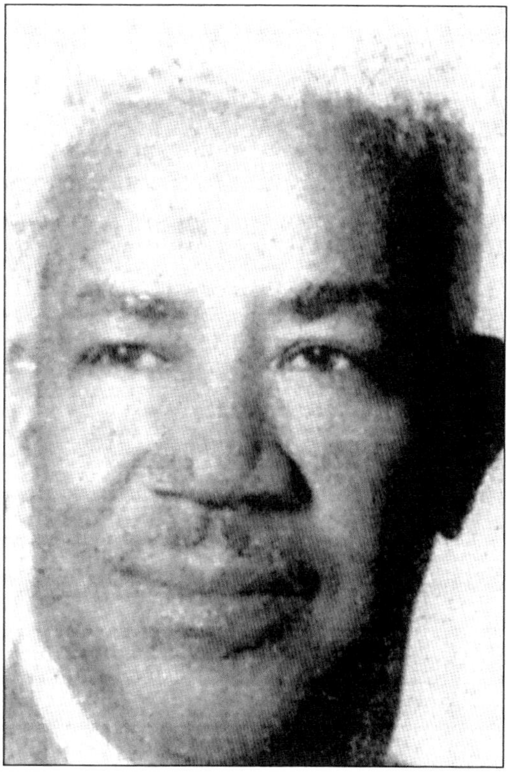

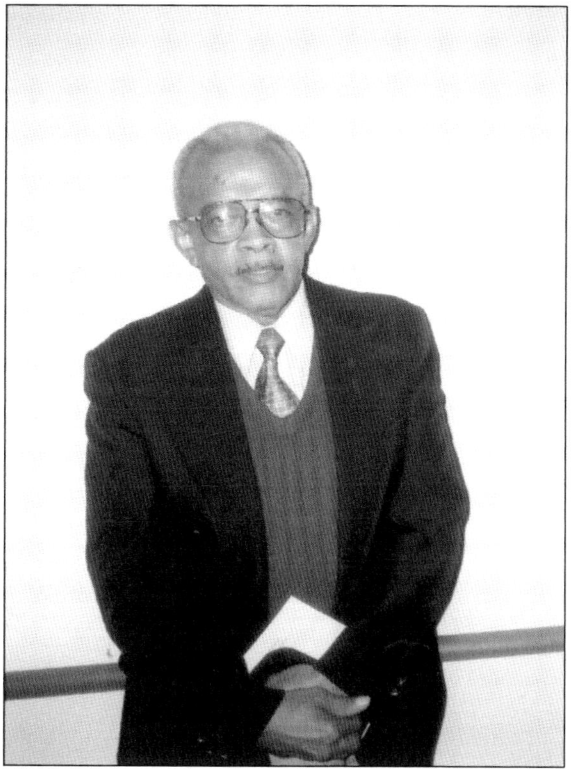

Rev. Charley M. Smith has served as pastor at Mount Olive Baptist Church for the past 11 years. Mount Olive Baptist Church, which was established in 1865, is located in the town of Dillwyn in Buckingham County. (Courtesy Charles W. White Sr.)

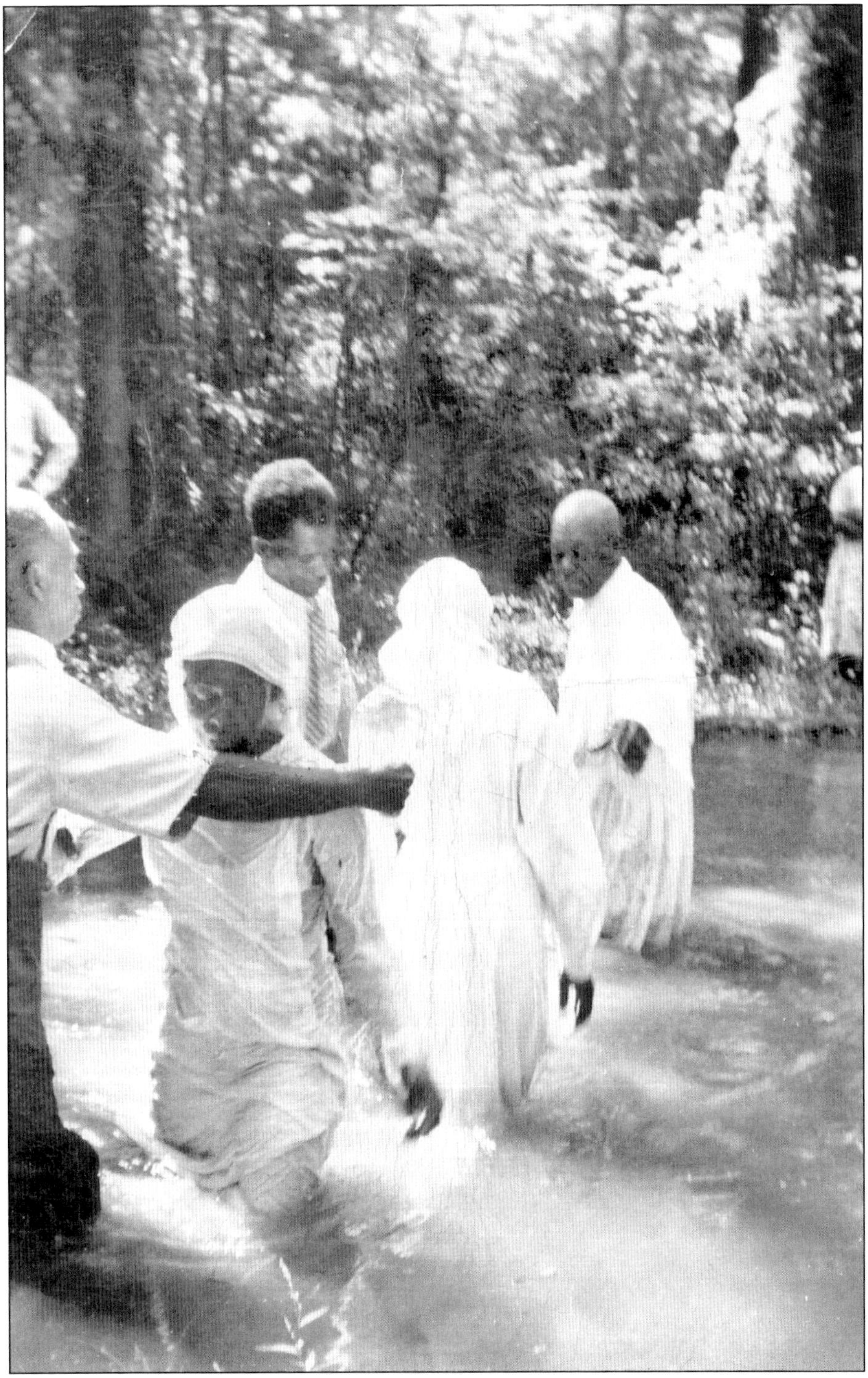

Taken in 1964, this photograph is of a traditional baptism at the Salem Baptist Church. The Salem Baptist Church was established in 1875 and is located in the James River District of Buckingham County. Historically, baptisms were administered in creeks and rivers; however, this tradition is rarely used today. (Courtesy Irene Cottrell Collection.)

This is a photograph of a vacation Bible school class at the Union Hill Baptist Church taken in the summer of 1960. The Union Hill Baptist Church, which was founded in 1868, is located the James River District of Buckingham County. (Courtesy John Laury Jr.)

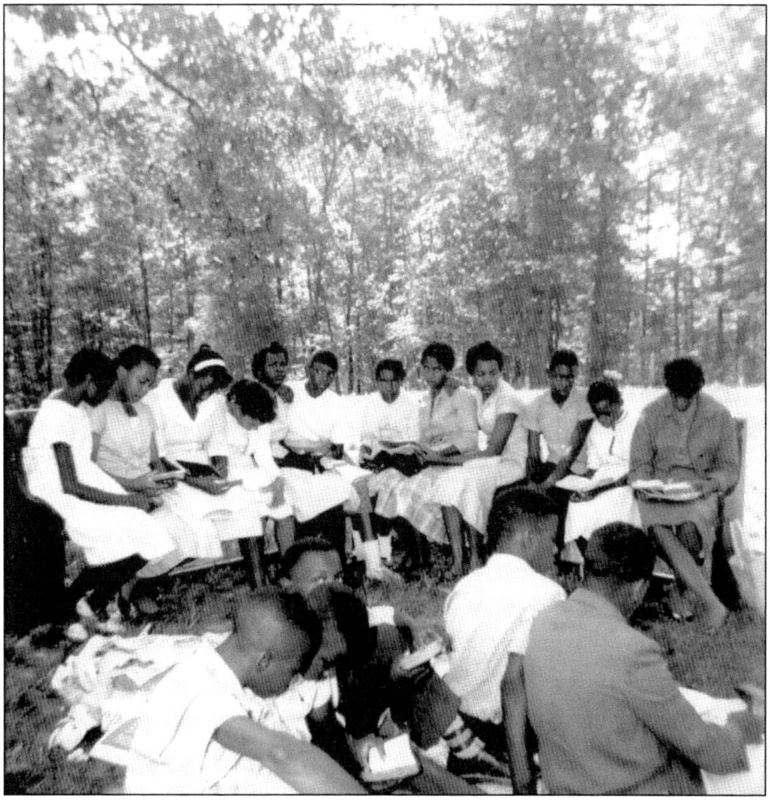

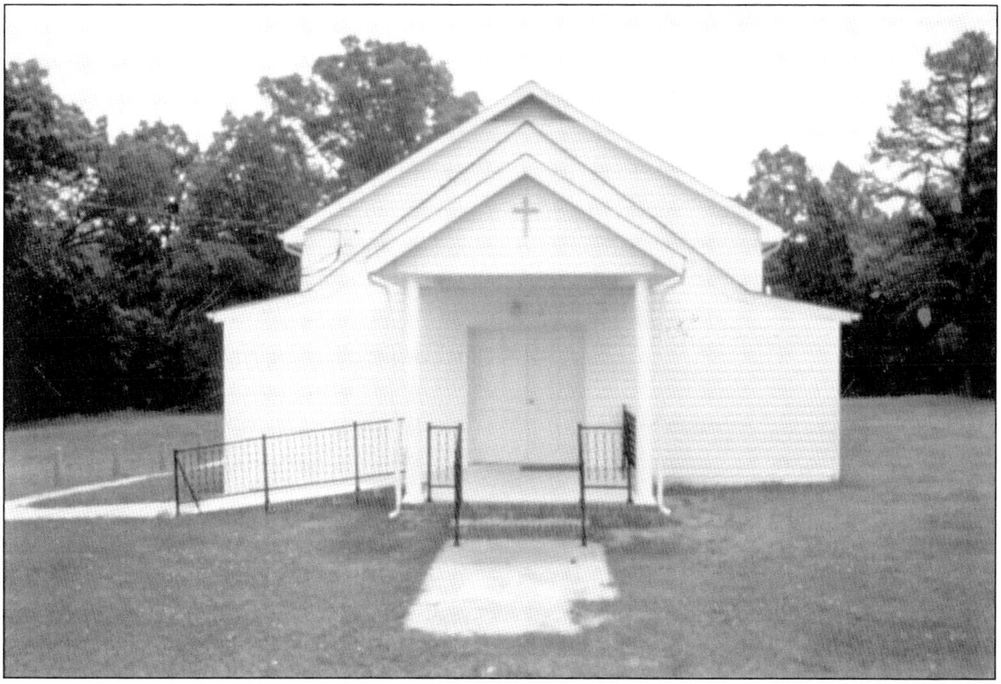

The Union Grove Baptist Church, shown above, was established in 1912 and is located in the James River District of Buckingham County. (Courtesy Charles W. White Sr.)

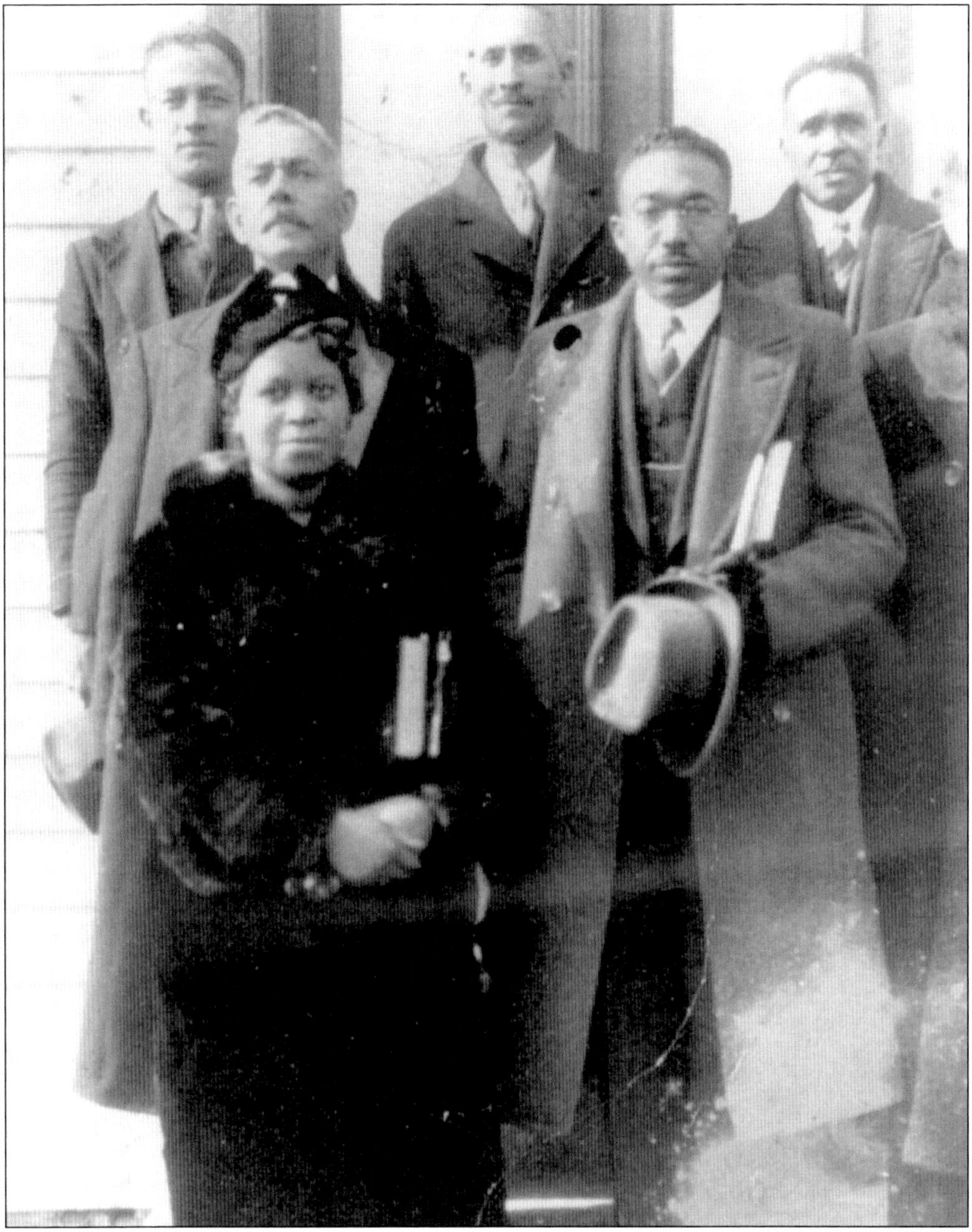

The First Liberty Baptist Church officers shown in this *c.* 1945 photograph are, from left to right, (first row) Mrs. Carrie Moseley; (second row) Deacon Nathaniel Morgan and Rev. Benjamin Bunn; (third row) Joseph Anderson, Deacon William Osborne, and Deacon Eddie Moseley. First Liberty Baptist Church, which was established in 1866, is located in the Maysville District of Buckingham County. (Courtesy Janie M. Osborne.)

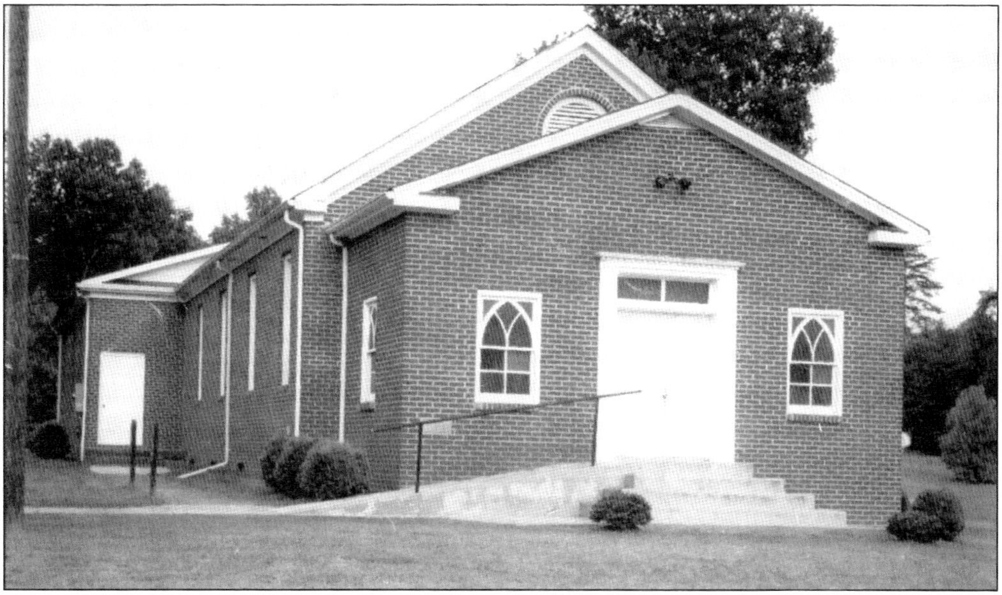

The Fork Union Baptist Church, pictured here, was founded in 1868. It is located in Buckingham, in the Maysville District of Buckingham County. (Courtesy Charles W. White Sr.)

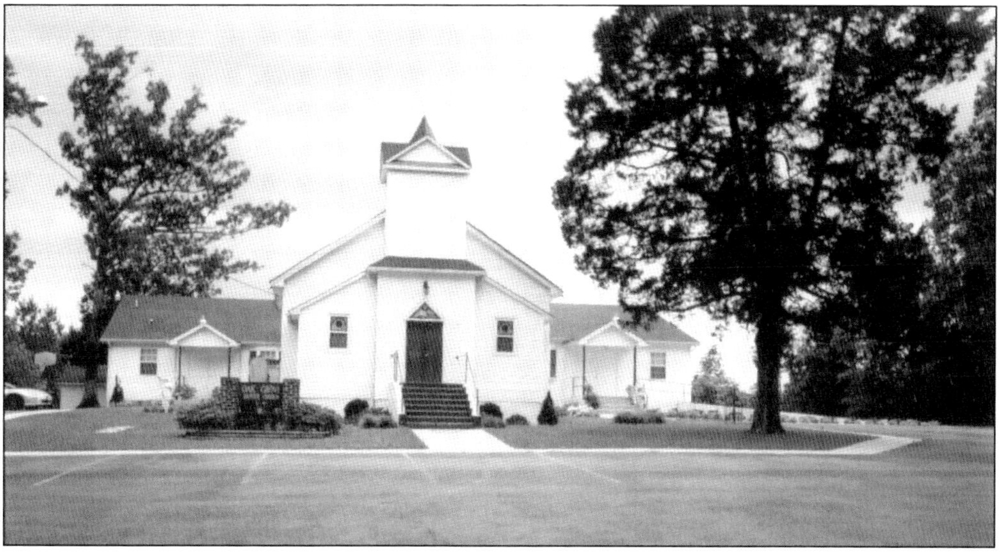

Shown in the photograph above is the Oak Grove Baptist Church, which is located in the Curdsville District of Buckingham County. Oak Grove Baptist Church was established in 1871. (Courtesy Charles W. White Sr.)

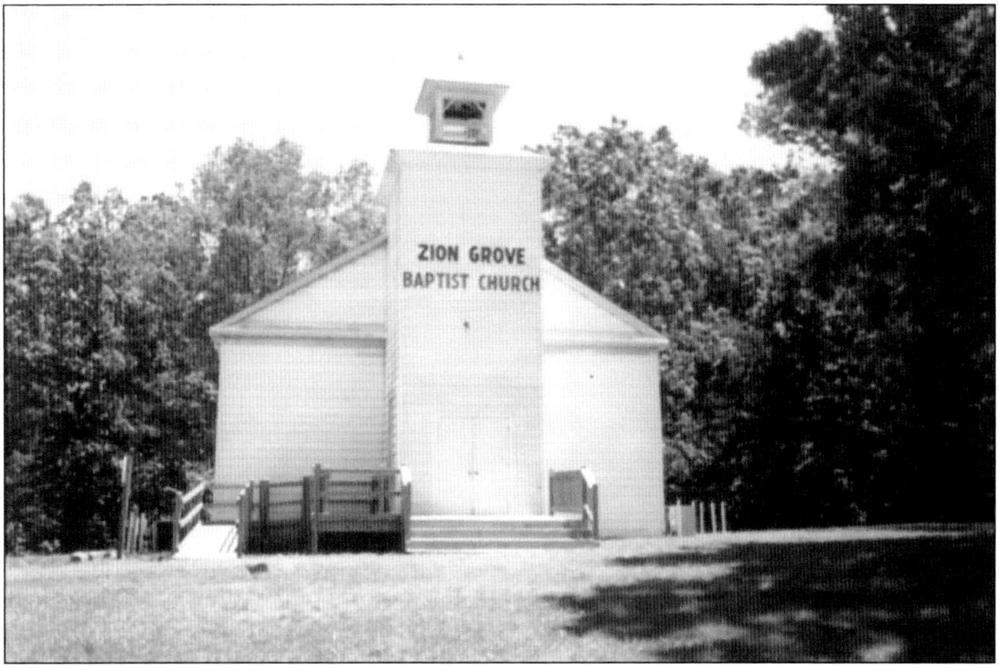

The Zion Grove Baptist Church, shown in this photograph, is located in the Marshall District of Buckingham County. The Zion Grove Baptist Church was established in 1871. (Courtesy Charles W. White Sr.)

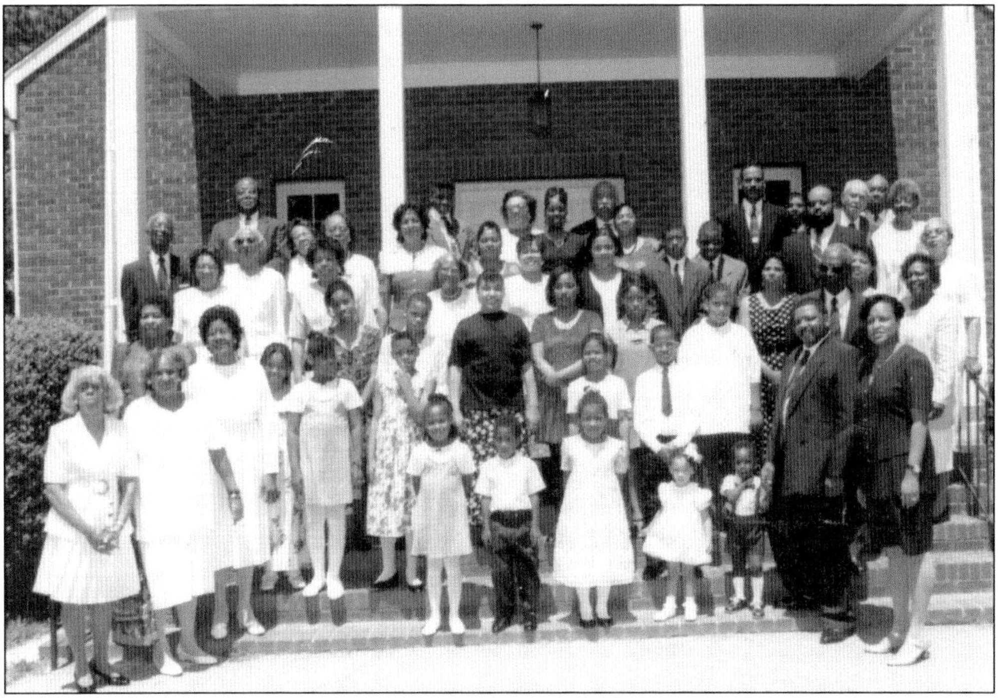

Several members of the Jerusalem Baptist Church stand in front of their church entrance. The Jerusalem Baptist Church, which was established in 1896, is located in the James River District of Buckingham County. (Courtesy Charles W. White Sr.)

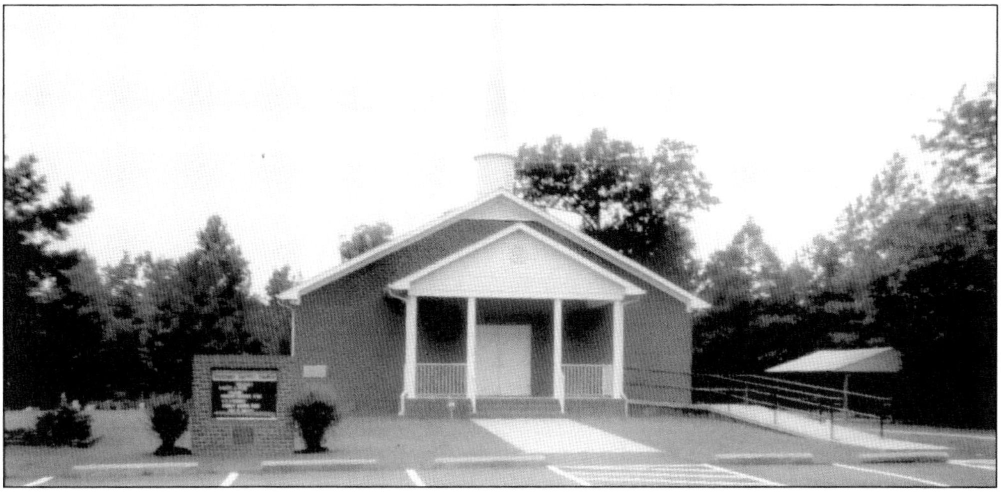

The Ridgeway Baptist Church (Scottsville) was established *c.* 1870. It is located in the Slate River District of Buckingham County. (Courtesy Charles W. White Sr.)

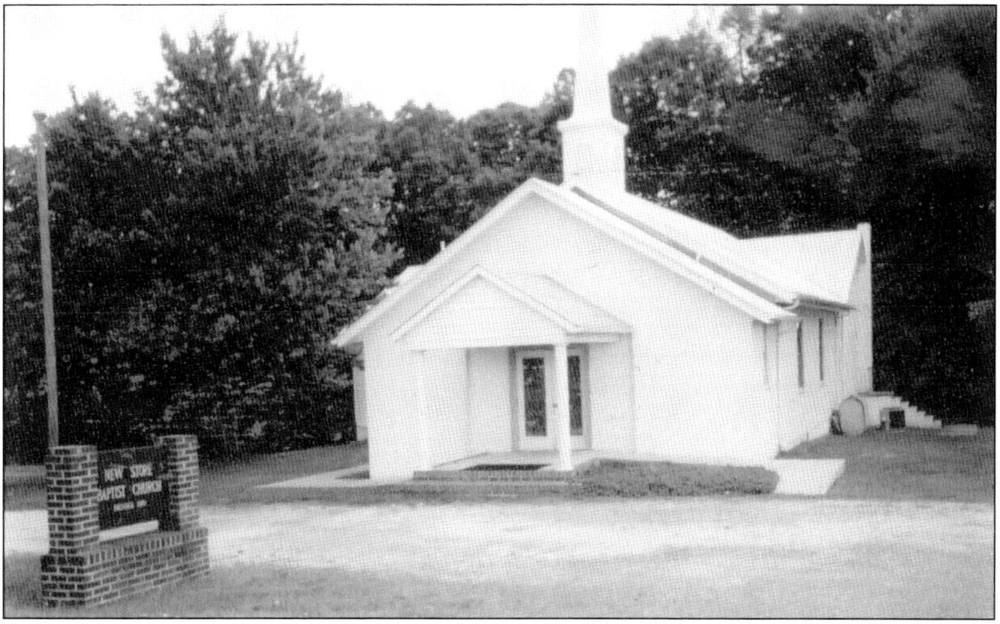

The New Store Baptist Church, located in the Francisco District of Buckingham County, was founded in 1870. (Courtesy Charles W. White Sr.)

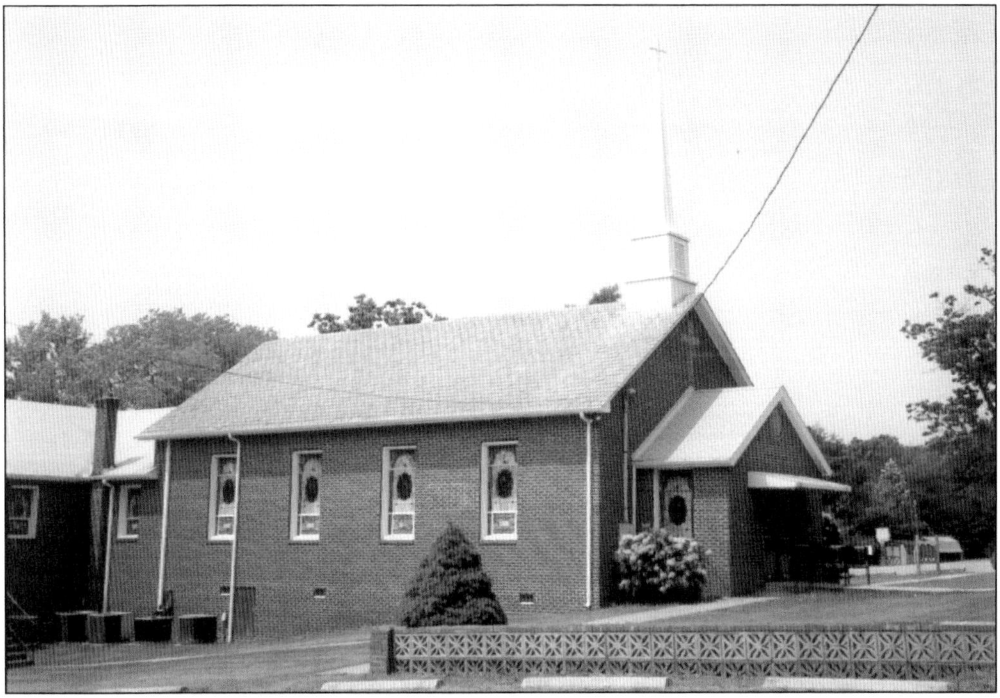

The Baptist Union Baptist Church, shown in this photograph, was established in 1868 with Rev. Samuel Harris as its first pastor. The Baptist Union Baptist Church is located in the Marshall District of Buckingham County. (Courtesy E. Renée Ingram.)

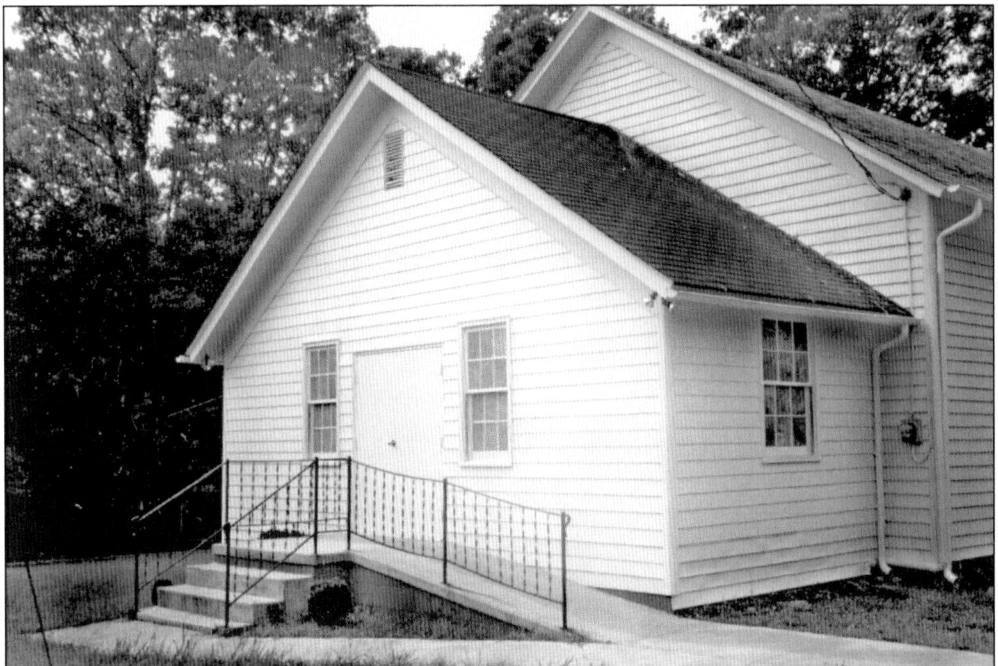

The New Hope Baptist Church, pictured here, was established in 1881 and is located in Gold Hill in the Marshall District of Buckingham County. (Courtesy E. Renée Ingram.)

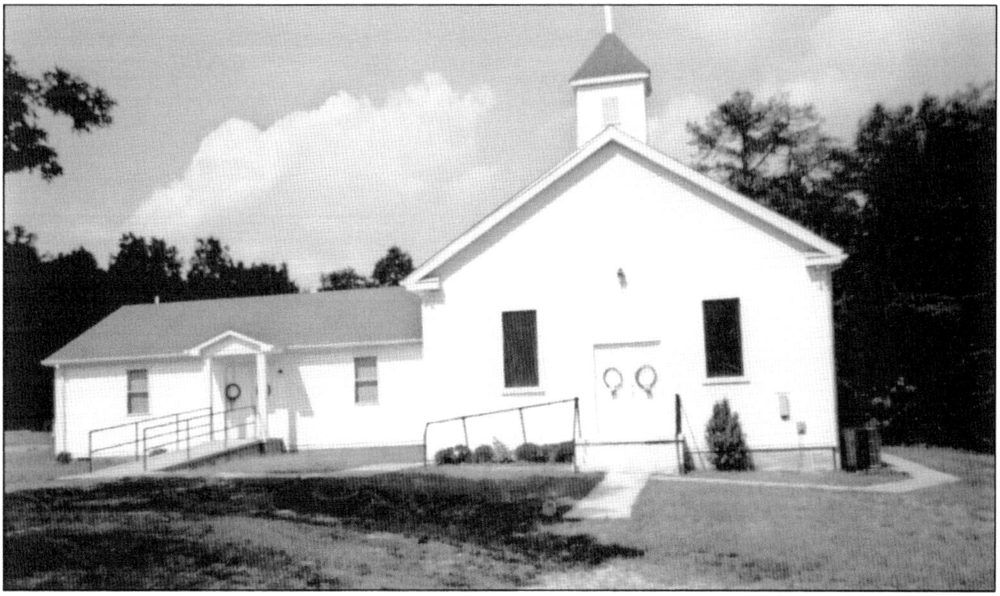

This is a photograph of the Holy Trinity Baptist Church, which was established in 1915. The Holy Trinity Baptist Church is located in Willis Mountain in the Curdsville District of Buckingham County. (Courtesy Charles W. White Sr.)

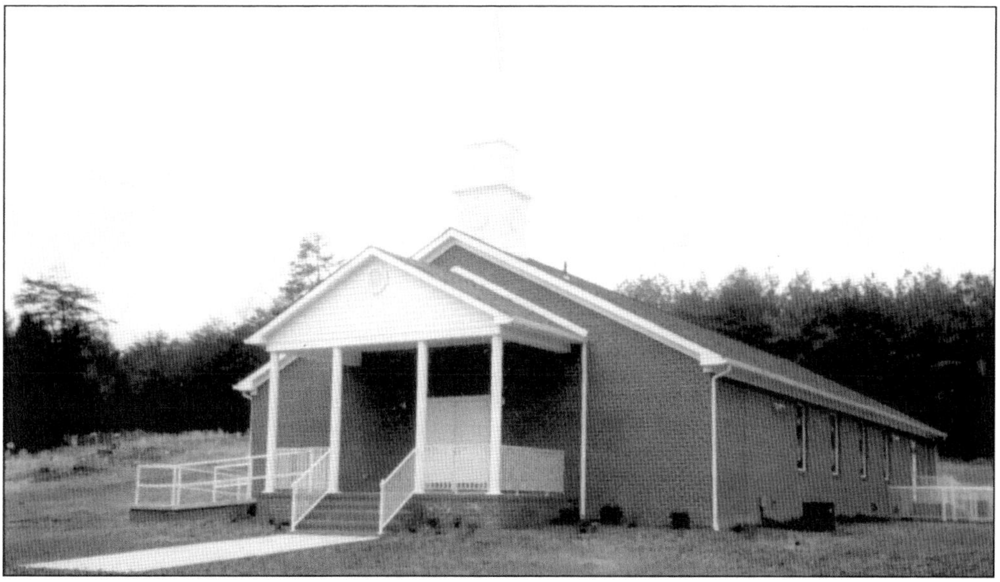

Shown above is the Mourner's Valley Baptist Church, which was established in 1882. This church is located in the Maysville District of Buckingham County. (Courtesy Charles W. White Sr.)

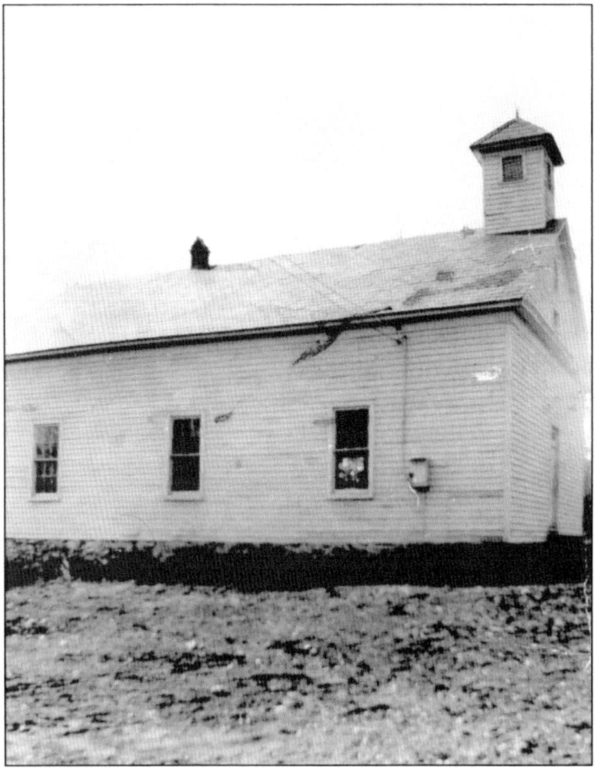

The Third Liberty Baptist Church's first building, seen here, was a wooden structure. This church was founded in 1865. (Courtesy Edith Jones.)

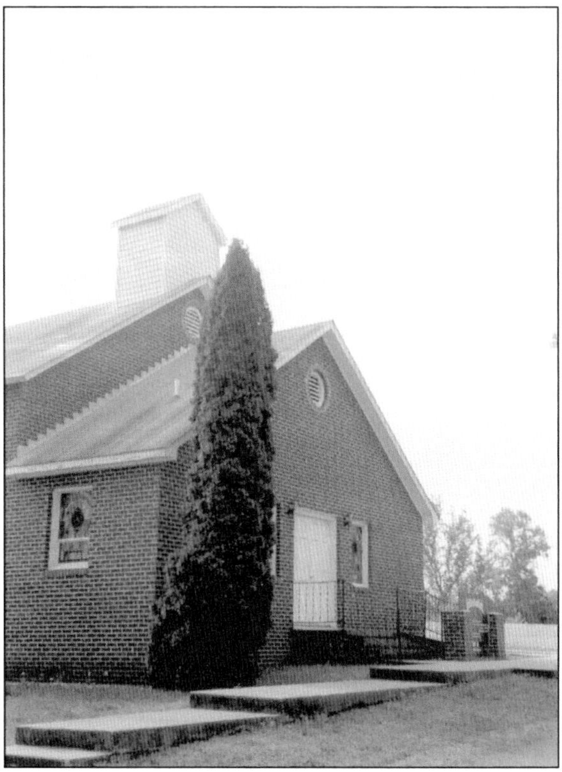

This is a photograph of the Third Liberty Baptist Church, which is located in New Canton in the Marshall District of Buckingham County, as it appears today. (Courtesy E. Renée Ingram.)

Four

Reflections on Our Education

The only way to get equality is for two people to get the same thing at the same time at the same place.

—Thurgood Marshall (1908–1993)

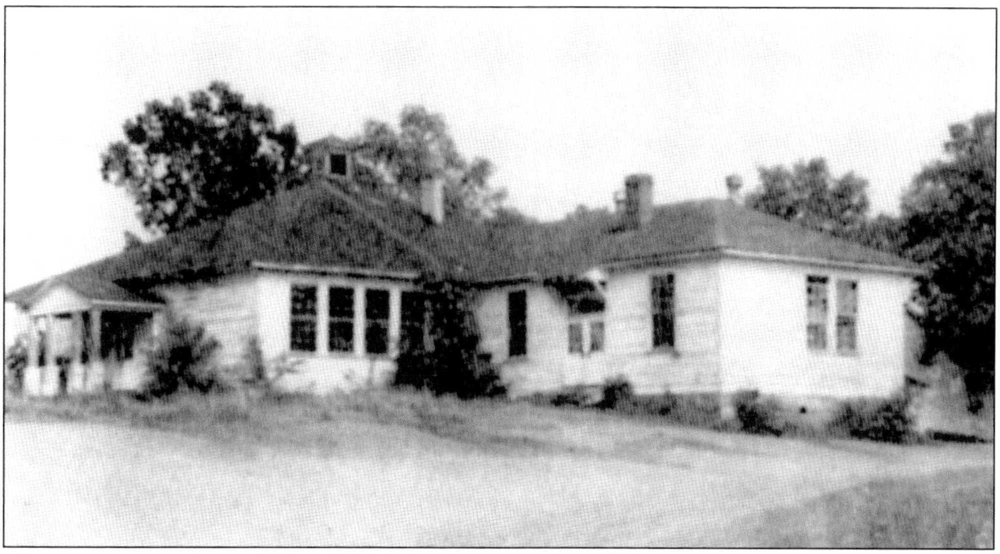

The Buckingham County Training School, which opened in 1924, was the first high school for African American students in the county. This school faced many challenges in being built with a cost of $6,100. The county's school board stated that it would not provide funding, and the $1,100 Rosenwald matching funds for the school would have to be raised by the parents. Under the leadership of Rev. Stephen J. Ellis and the newly organized countywide League for School Improvements, the funds were raised. The school opened in 1924, with Thomas L. Dabney as its principal, and served the community until it closed in 1953. (Courtesy Charles W. White Sr.)

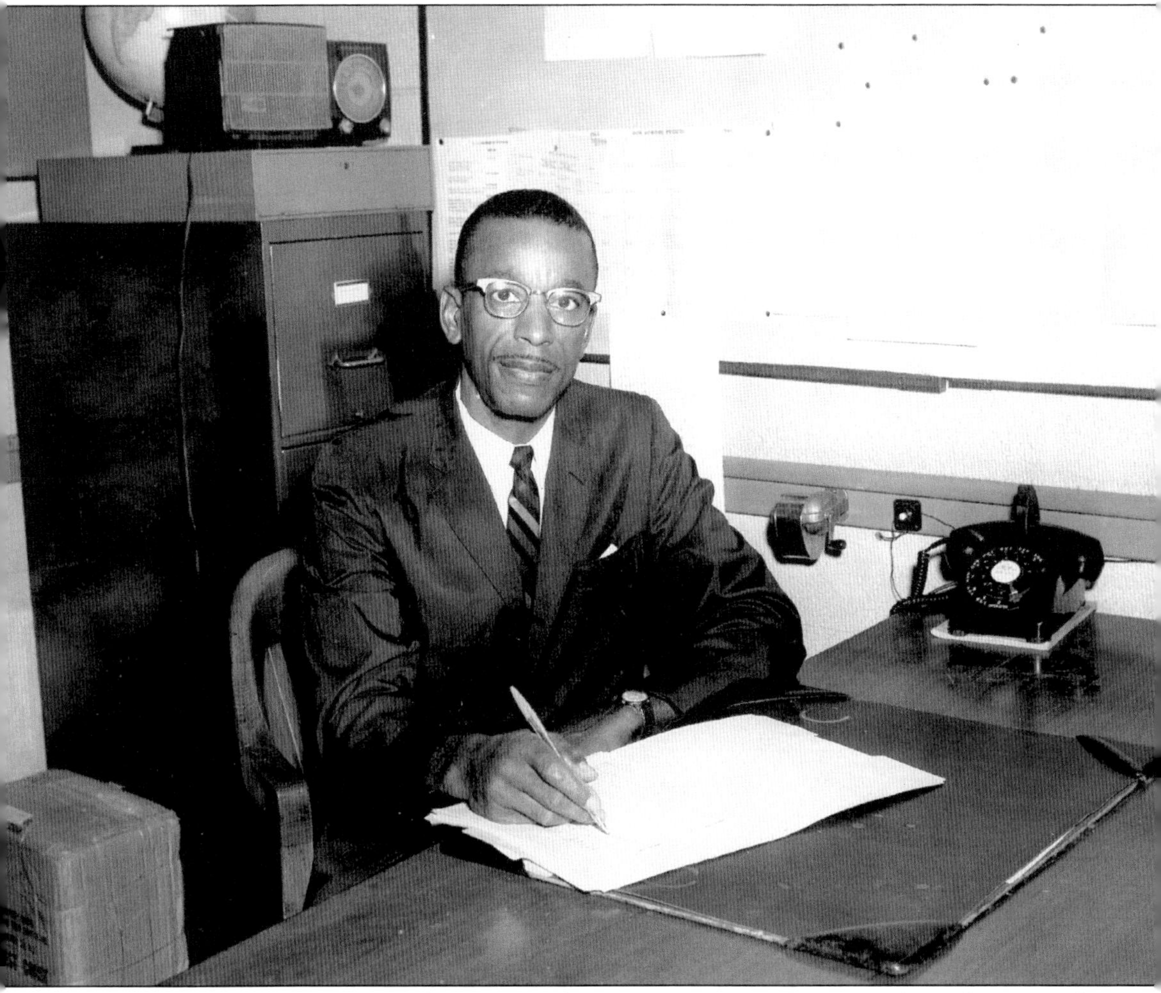

George Frank Harris, son of George and Annie Harris, was born in a log cabin near the Glenmore area of the James River District in Buckingham County. George Frank Harris was educated in the county school system and graduated from the Buckingham County Training School in 1934. He graduated from the School of Agriculture at Virginia State College (Virginia State University) and held a teaching position in Gloucester County, Virginia. Eventually George Frank Harris returned to Buckingham County, became one of the leading black educators, and held the second highest administrative position in the county public school system. In addition to serving in the public school system, Harris held several civic leadership positions in the county, including president of the Association for Study of Afro-American Life and History. (Courtesy George Frank Harris.)

Jeanette (Logan) White, born in March 1891 in the Marshall District of Buckingham County, was the only daughter of Archer and Mary F. Logan. She taught elementary school in the county. Many of the elementary schools were only open for five months out of the year; however, teachers volunteered to keep schools open for an extended period of time. Many teachers, including Mrs. White, worked for several months without pay from the county school board. (Courtesy Richard A. Stanton III.)

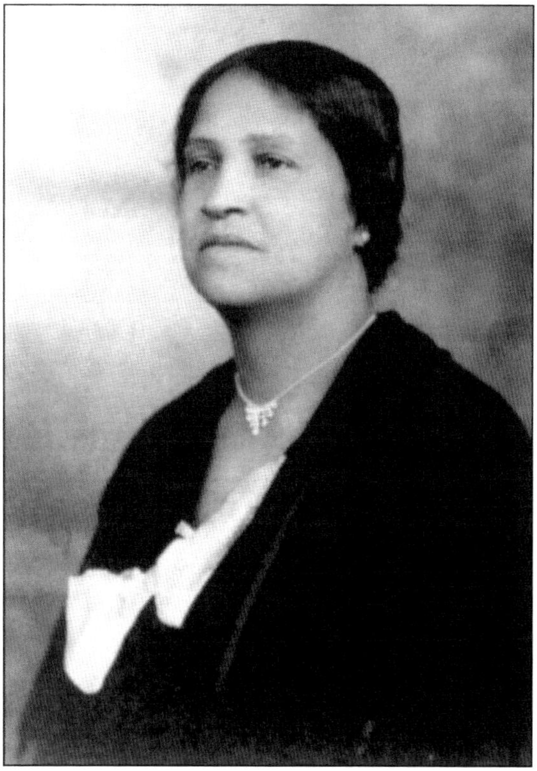

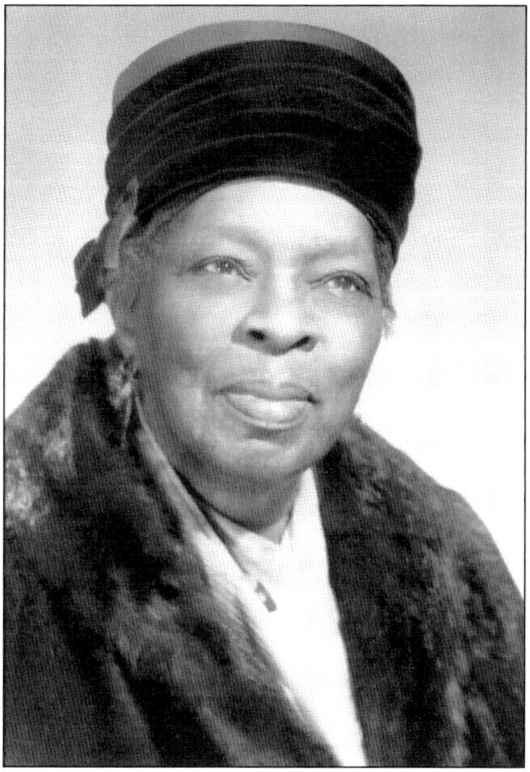

Pictured here is Queen E. Ragland, who taught at the Beesville School, which was located in the Slate River District of Buckingham County. (Courtesy Charles W. White Sr.)

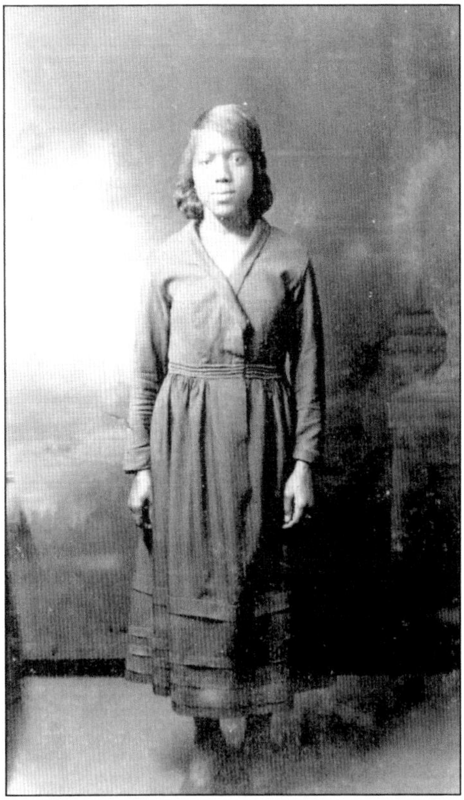

Pictured here is Annie Morris Clarke in 1930. Annie Morris Clarke was a photographer and teacher at the Deep Bottom School, which was located in the Marshall District of Buckingham County. (Courtesy Charles W. White Sr.)

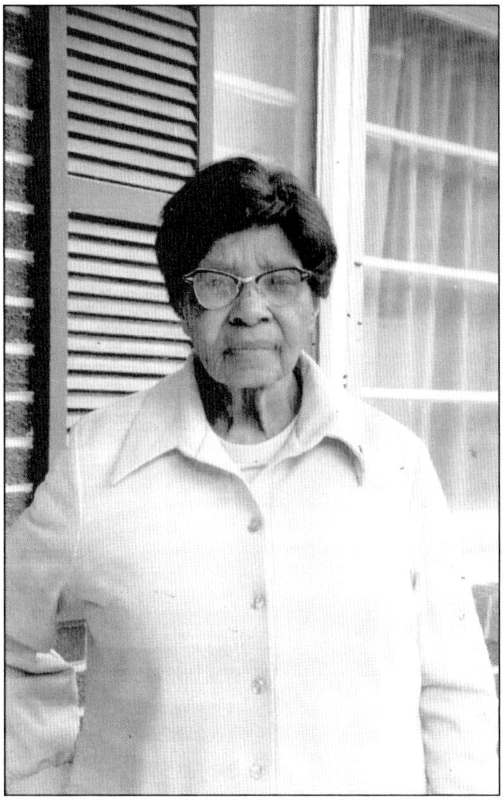

Nellie M. Jones, shown here, taught at the Union Grove School, which was located in the James River District of Buckingham County. (Courtesy Charles W. White Sr.)

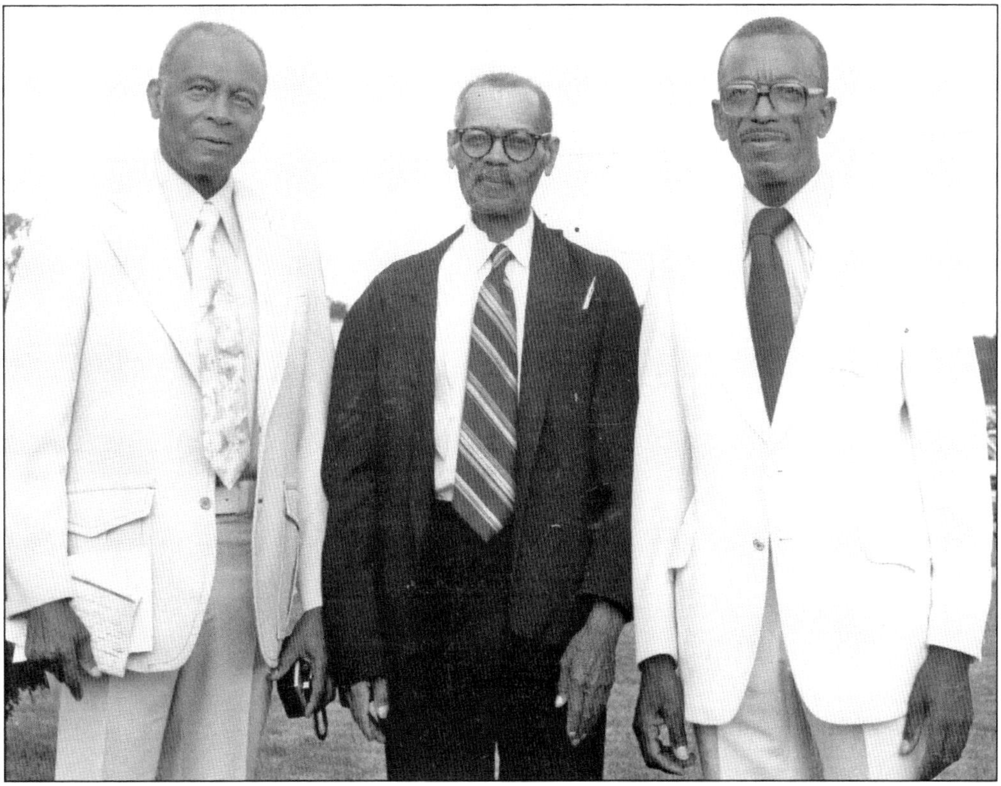

This is a photograph of the reunion of the Buckingham County Training School in 1977. Pictured from left to right are Richard Pegram, former teacher; Thomas L. Dabney, Buckingham County Training School's first principal; and George Frank Harris, Buckingham County Training School's last principal. (Courtesy George Frank Harris.)

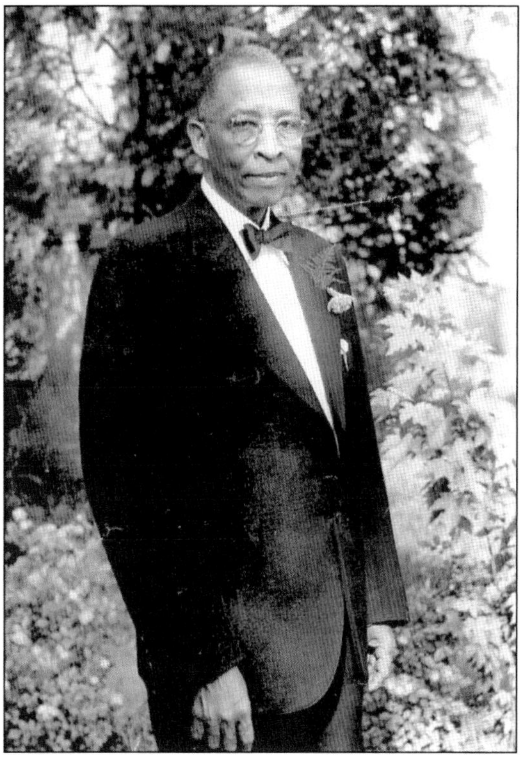

Charles W. Yearwood was a retired principal from Clifton Forge, Virginia, when he moved to Buckingham County. The Harvard University–trained educator served as a teacher and principal at Chestnut Grove School. He was a man ahead of his time who refused to accept second-class citizenship and taught adults and students the same. (Courtesy Charles W. White Sr.)

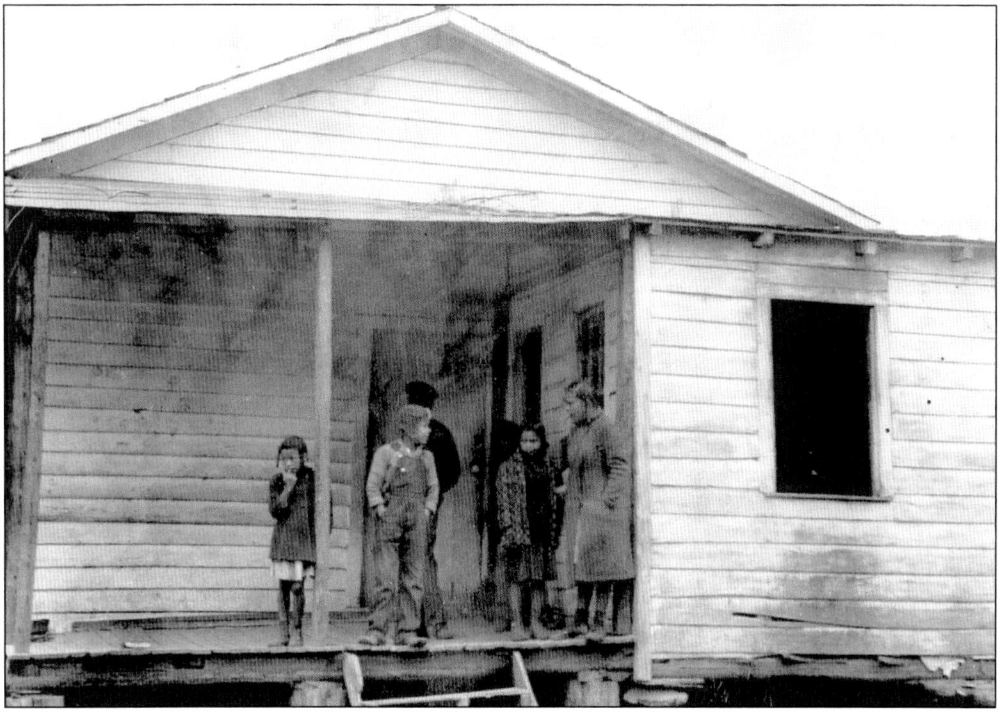

The Diana Mills School is pictured here in 1949. The Diana Mills School, a one-room wooden structure, was located in the Marshall District of Buckingham County. (Courtesy Charles W. White Sr.)

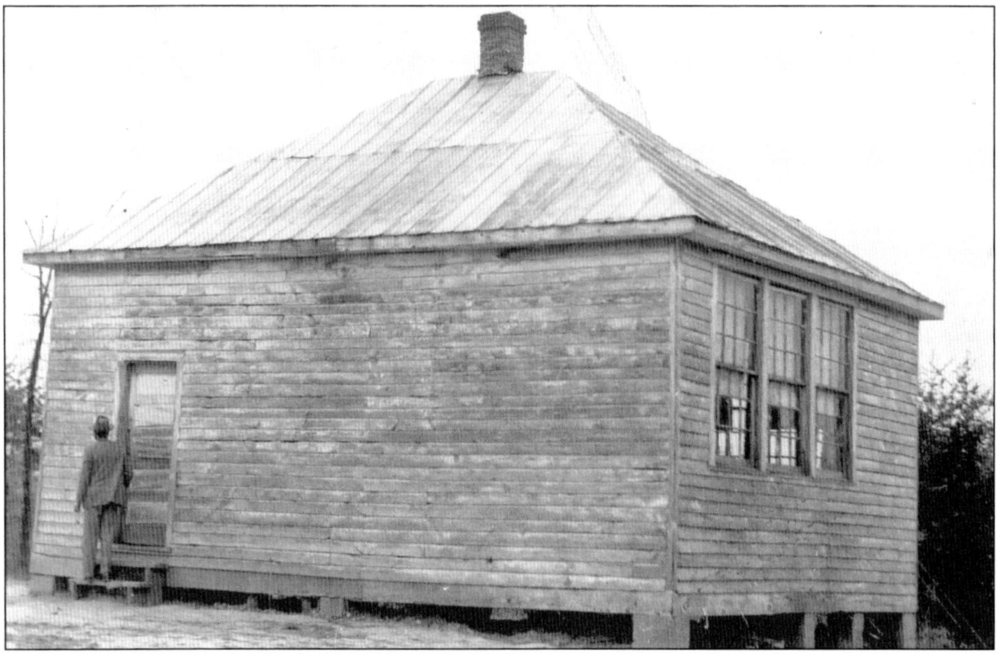

Located in the Curdsville District of Buckingham County was the Saratoga School, another one-room wooden structure. This photograph of the Saratoga School was also taken in 1949. (Courtesy Charles W. White Sr.)

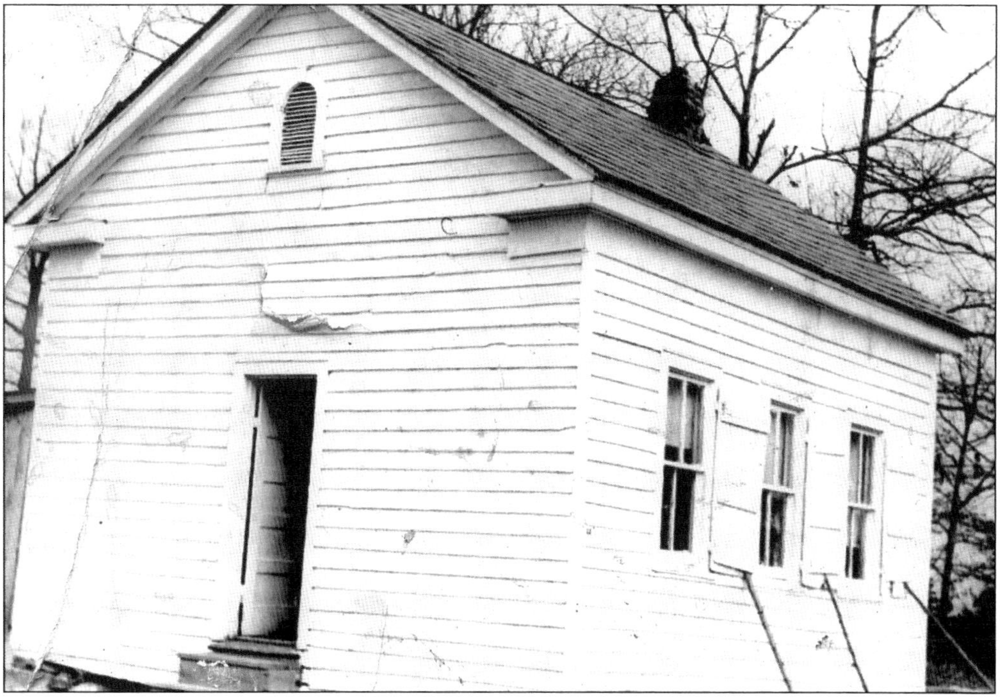

This is a photograph of the Petersville School taken in 1949. The Petersville School was located in Gold Hill in the Marshall District of Buckingham County. (Courtesy Charles W. White Sr.)

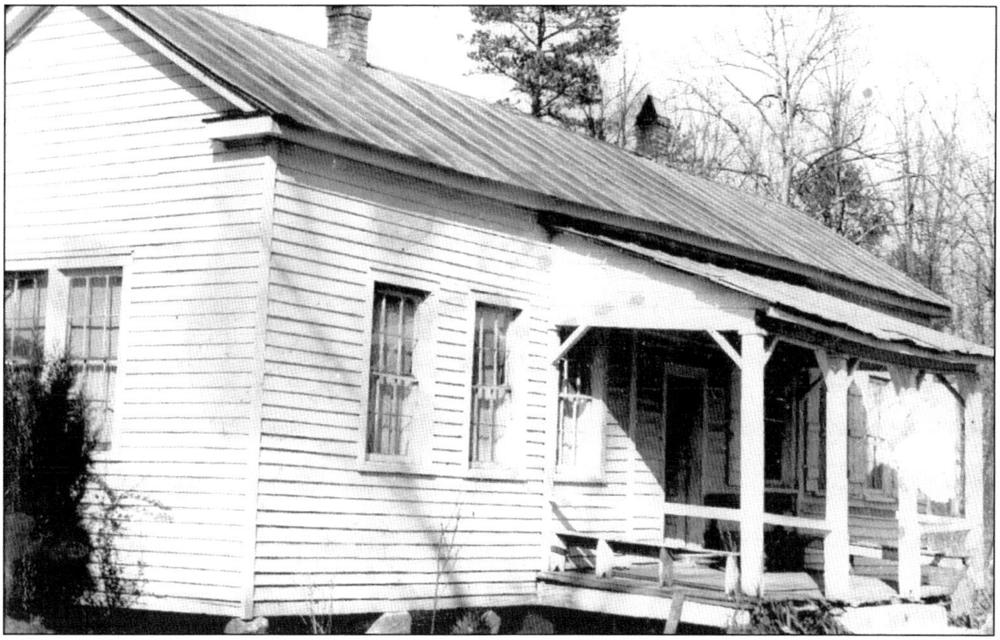

The Ridgeway School, shown here in 1949, was a two-room wooden structure. The Ridgeway School was located in the Slate River District of Buckingham County and was among the first African American junior high schools in the commonwealth of Virginia. (Courtesy Charles W. White Sr.)

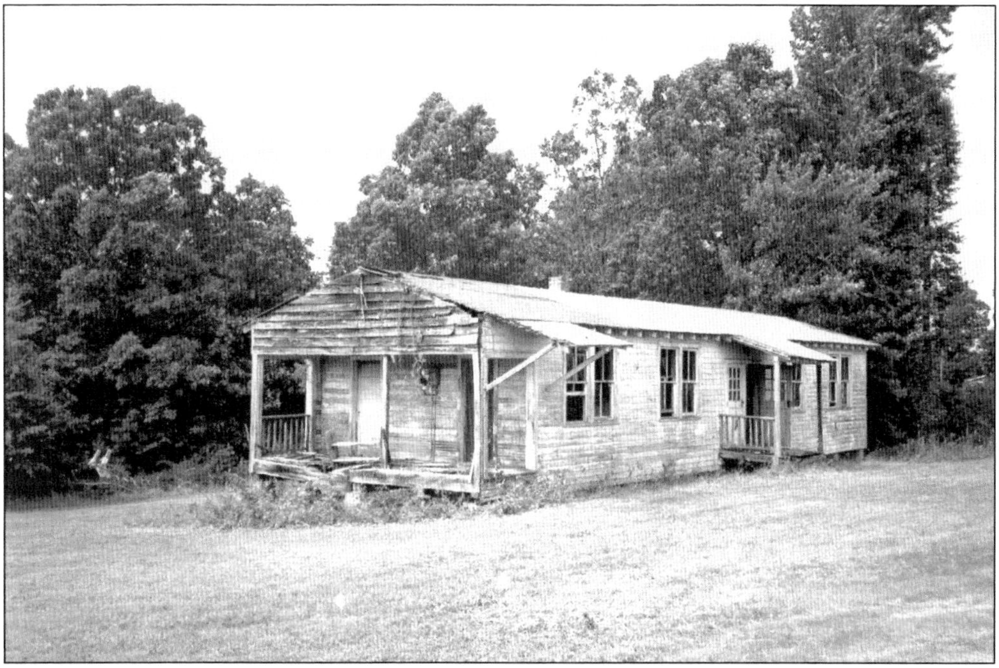

Prior to restoration, the Deep Bottom School, which was a two-room wooden structure, was in poor condition. The Deep Bottom School was located in the Marshall District of Buckingham County. (Courtesy Charles W. White Sr.)

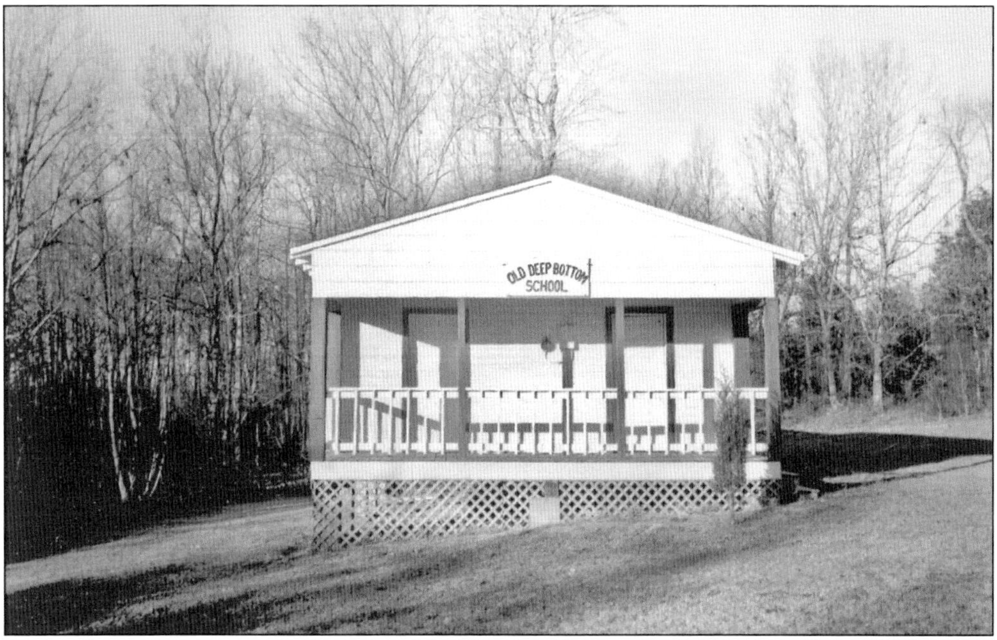

This is a photograph of the restored Deep Bottom School as it appears today. The Baptist Union Baptist Church is currently using this structure for multiple purposes. (Courtesy E. Renée Ingram.)

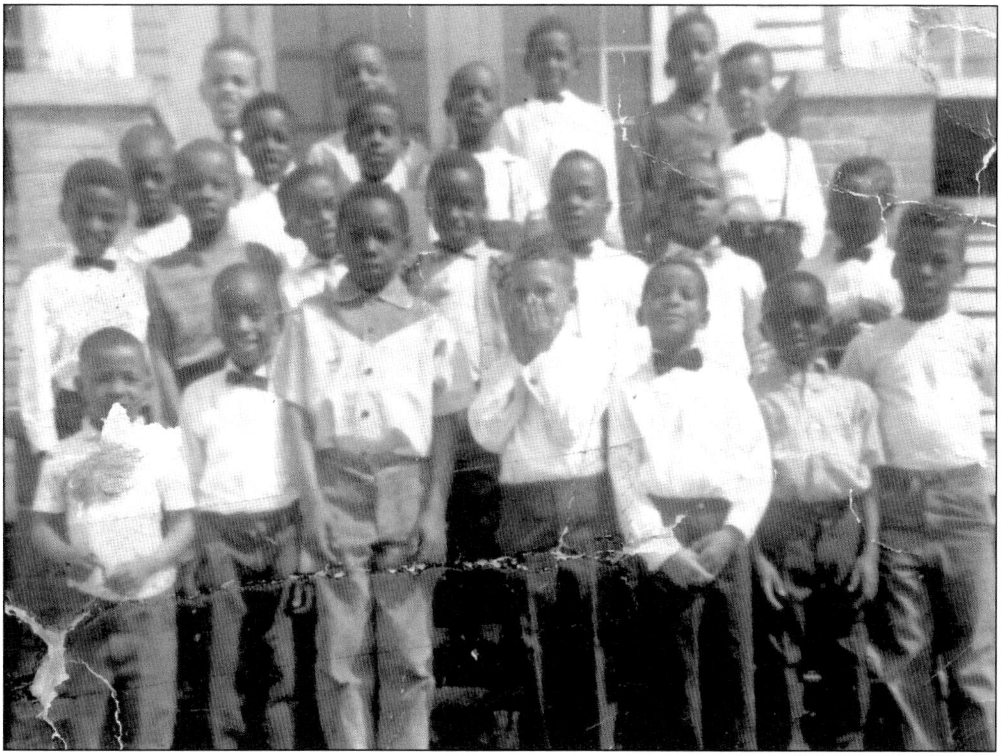

The Stephen J. Ellis Elementary School male students are pictured here, *c.* 1955. The Stephen J. Ellis Elementary School was located in the town of Dillwyn in Buckingham County. (Courtesy Irene Cottrell Collection.)

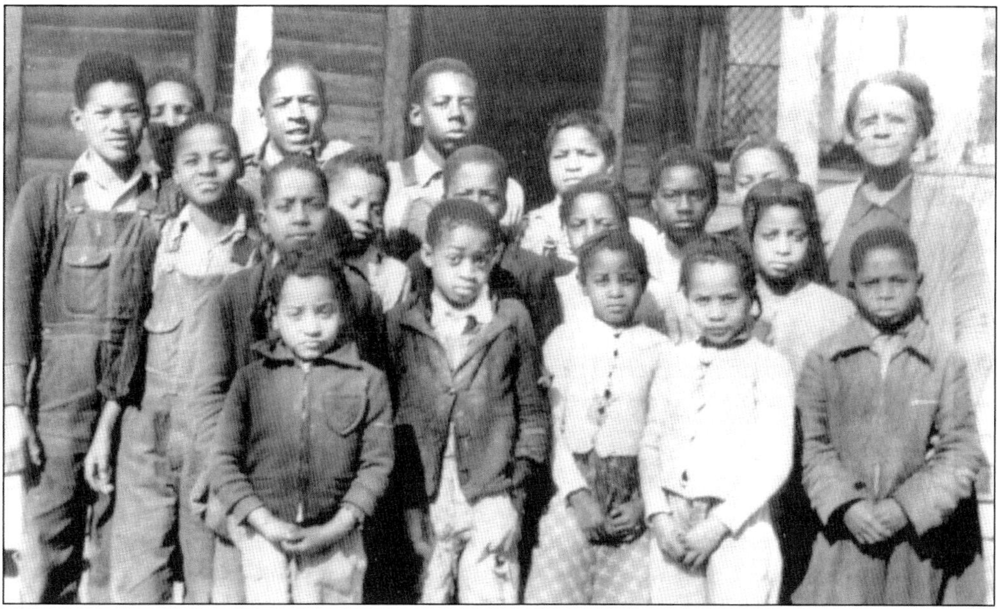

Pictured here are Red Bottom Elementary School students with their teacher, Mrs. Pauline Brown Wayne, in 1946. The Red Bottom Elementary School was located in the James River District of Buckingham County. (Courtesy Dorothy Bowling.)

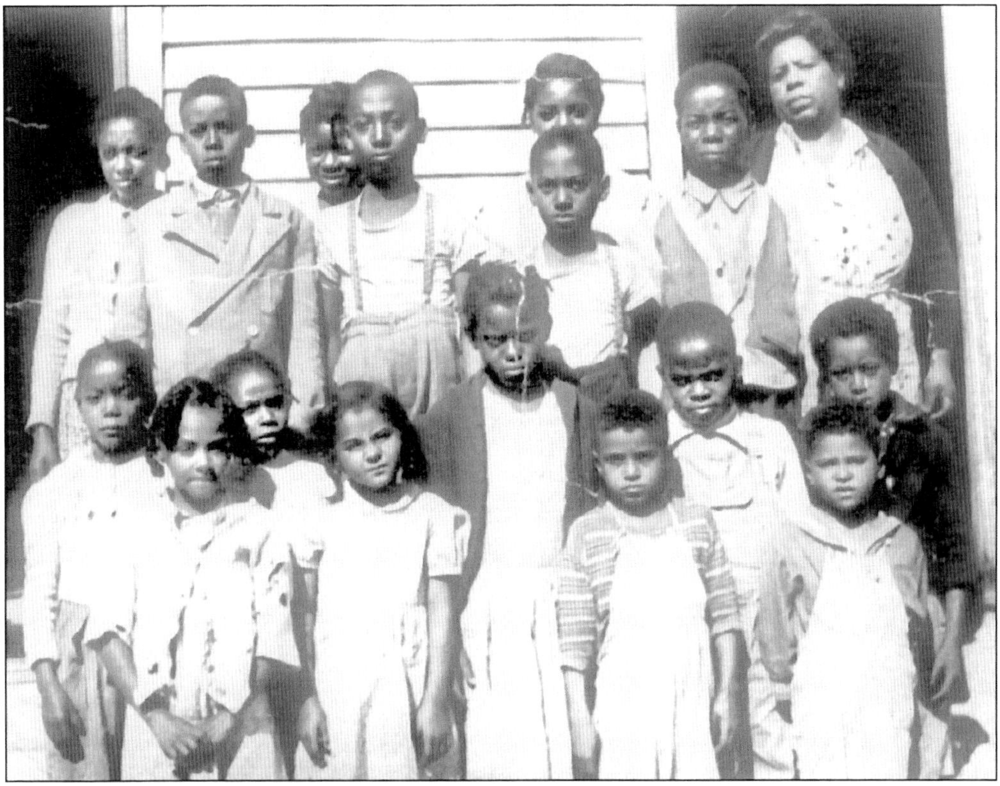

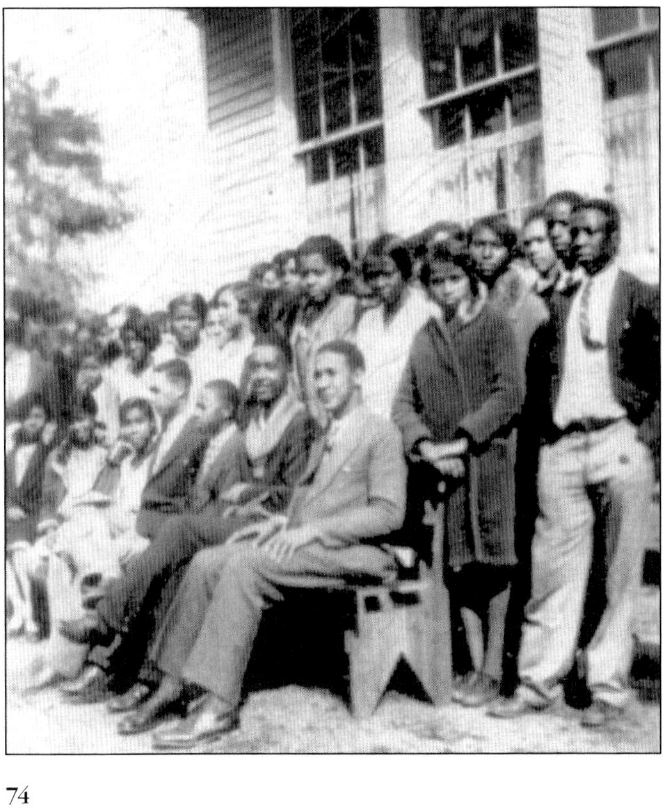

The Carters Field Elementary School students are shown here with their teacher, Mrs. Mary E. Austin Logan, who is standing in the back row at the far right. The Carters Field Elementary School was located in the James River District. (Courtesy Harvey W. Shelton.)

The Buckingham County Training School Class of 1931–1932 has a future principal, George Frank Harris, standing second from right. Harris was in the eight grade at the time this photograph was taken. (Courtesy George Frank Harris.)

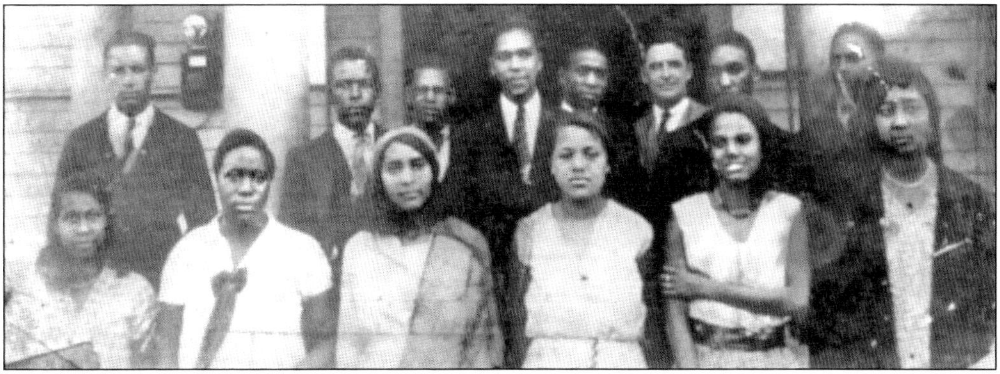

Pictured here is the Buckingham County Training School class of 1934 on their graduation day. (Courtesy Charles W. White Sr.)

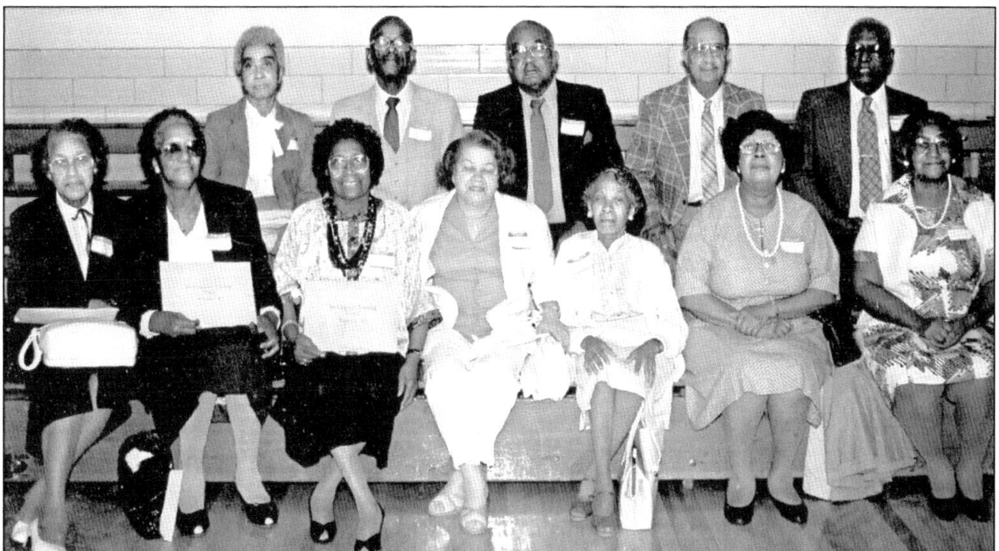

Members of the Buckingham County Training School class of 1934 are shown here at their class reunion in 1987. (Courtesy George Frank Harris.)

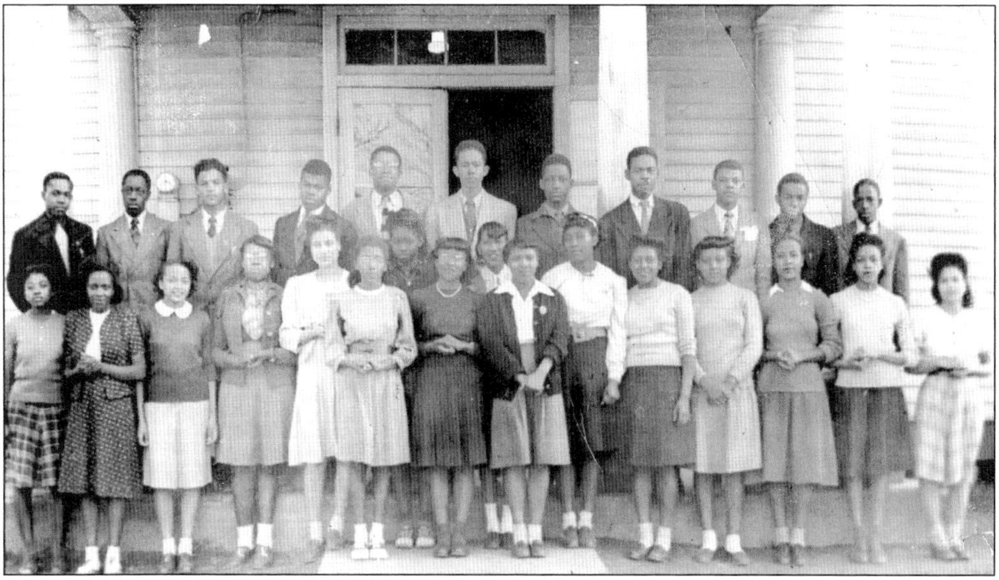

Pictured here is the Buckingham County Training School class of 1948. (Courtesy George Frank Harris.)

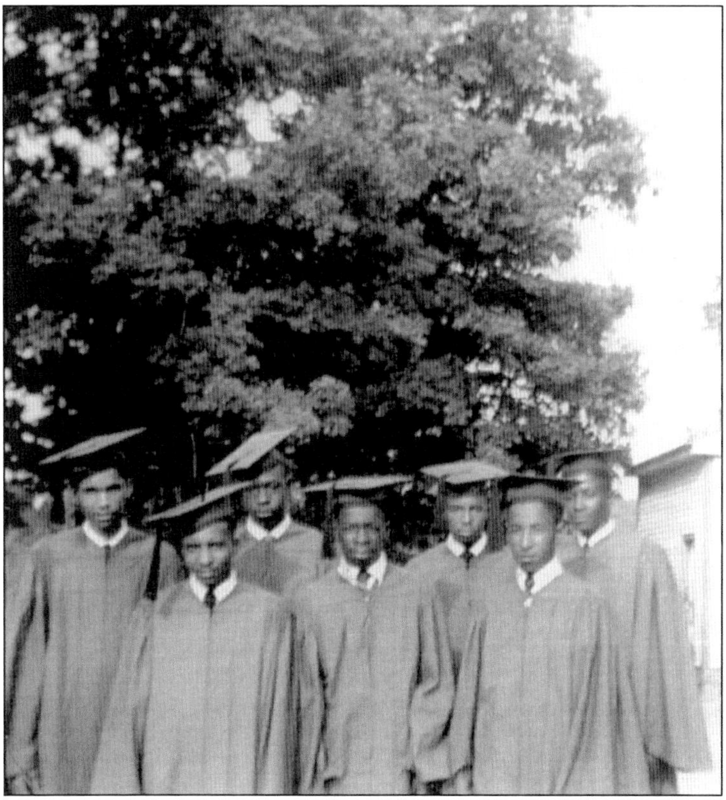

It is graduation day for the class of 1951 at the Buckingham County Training School. Shown here are the male graduates in their caps and gowns. (Courtesy Nannie M. Woodson.)

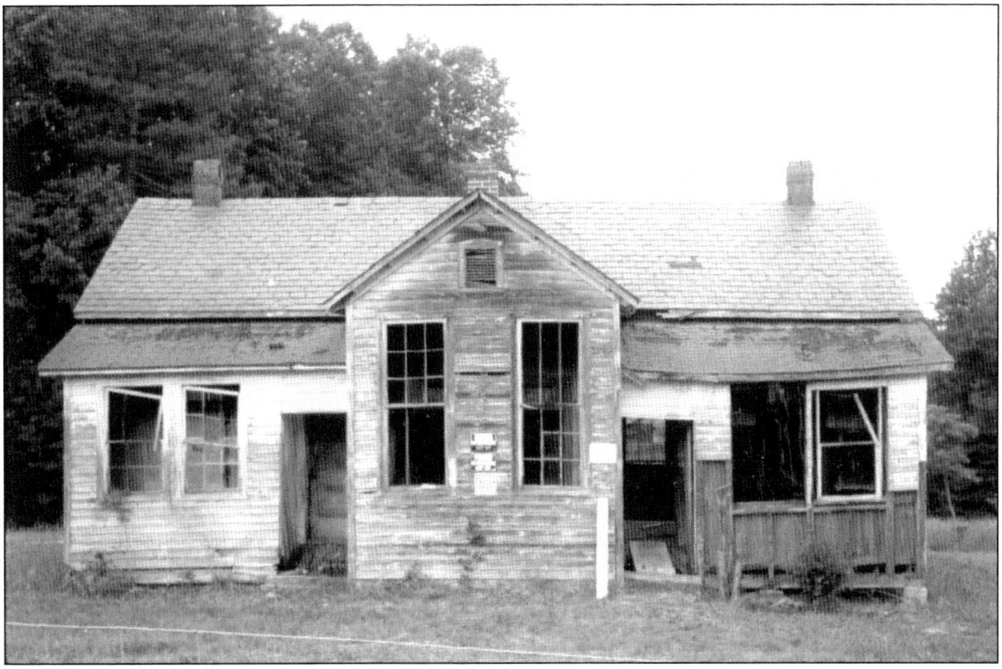

This is a photograph of the Liberty School taken before its restoration. The Liberty School was a two-room structure built in 1926 near the Third Liberty Church in New Canton, in the Marshall District of the county. This school was built with the assistance of Rev. John Buchanan Riddle, uncle of Carter G. Woodson, and patrons. The Rosenwald fund provided $700 toward the construction of Liberty School. The cost of this historic structure was $2,460. (Courtesy Marjorie Chambers.)

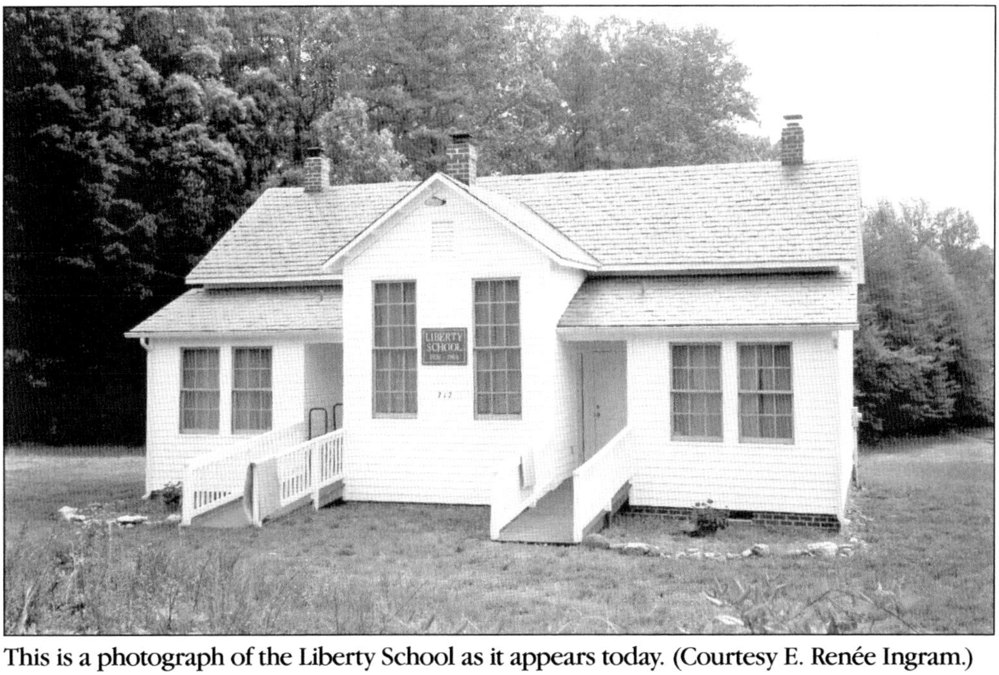

This is a photograph of the Liberty School as it appears today. (Courtesy E. Renée Ingram.)

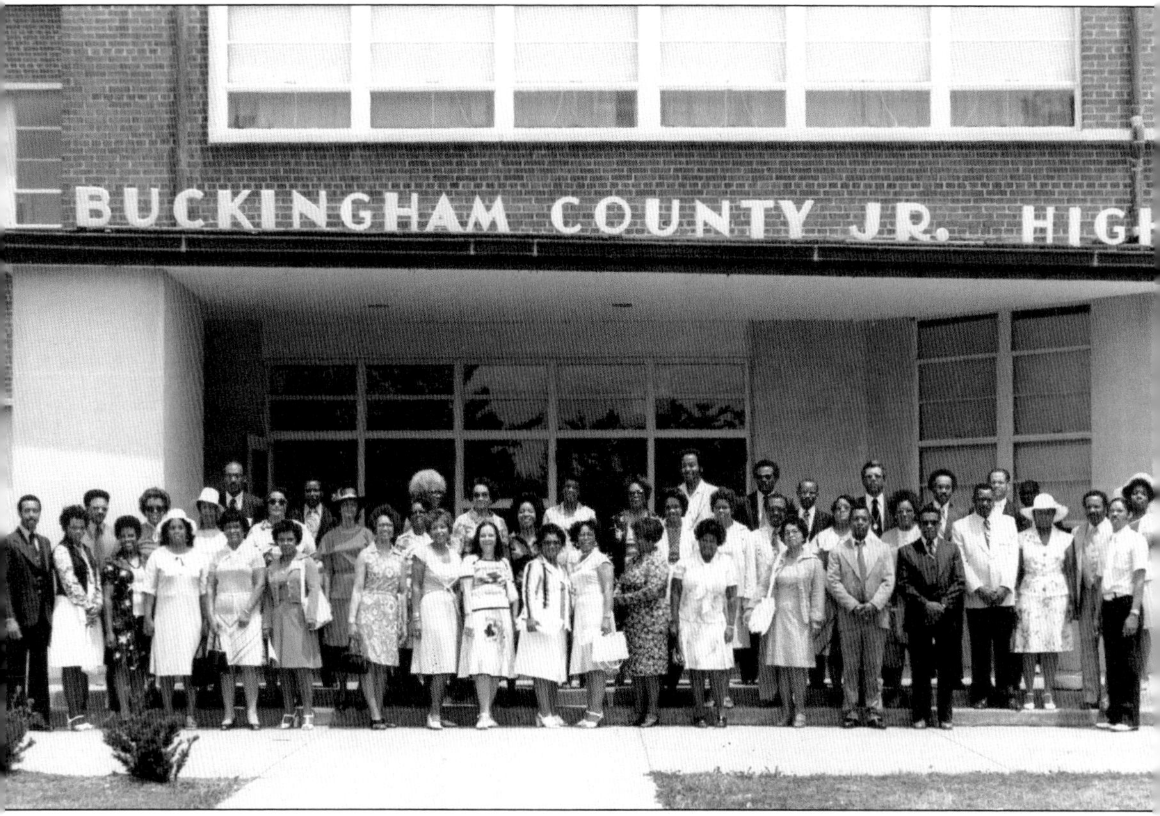

The school reunion of the Buckingham County Junior High School (formerly the Carter G. Woodson High School) is shown here, *c.* 1980. (Courtesy Arlene Bolling Woodson.)

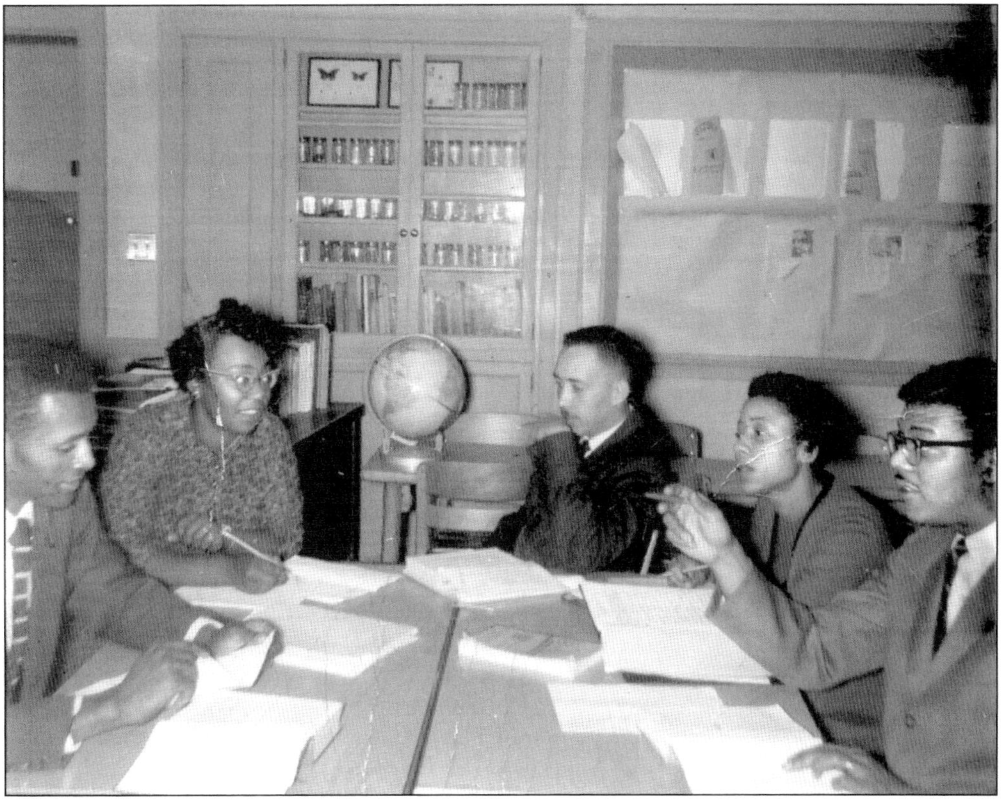

Members of the faculty committee meet at the Carter G. Woodson High School, *c.* 1968. Shown here from left to right are co-author Charles W. White Sr., Mary Brannon, Albert Dowe, Betty Myrick, and William Parks. (Courtesy Charles W. White Sr.)

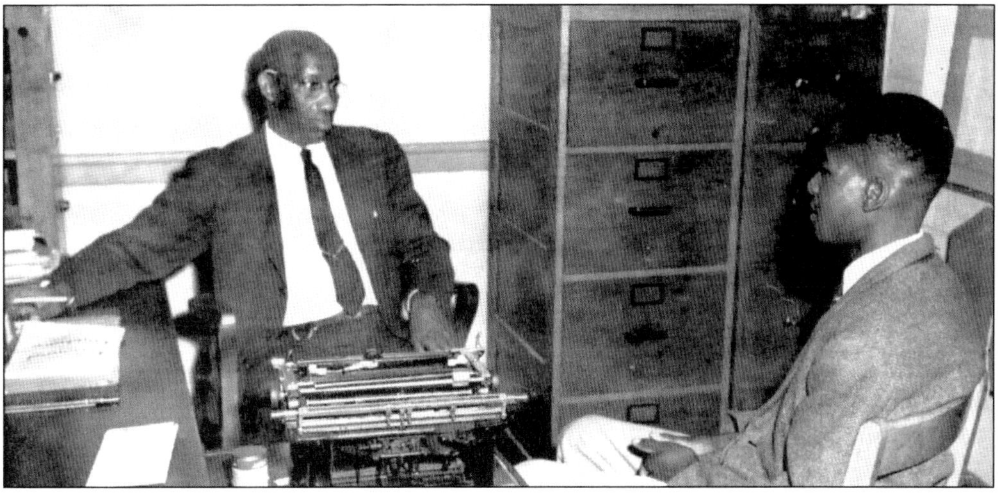

Guidance counselor Rev. William J. Kerr is shown here in his office with student Elbert Horsley at the Carter G. Woodson High School. (Courtesy *The Yellow Jackets*, 1957 Carter G. Woodson High School yearbook.)

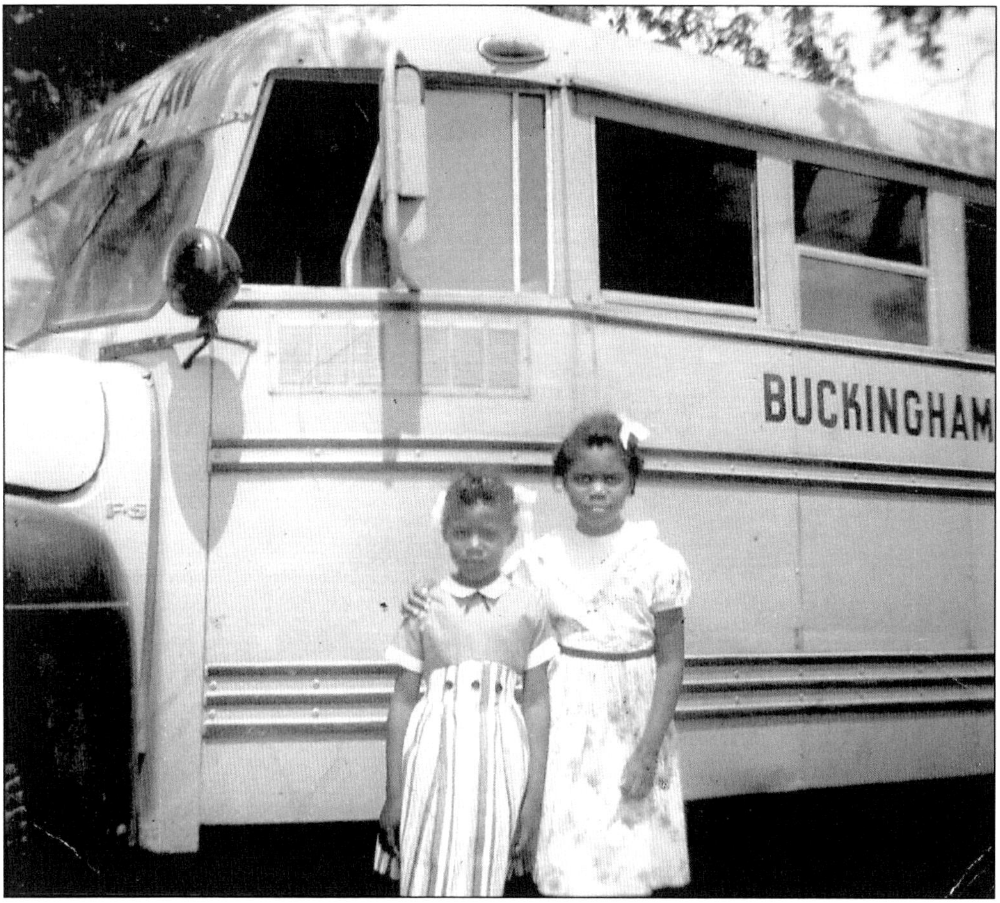

Thelma Cottrell and her friend Gloria Jones are standing by a Buckingham school bus waiting to go to school in 1957. (Courtesy Irene Cottrell Collection.)

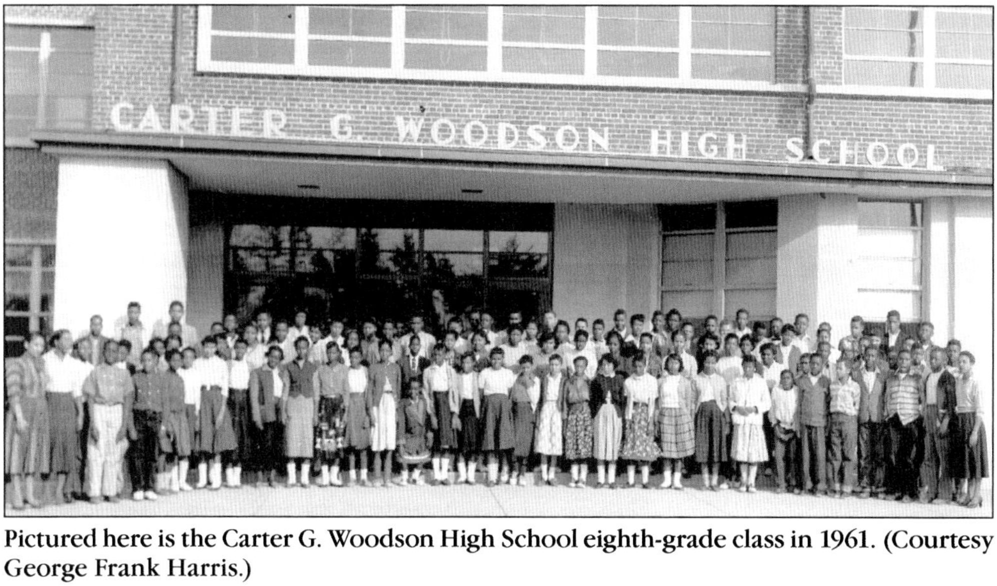

Pictured here is the Carter G. Woodson High School eighth-grade class in 1961. (Courtesy George Frank Harris.)

Four seniors from the Carter G. Woodson High School are shown here in 1957. From left to right are Elva Miller, Richard Carey, Eleanor Carter, Herbert Taylor, and Pauline Davis. (Courtesy George Frank Harris.)

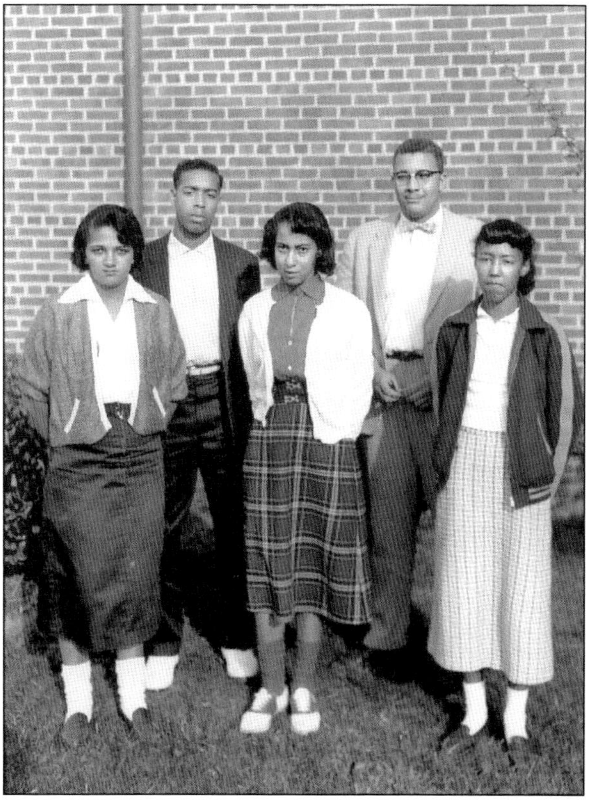

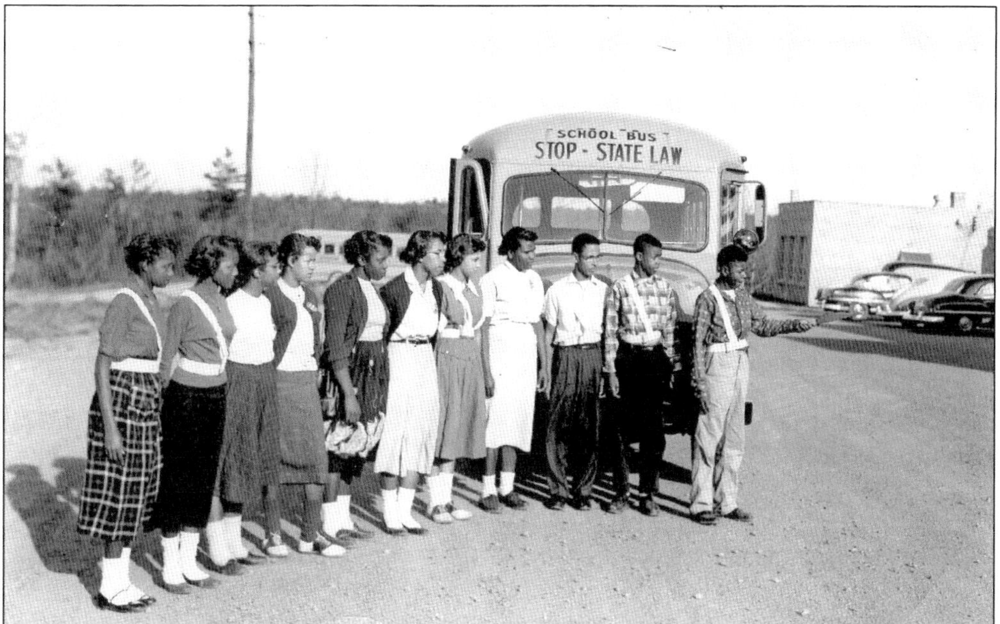

Pictured here is the Carter G. Woodson High School Safety Patrol, *c.* 1957. One student is providing instructions on loading and unloading students from the school bus as part of their safety exercise. (Courtesy George Frank Harris.)

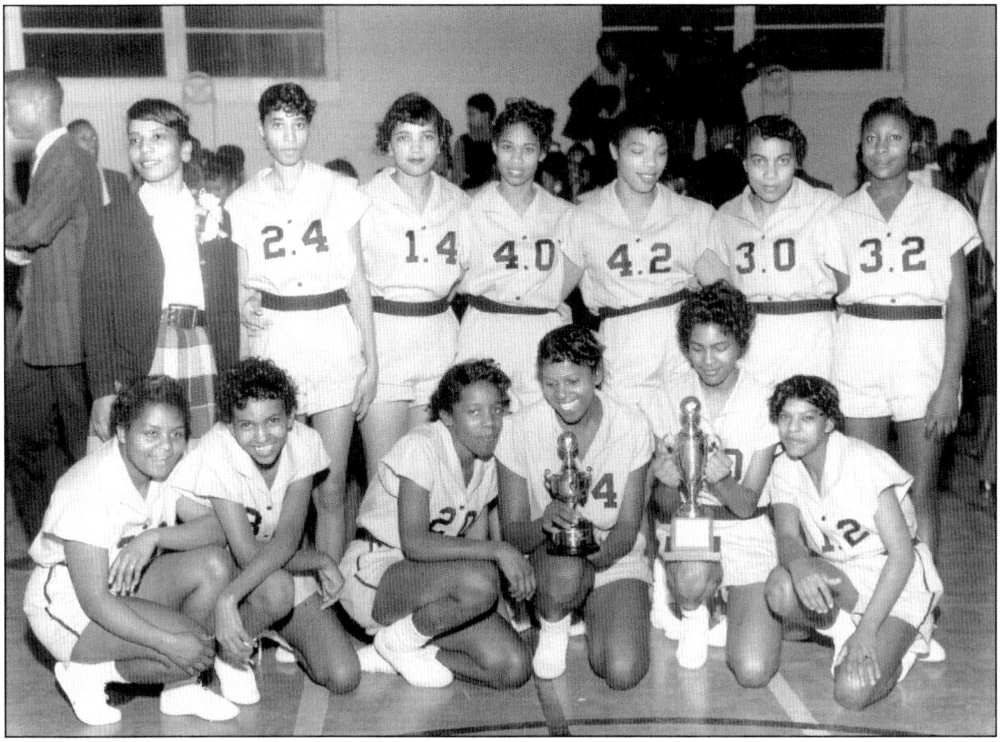

Pictured here is the Carter G. Woodson High School girls' championship basketball team, *c.* 1965. (Courtesy George Frank Harris.)

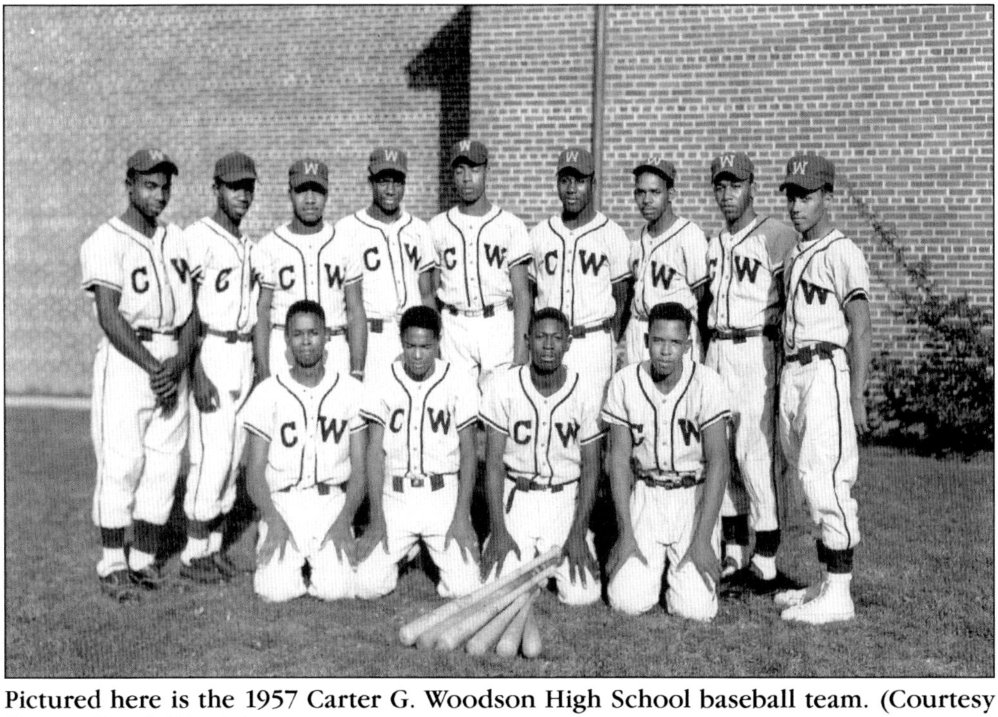

Pictured here is the 1957 Carter G. Woodson High School baseball team. (Courtesy George Frank Harris.)

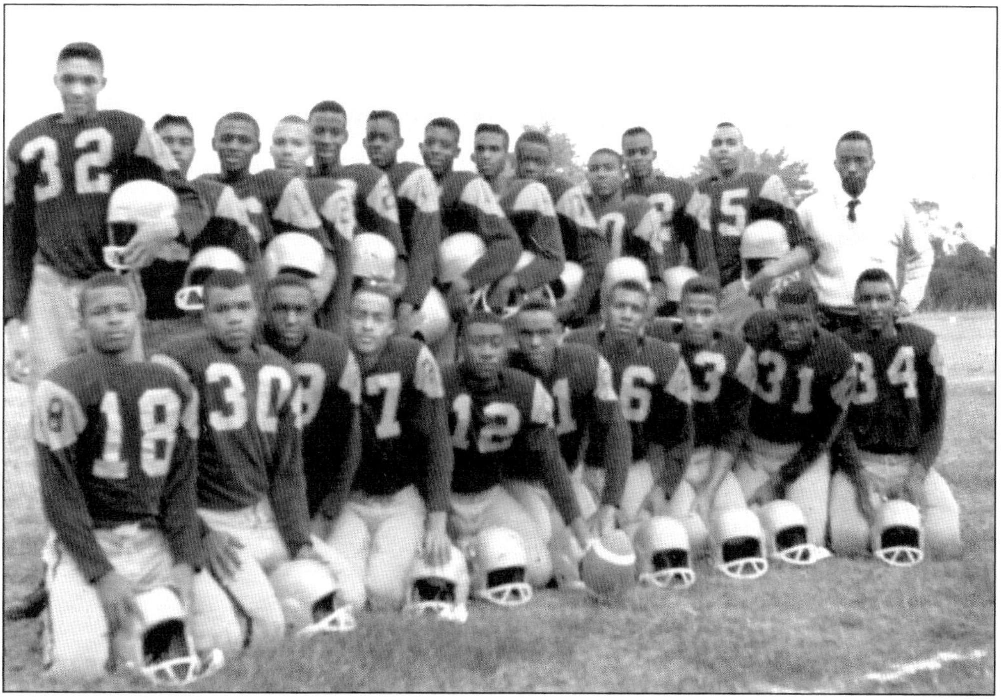

The Carter G. Woodson High School 1962 football team is shown here with their coach, Alfred Wilson (standing far right). (Courtesy of George Frank Harris.)

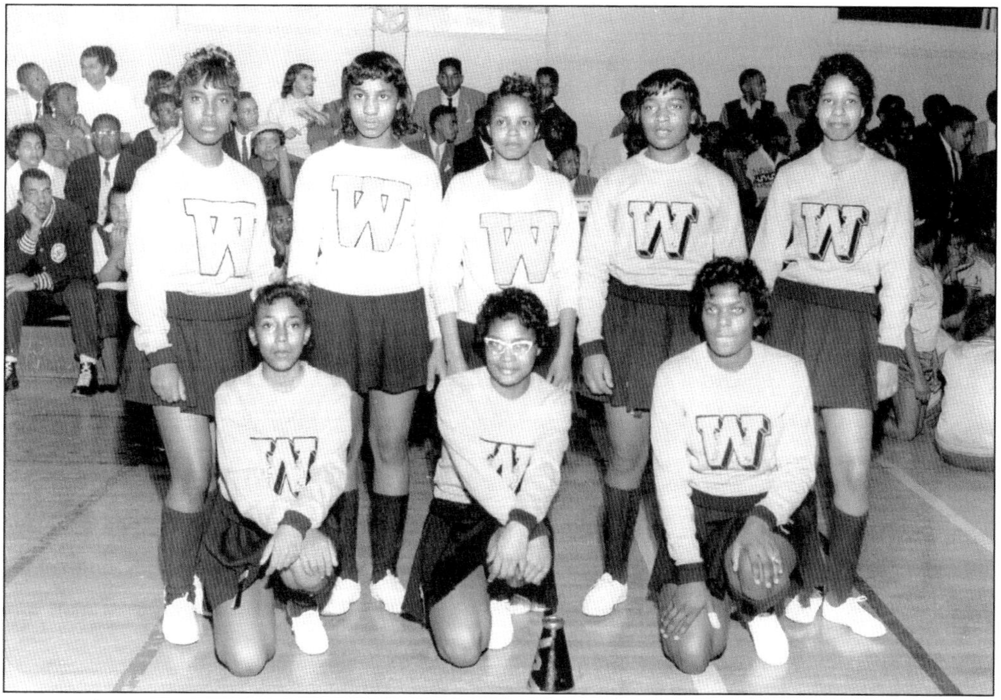

Pictured here are the Carter G. Woodson High School cheerleaders. (Courtesy George Frank Harris.)

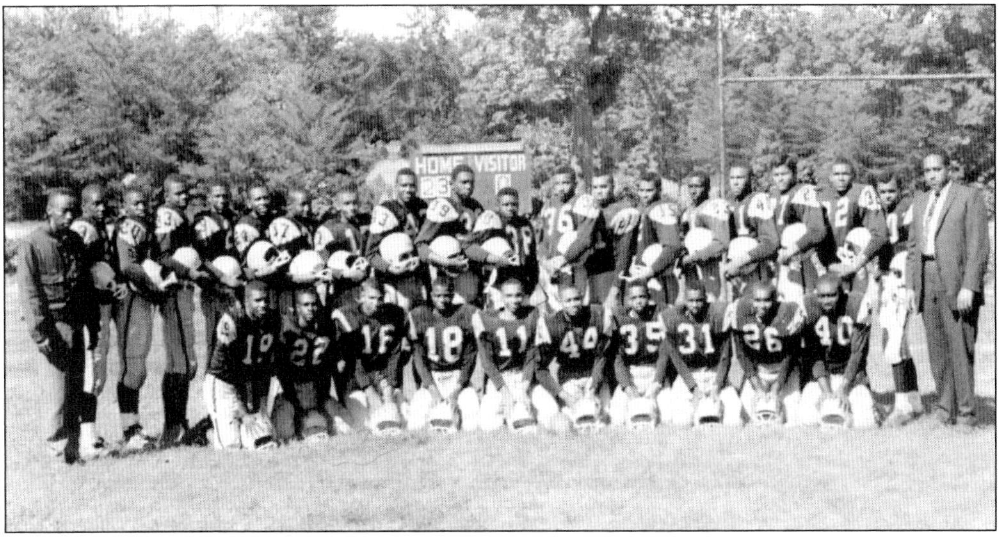

The 1966 Woodson Yellow Jackets from the Carter G. Woodson High School are shown here with their coach A. D. Wilson (standing far left) and coach F. D. Johns (standing far right). (Courtesy Charles W. White Sr.)

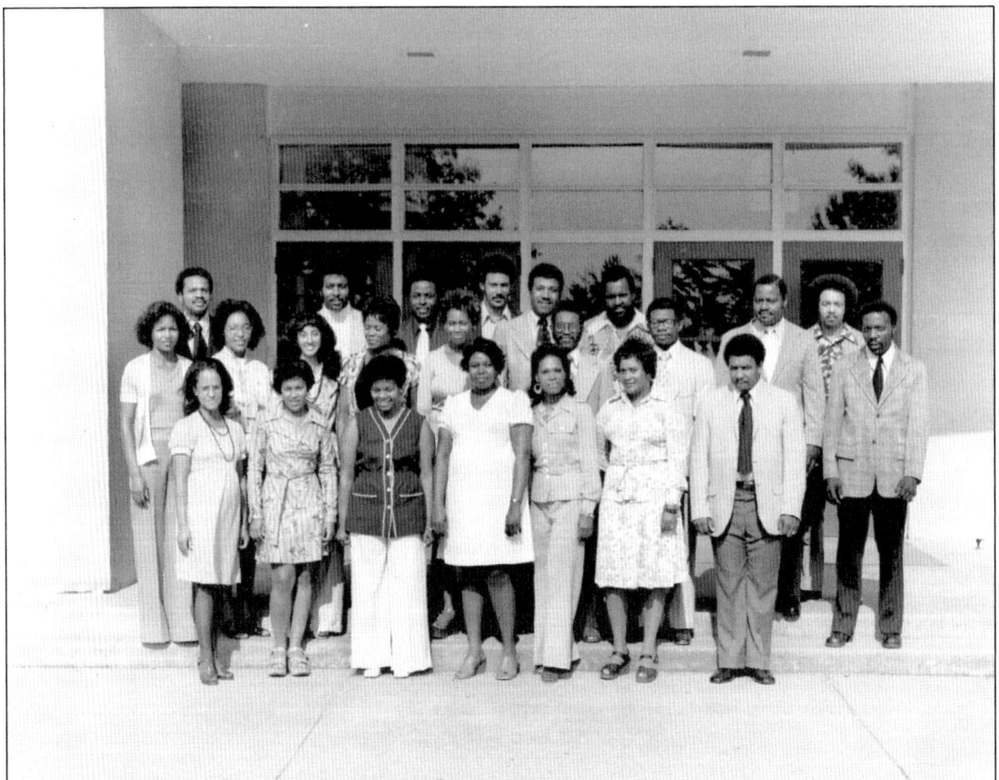

Pictured here are members of the Carter G. Woodson class of 1965 at their 10-year class reunion. (Courtesy George Frank Harris.)

Five

A Glimpse of Our Military Service

I would fight for my liberty so long as my strength lasted,
and if the time came for me to go, the Lord would let them take me.

—Harriet Tubman (*c.* 1820–1913)

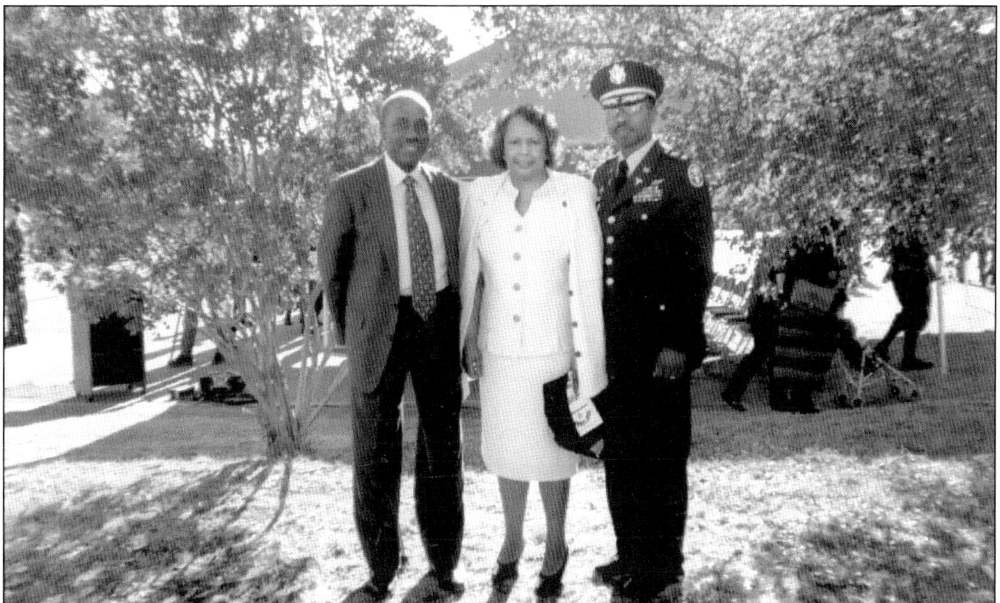

Pictured here is Dr. (Col.) Clyde A. Turner Jr. of Buckingham County with his parents, Clyde and Celestine (Anderson) Turner. Dr. Turner, chief of the Emergency Medicine Department at Fort Hood, Killeen, Texas, has just received his wings in this picture. In 2001, Dr. Turner received an Army Commander's Coin for his achievements in emergency medicine at Darnall Army Community Hospital, which is known for being the busiest emergency center in the Armed Forces. (Courtesy Celestine Anderson Turner.)

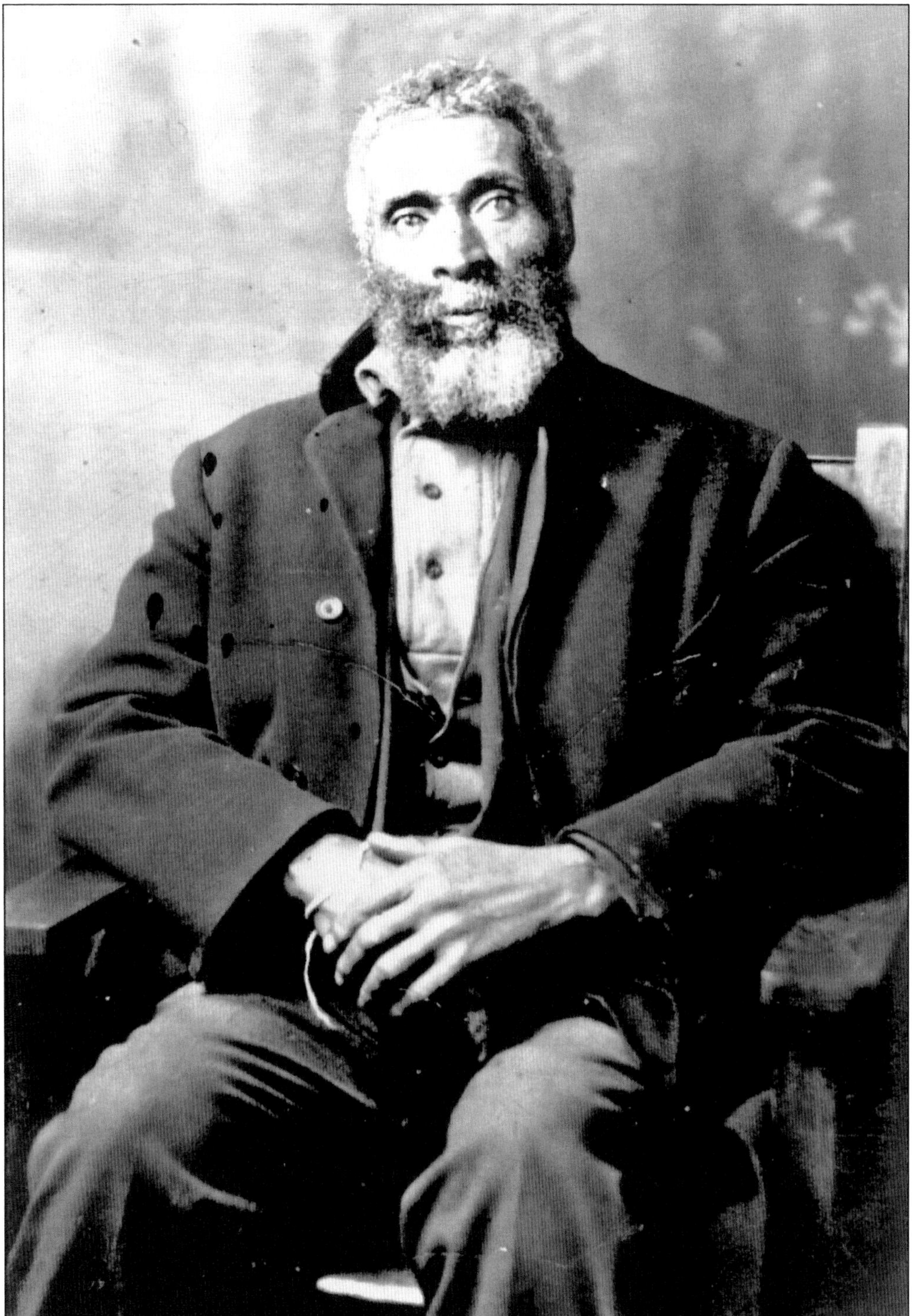

Andrew Miller, a Confederate army laborer in the Civil War, was born about 1848. Andrew Miller was from the Slate River District of Buckingham County. (Courtesy Eugene T. Miller Jr.)

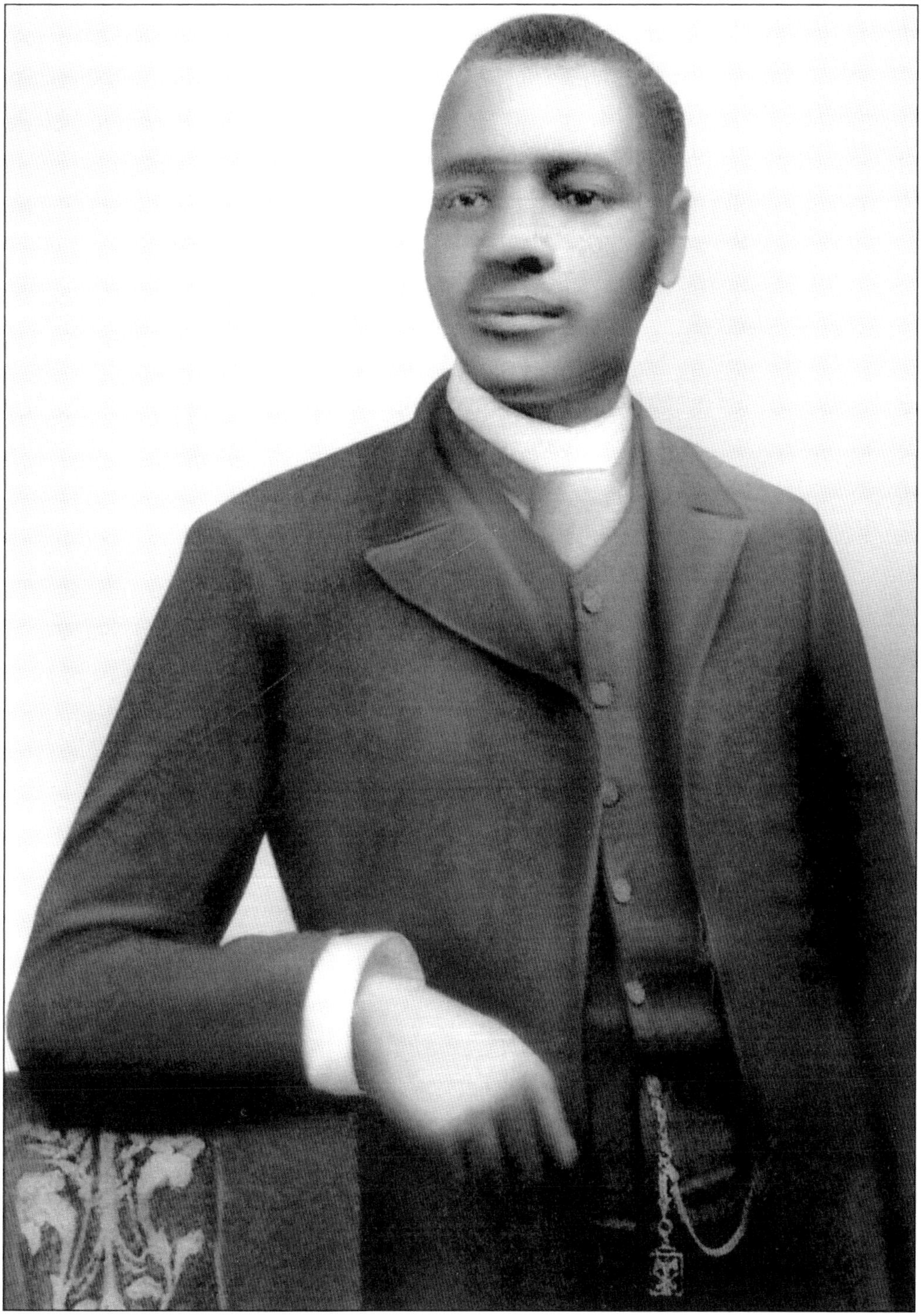

Pictured here is Sgt. Joseph S. Goolsby, a buffalo soldier. Goolsby was born in 1867 in the Maysville District of Buckingham County. In 1888, he enlisted with the distinguished 10th U.S. Cavalry, D Troop, and served for five years. (Courtesy Charles W. White.)

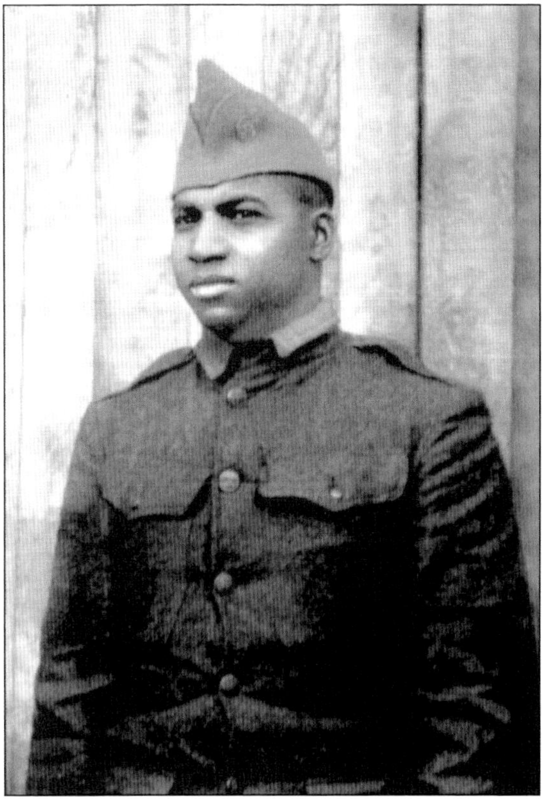

Pvt. Ulysses S. Washington Sr. served in the U.S. Army during World War I. (Courtesy Otto K. Washington.)

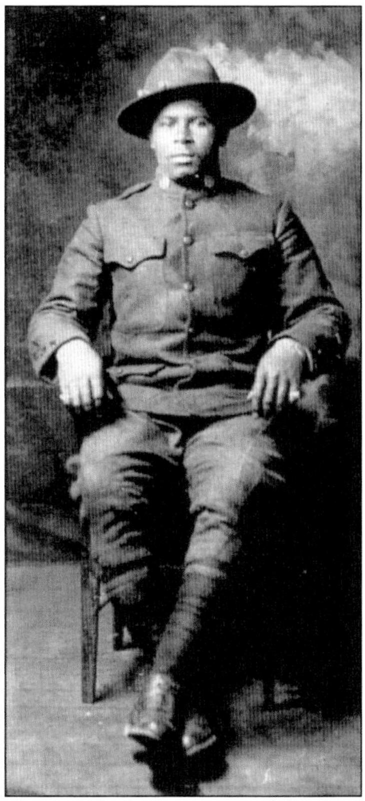

Pictured here is Pvt. Phillip Moseley. Private Moseley served in the U.S. Army during World War I. (Courtesy Nannie M. Woodson.)

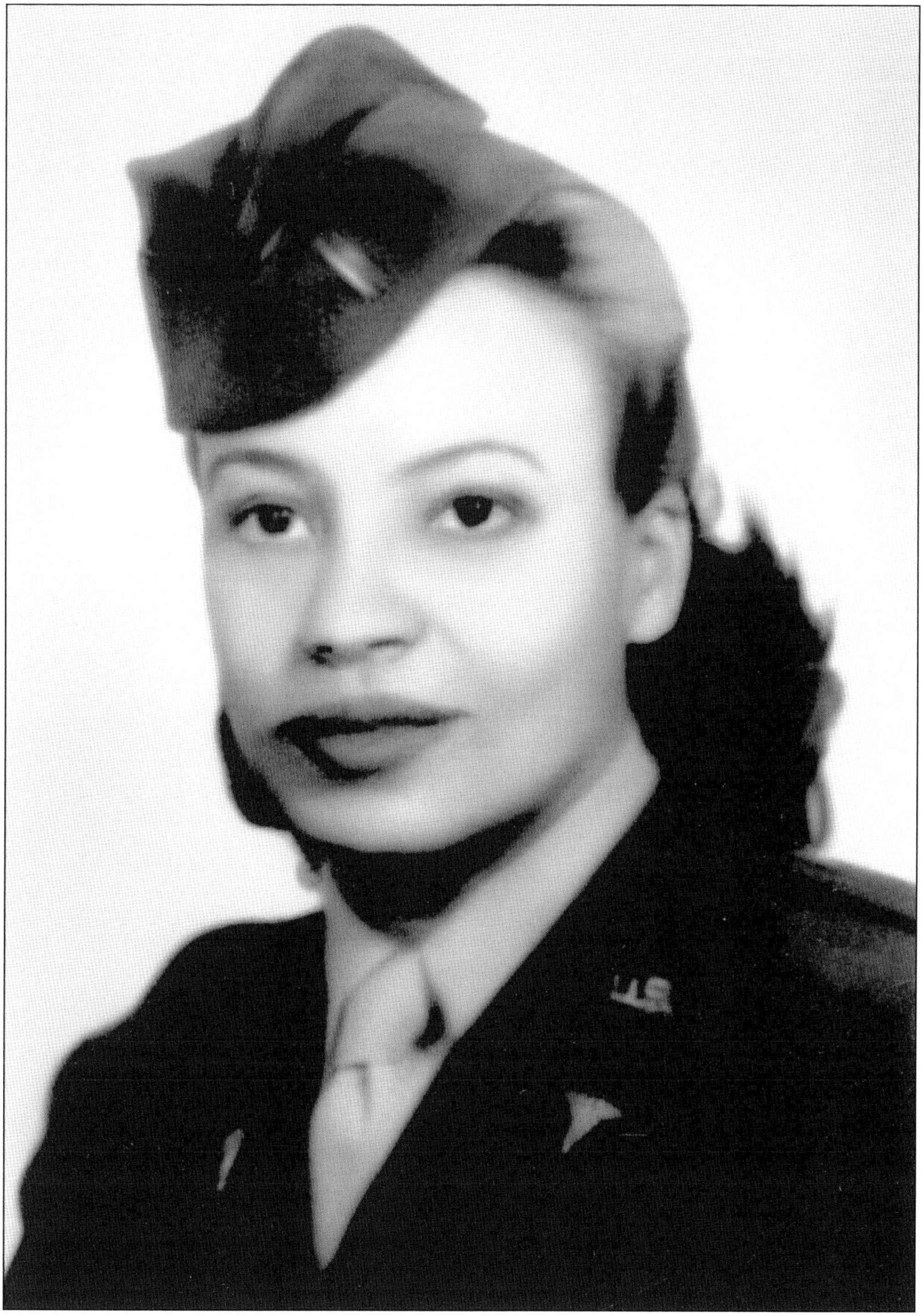

First Lt. Vivian Eldridge was one of the few commissioned African American female officers in the U.S. Army during World War II. Eldridge was born about 1922 in the Curdsville District of Buckingham County and was the eldest child of Ampie and Hazel Eldridge. (Courtesy Charles W. White Sr.)

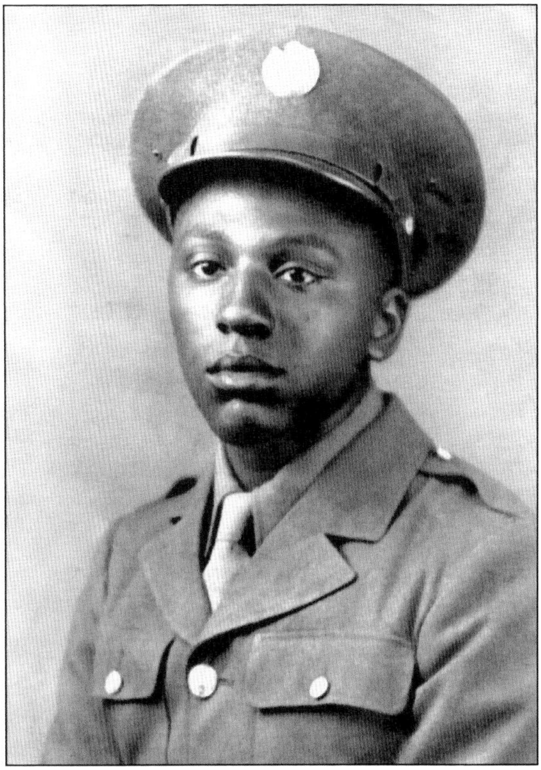

Pvt. Reuben Chambers served in the U.S. Army during World War II. (Courtesy Irene Cottrell Collection.)

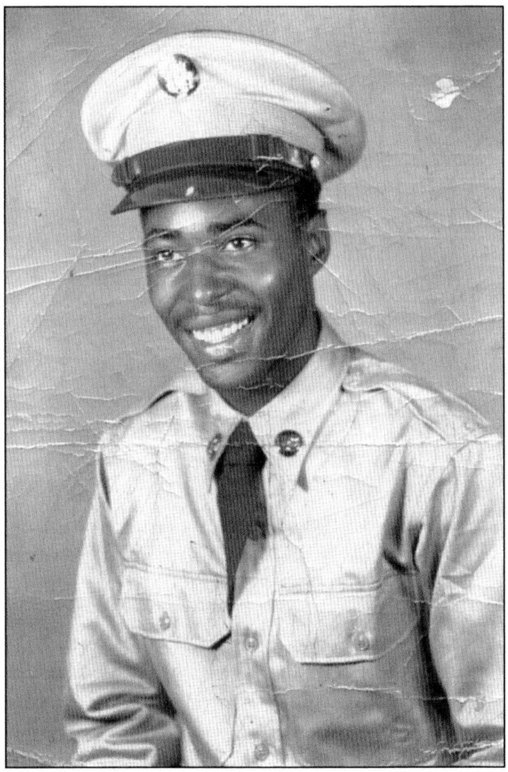

Pictured here is Cpl. Leslie O. Gregory. Tragically Corporal Gregory was killed during an engagement on Pork Chop Hill during the Korean War. (Courtesy Charles W. White Sr.)

Cpl. Walter Herbert Patterson, shown here, was in the U.S. Army during World War II and served in the European Theater in Belgium and France. This combat veteran still resides in Buckingham County today. (Courtesy John Laury Jr.)

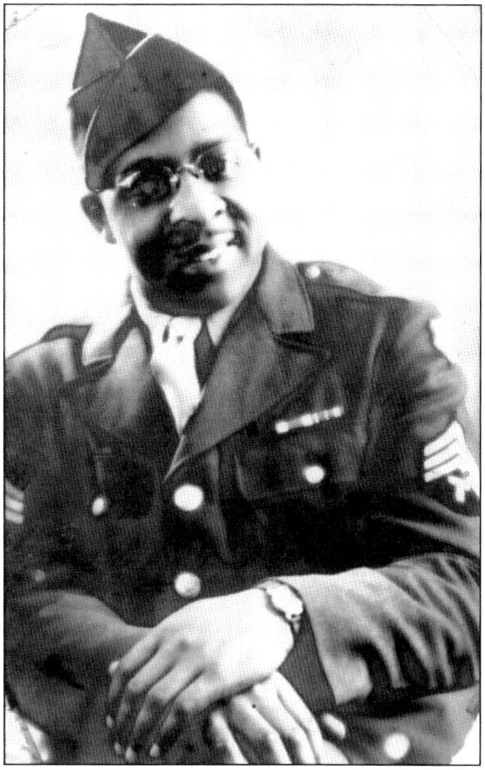

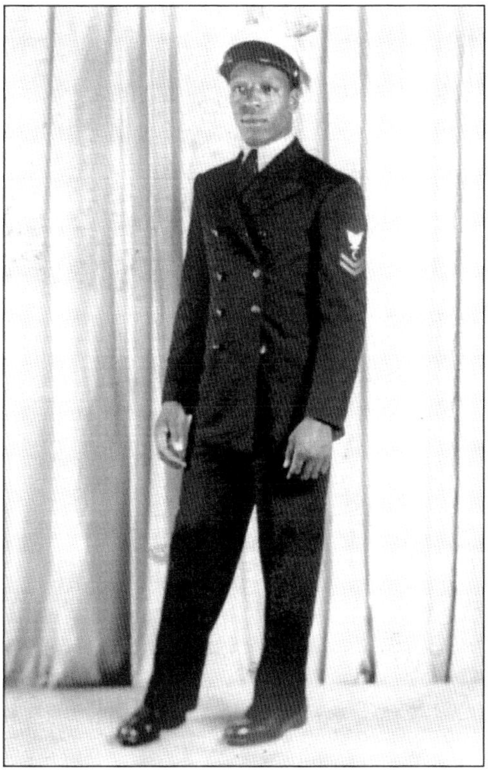

PO2 James Jones served as a steward in the U.S. Navy during World War II. (Courtesy of the Irene Cottrell Collection.)

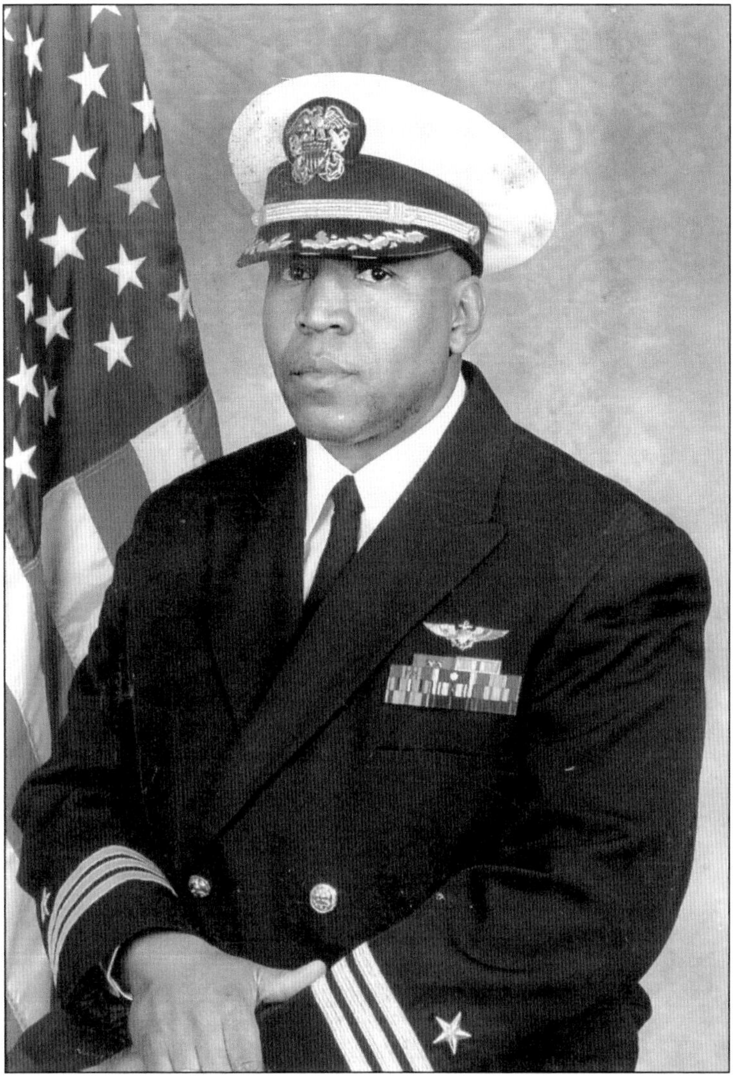

Comdr. Orestes D. Gooden served in the U.S. Navy. Gooden, son of Allen C. Gooden Jr. and Christine (Shelton) Gooden, was raised in the James River District and is a 1977 graduate of Buckingham County High School. He received a bachelor of science degree from Virginia State University (third generation legacy) and a master's of aeronautical science from Embry-Riddle Aeronautical University. Commander Gooden is a distinguished graduate of the Navy Electronics School and Naval Nuclear Power School and was commissioned an ensign after completing Officer Candidate School. Following completion of flight training, he was designated a naval aviator and received the coveted Wings of Gold. Qualified as an aircraft and mission commander, he has held numerous leadership positions and assignments with various commands. Commander Gooden's professional memberships include U.S. Naval Institute, Civil Air Patrol, Tuskegee Airmen Inc., American Association of Airport Executives, Organization of Black Airline Pilots, and Alpha Phi Alpha Fraternity, Inc. As a citizen sailor, Commander Gooden has enjoyed a civilian career as a manufacturing engineer with Ford Motor Company and Visteon Automotive Systems. He is currently a professor of aviation science at Elizabeth City State University. (Courtesy Joyce Gooden.)

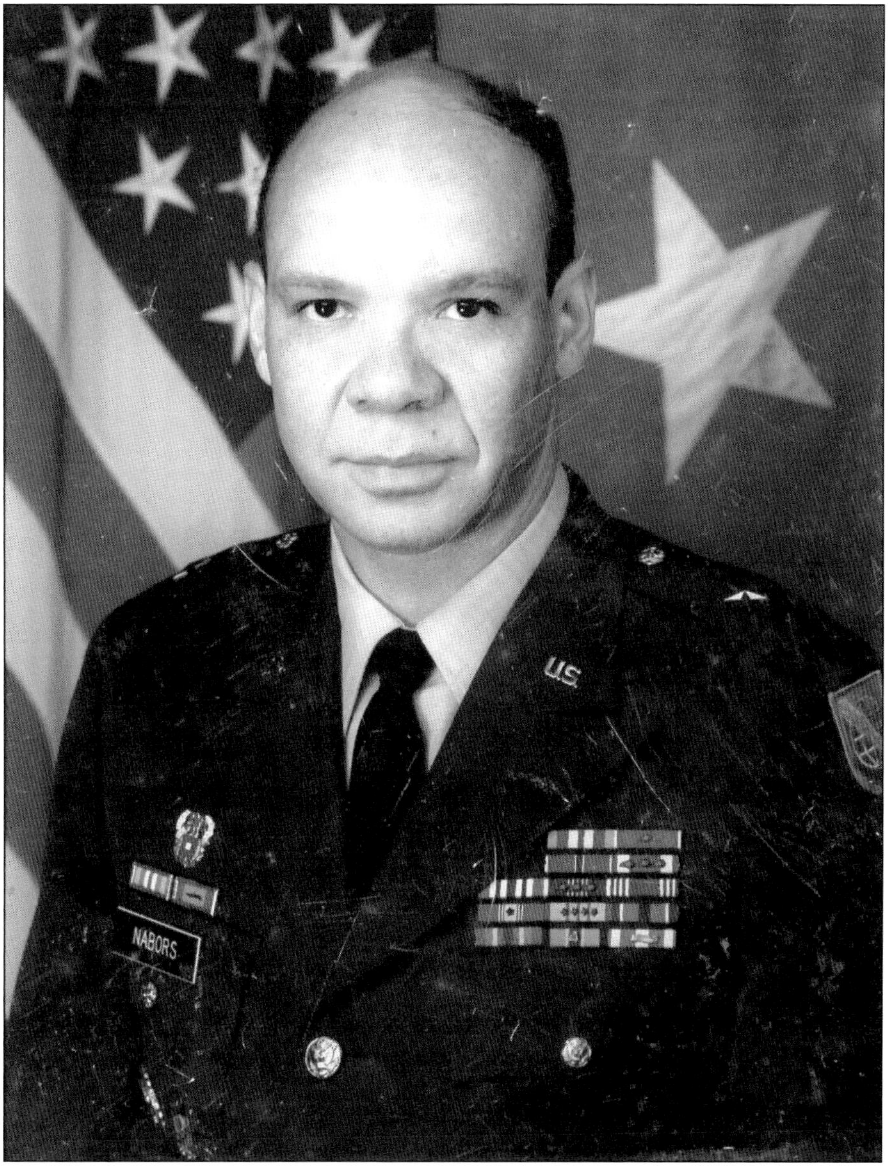

Maj. Gen. Robert L. Nabors, youngest son of Mansfield and Mabel Nabors of the Maysville District of Buckingham County, is a highly decorated U.S. Army officer who has received nearly 400 awards and honors and 38 official military awards and decorations. Major General Nabors received the Distinguished Service Medal, the military's third-highest award; Defense Superior Service Medal; Legion of Merit with four oak leaf clusters; Bronze Star Medal; and the Presidential Support Badge. Nabors's honorary awards include NAACP Roy Wilkins Award of Renown 2000. Nabors received a bachelor of science degree from the University of Arizona and an master of science degree in systems management from the University of Southern California. He served as a senior fellow in the National Security Affairs Program at Harvard University and is a graduate of the Senior Officials in National Security Program at Harvard. Nabors also is a member of the American Mensa Society. Nabors is presently senior vice president for EDS U.S. Government Solutions, with special responsibility for Homeland Security. (Courtesy of Michael Nabors.)

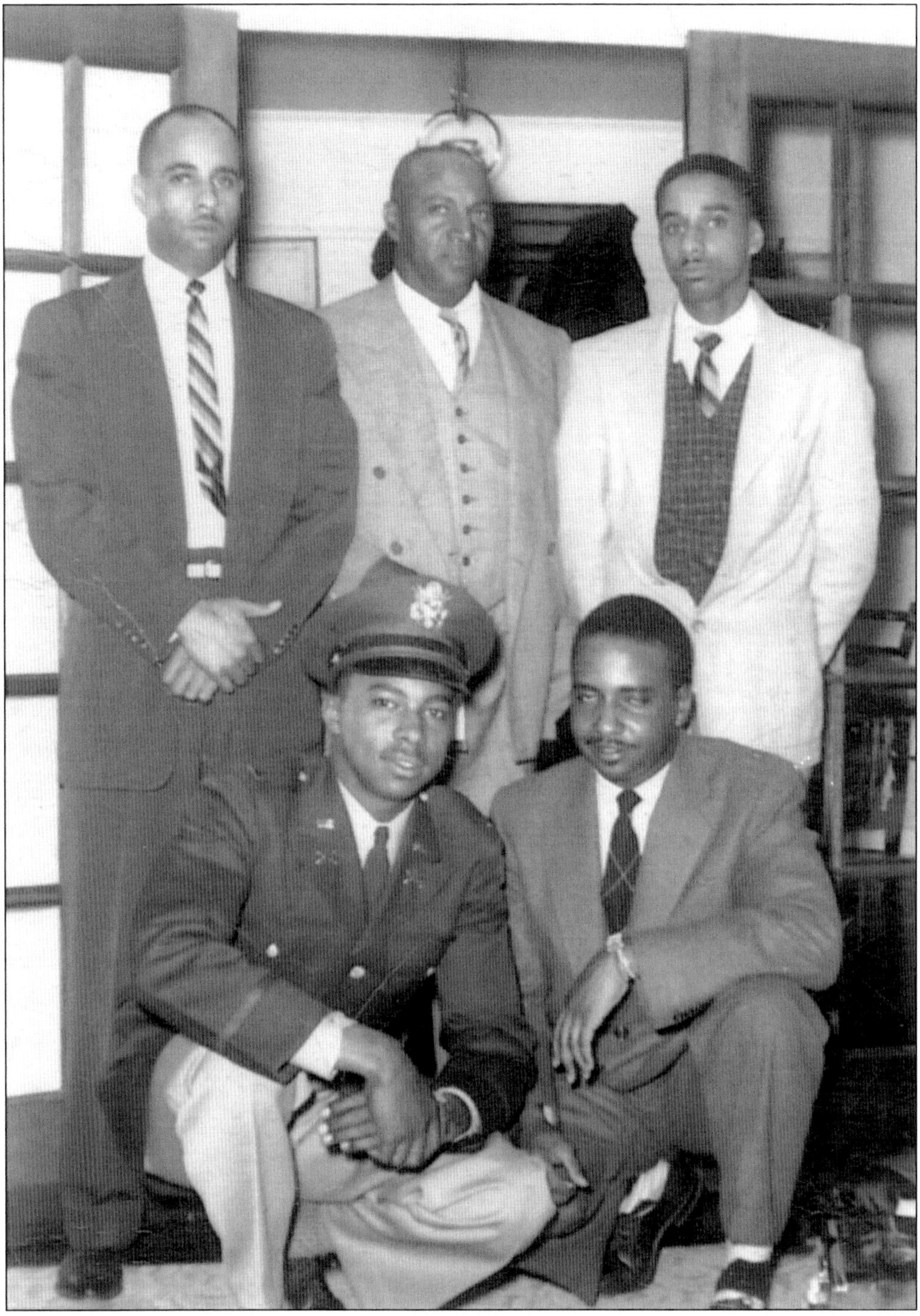

The Washington family has served in the military since the Civil War. Pictured here *c.* 1950, from left to right, are (first row) Korean War veterans Russell and Otto K.; (second row) Ulysses S. Jr., U.S. Navy, World War II; Ulysses S. Sr., U.S. Army, World War I; and Thomas, Army Air Force, World War II. (Courtesy Otto K. Washington.)

Six

Civic and Social Organizations

I have found that among its other benefits, giving liberates the soul of the giver.

—Maya Angelou (born 1928)

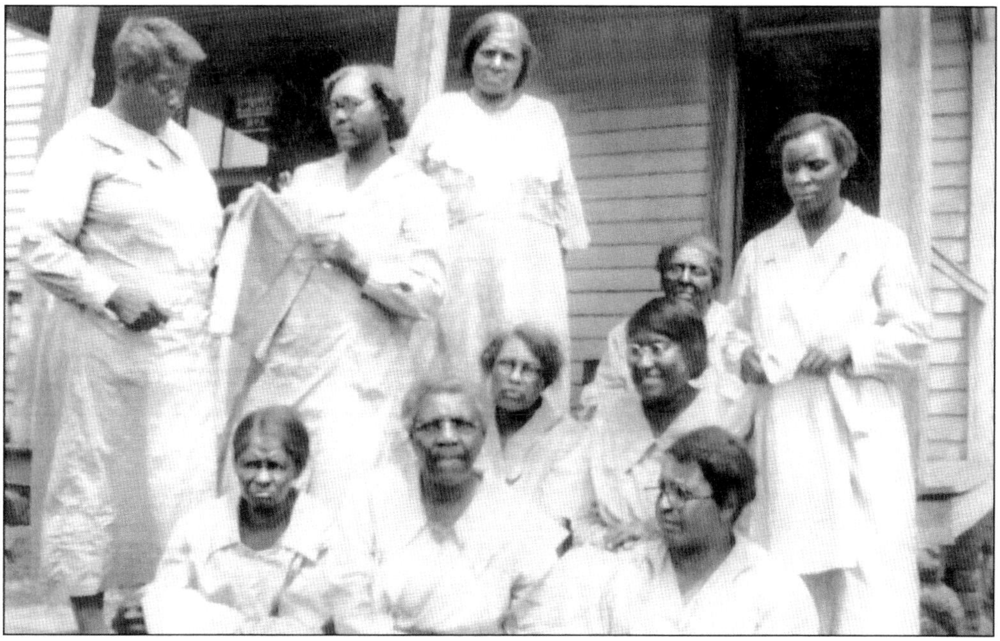

Pictured here are members of the Homemaking Club in the 1930s. As farming became more of a business enterprise and the problems of agriculture became more complex, a need for some special training in the field of agriculture and county life was evident. The establishment of homemaking clubs was an opportunity to demonstrate to the community the value of good farming practice. (Courtesy the Gooden family.)

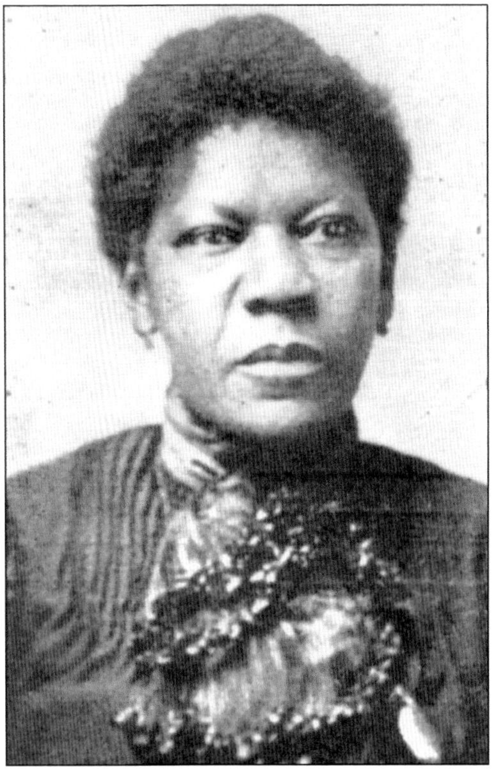

The Slate River Woman's Convention was an auxiliary to the Slate River Baptist Association of Central Virginia, established in 1925. The convention was established by Louisa Smith (left), founder and first president; Mary E. Redwood (below left), founder; and Sallie Miller (below right), founder. (Courtesy University of Virginia.)

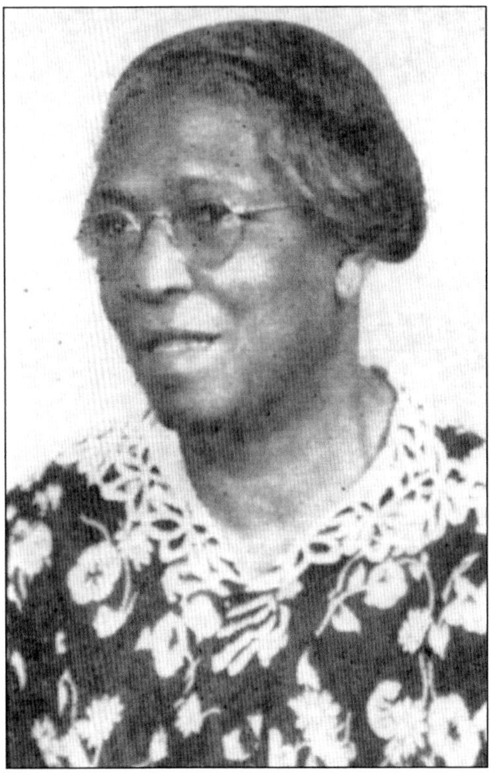

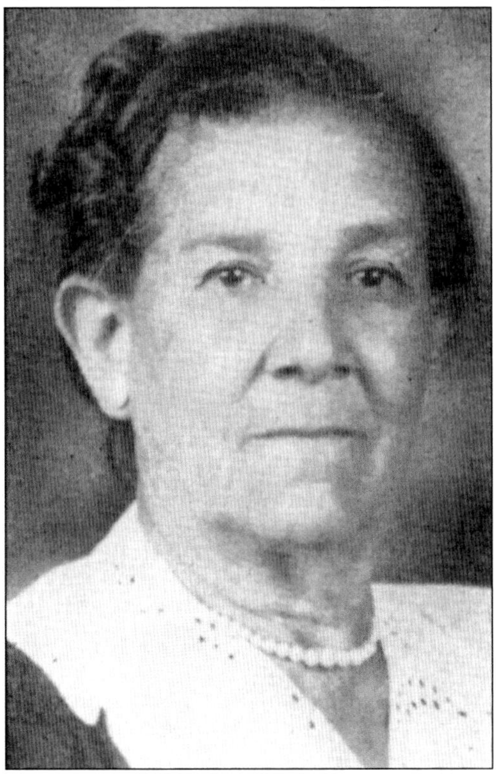

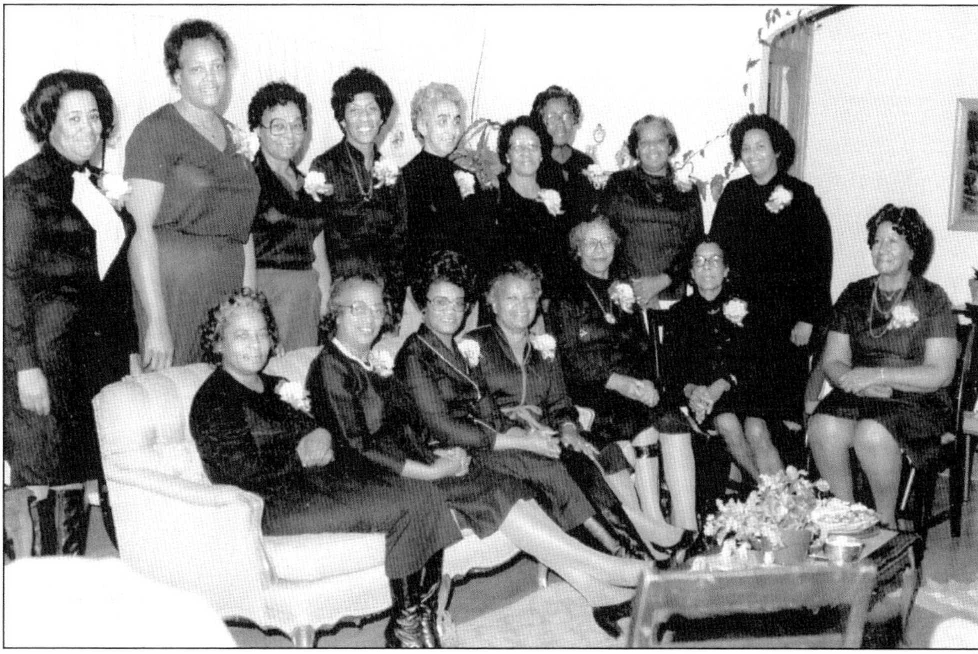

On January 21, 1956, Club XXV was organized by a group of concerned African American women to assist the less fortunate. The organization elected Carol P. Jones as its first president, with Americus B. Harris as vice president, Ophelia Shelton as secretary, Estherlynn Allen as treasurer, and Mary E. K. Logan as chaplain. As Club XXV evolved, the organization expanded its focus on education, family life, community improvement, civic participation, and recreation. Club XXV selected the carnation as its flower and green and white as its colors. (Courtesy Charles W. White Sr.)

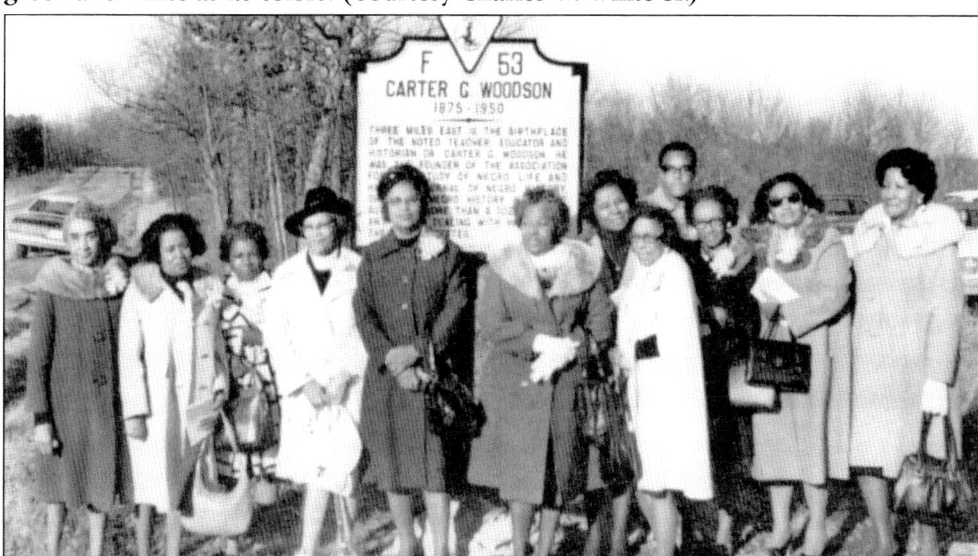

Pictured here are members of Club XXV at the dedication ceremony of the Dr. Carter G. Woodson state historic highway marker in 1976. The marker is located on U.S. Highway 15. Dr. Woodson's birthplace is three miles east of the marker. (Courtesy Charles W. White Sr.)

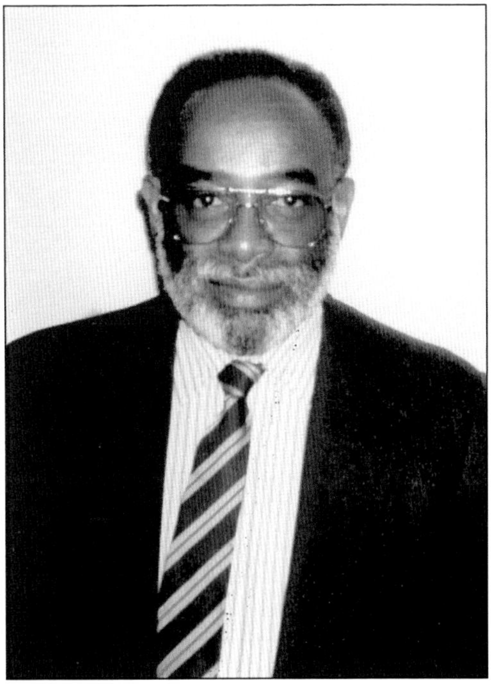

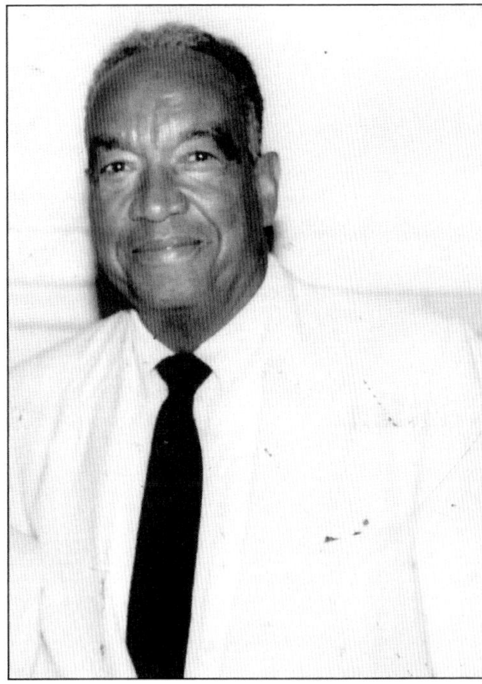

Shown on the left is James Jones, the current president of the NAACP–Buckingham County Branch. The late Douglas Patterson, who was past president of the NAACP–Buckingham County Branch, is shown on the right. The Buckingham branch of the NAACP was established by African American community leaders and parents. They wanted county officials to address their concerns regarding education for Buckingham County's African American children, who were being ignored at the time. (Courtesy Charles W. White Sr.)

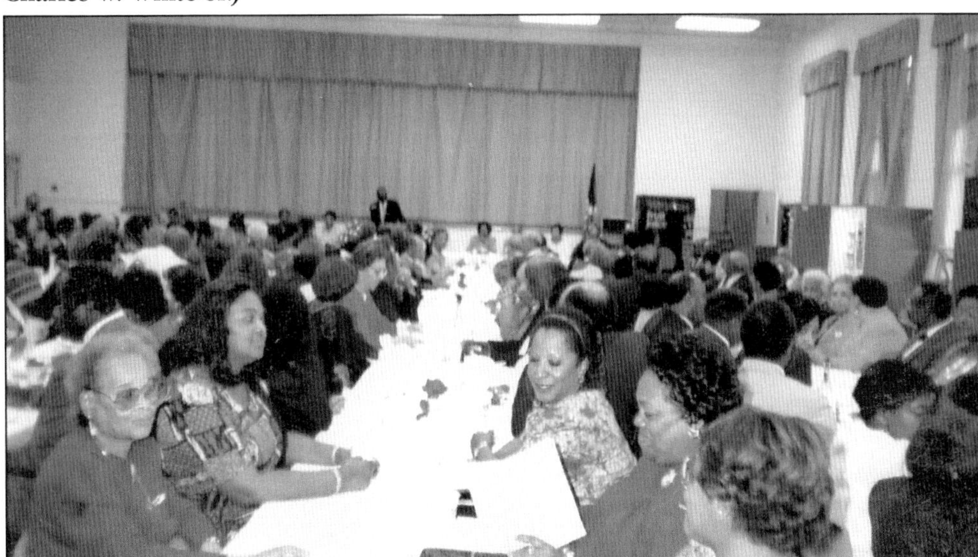

Pictured here are attendees at the Buckingham County Branch of the NAACP Freedom Fund banquet. This banquet is one of the organization's largest events in the county. (Courtesy Charles W. White Sr.)

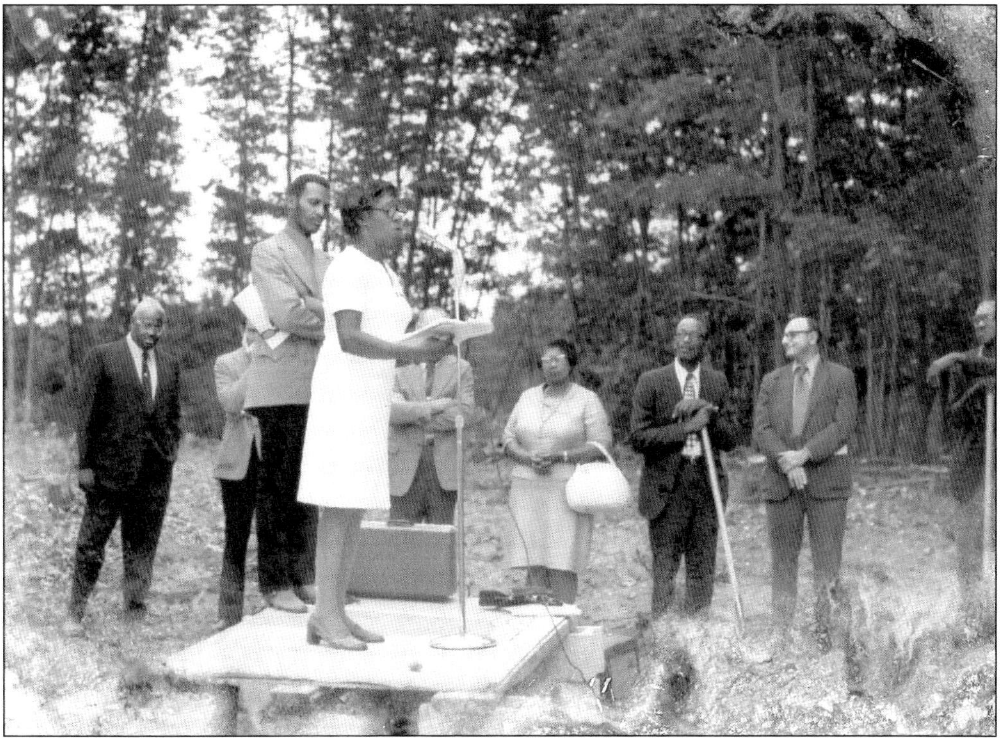

The groundbreaking ceremony of the Central Virginia Community Health Center, located in New Canton in the Marshall District, was held *c.* 1970. The center provides a variety of health care services to the residents throughout Southside Virginia. (Courtesy Charles W. White Sr.)

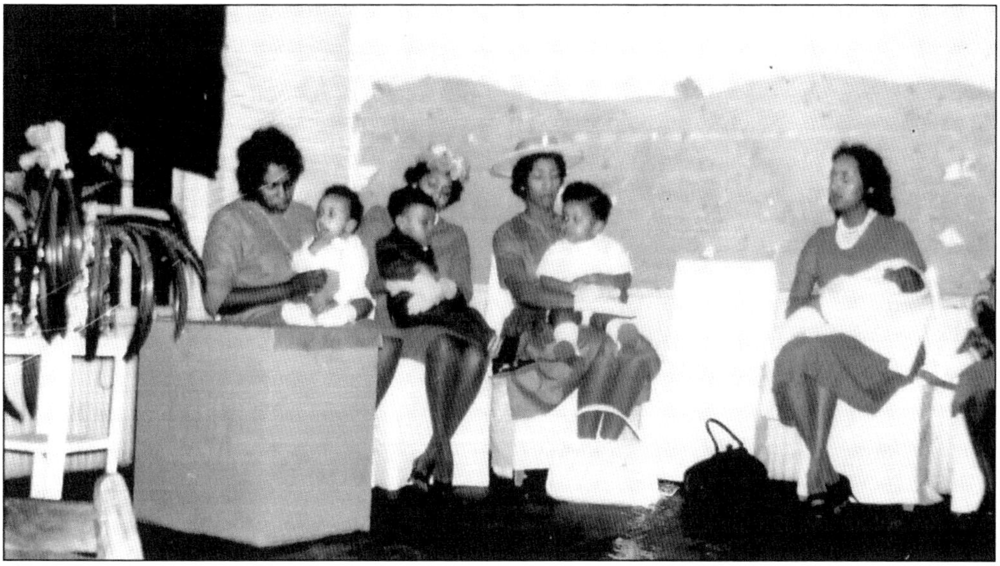

Pictured here are contestants in the Buckingham County Baby Contest, which was a fund-raiser to purchase school supplies. The event was held at the Stephen J. Ellis Elementary School in the 1960s. (Courtesy Charles W. White Sr.)

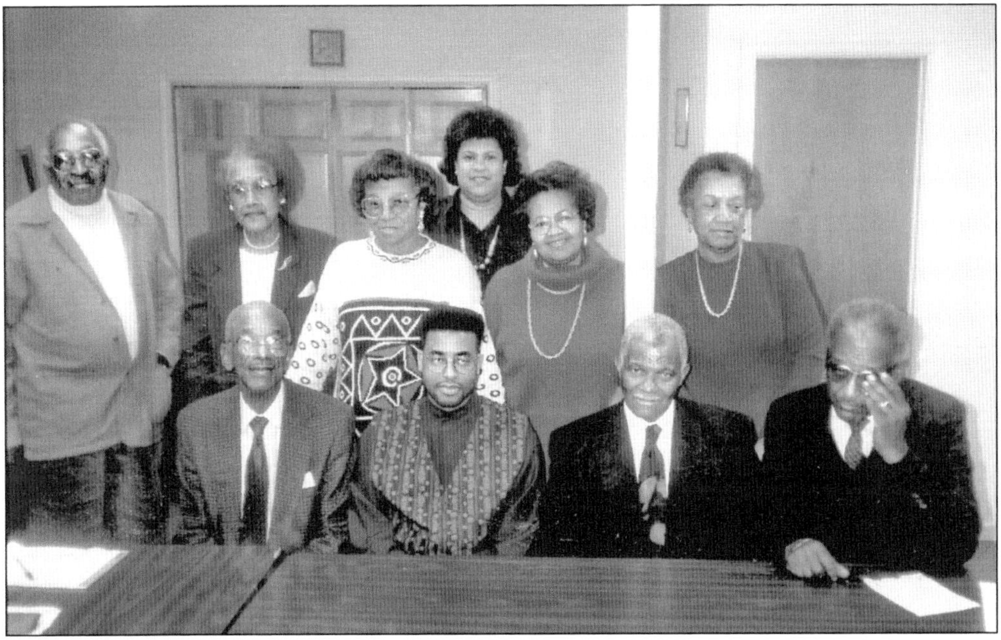

Members of the Buckingham County Afro-American Life and History Society shown here include co-author Charles W. White Sr. (seated far right), who is president of the Buckingham County Afro-American Life and History Society. (Courtesy Charles W. White Sr.)

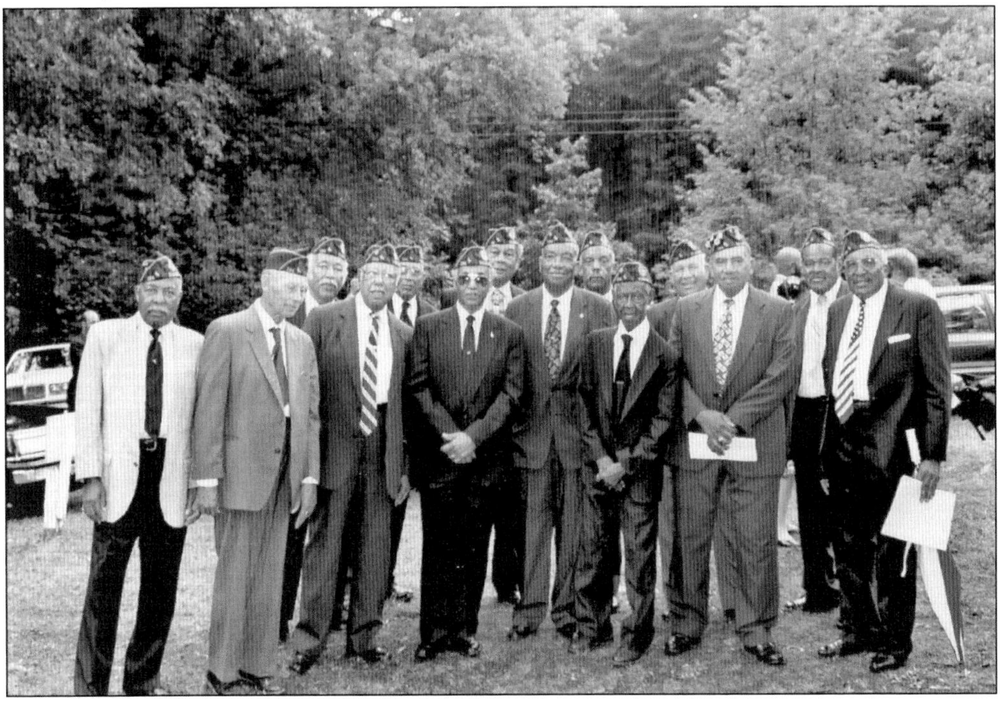

Pictured here are members of the American Legion Post 134. In 2003, the American Legion Post 134 received the coveted Golden Eagle Award at the 10th District American Legion Convention. (Courtesy Charles W. White Sr.)

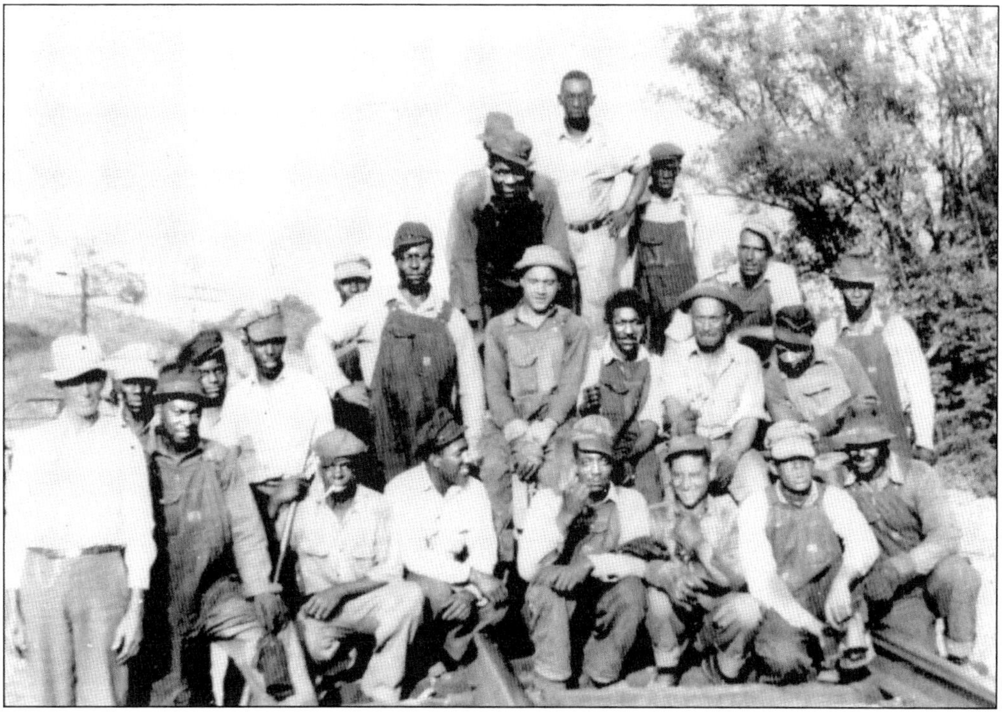

This is a photograph of a crew of railroad track maintenance workers taken in 1943. Many of the workers were from Buckingham County. (Courtesy Charles W. White Sr.)

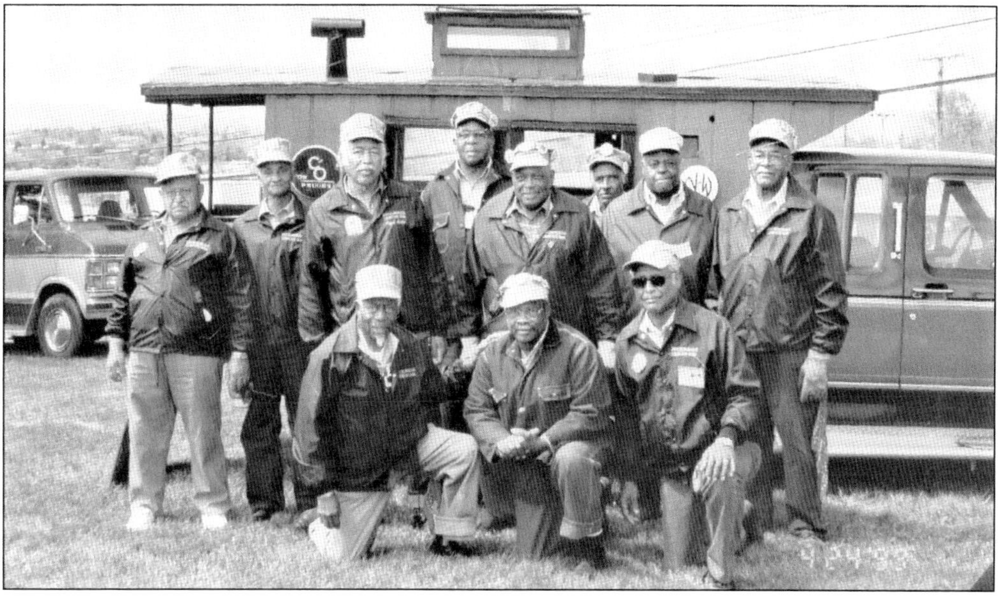

Shown here are the re-enactors of the Buckingham Lining Bar Gang, which is currently in its 15th season of performing. This group was established in 1990, following a reunion of former railroad employees organized by the Virginia Foundation for the Humanities' Piedmont Humanities Council and the Virginia Folklife Program. The re-enactors are steeped in the "worksong" and occupational tradition of Virginia's old railroad workers and have performed throughout the United States. (Courtesy Charles W. White Sr.)

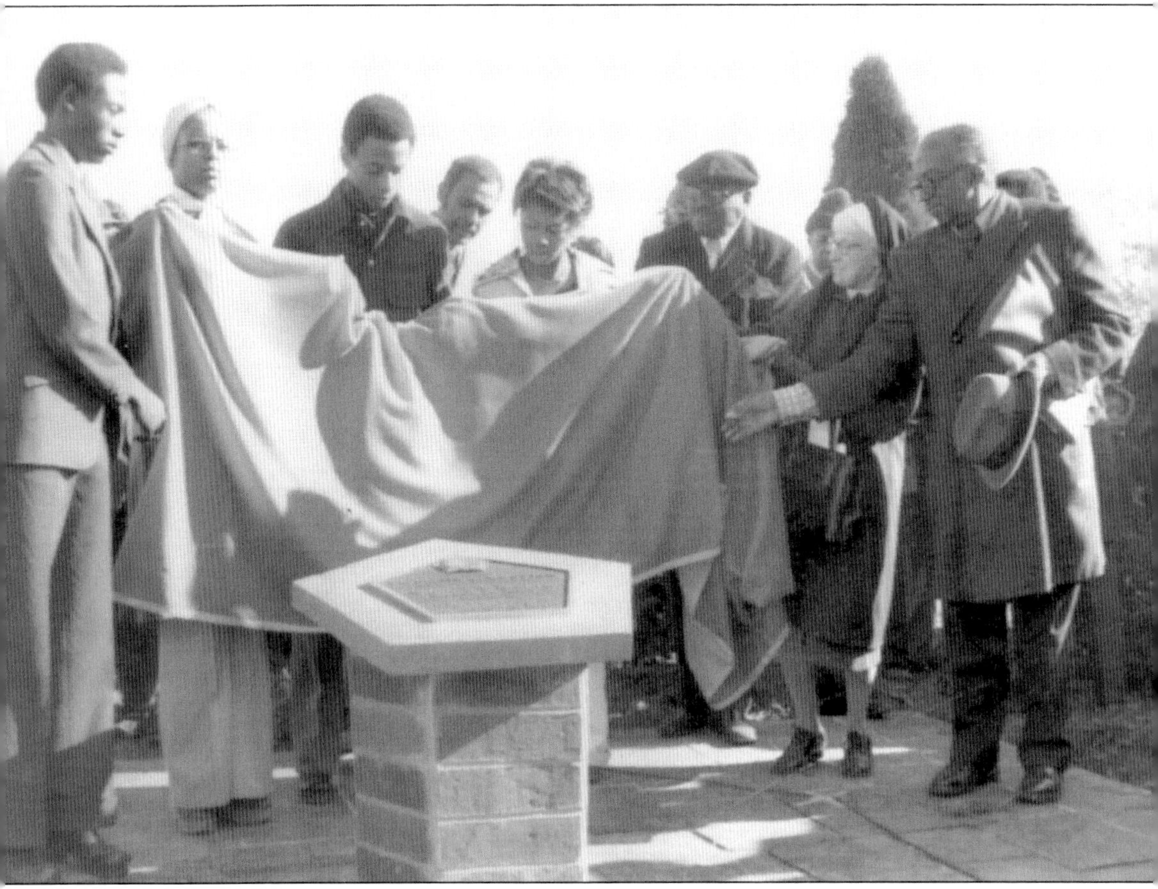

This photograph was taken at the unveiling of the Carter G. Woodson Birthplace Marker on December 19, 1975, to commemorate the 100th birthday of Dr. Woodson. The marker is located in New Canton in the Marshall District of Buckingham County. (Courtesy George Frank Harris.)

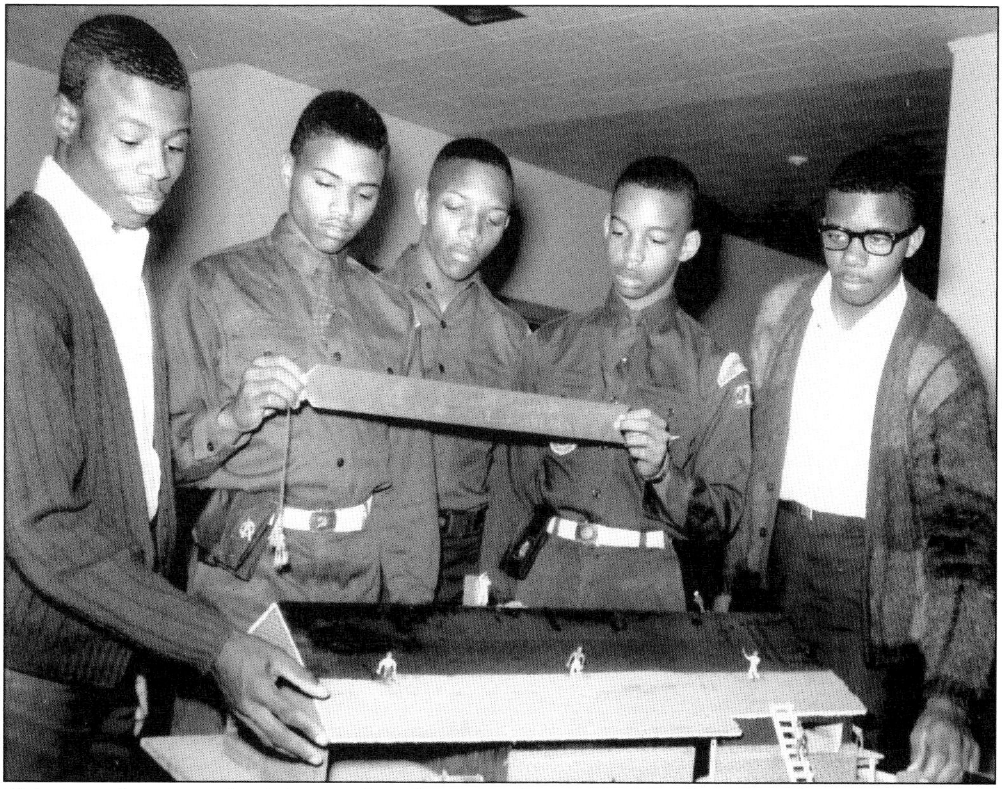

This is a photograph of the Buckingham Explorer Scouts taken *c.* 1965. The Scouts are shown here with the banner they won in a Post Specialty Contest in the category of building. (Courtesy George Frank Harris.)

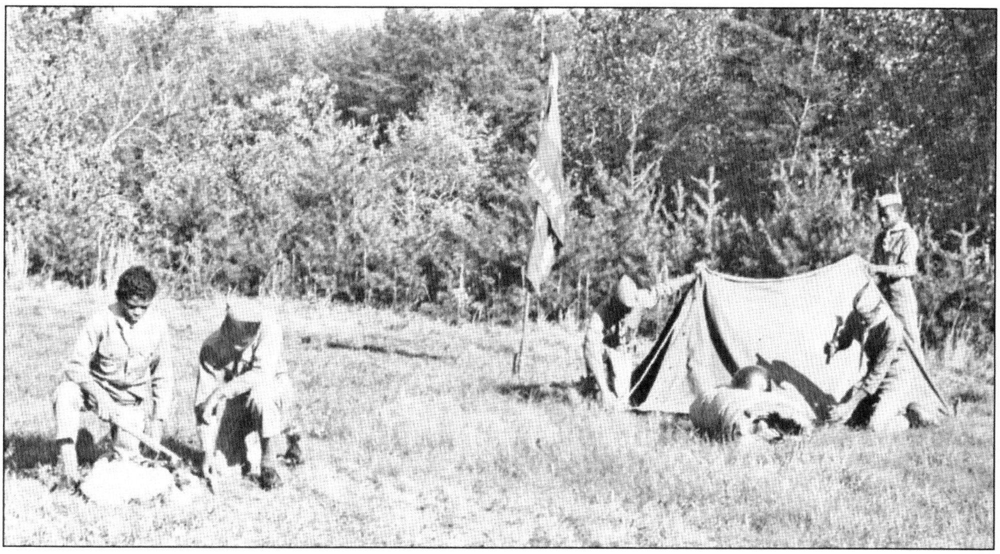

The Buckingham Boy Scouts show their skills in 1967 by setting up tents under their Scout leader's direction. The Boy Scouts of America was incorporated in 1910 to provide a program for community organizations that offer effective character, citizenship, and personal fitness training for youth. (Courtesy Charles W. White Sr.)

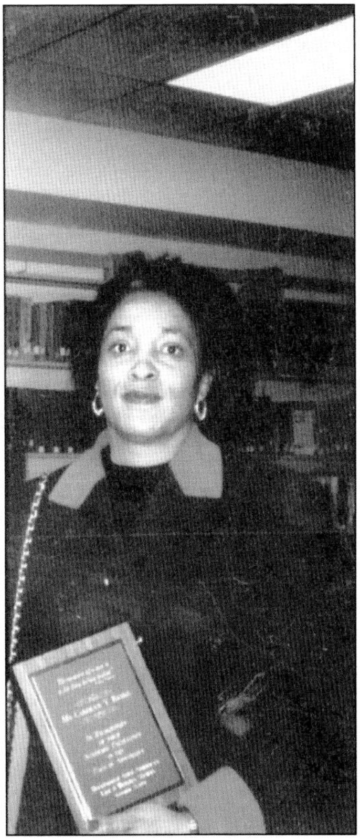

In 1997, the Buckingham County Afro-American Life and History Society presented a plaque to Carolyn Y. Banks for her academic excellence during the height of integration. Carolyn Y. Banks was Buckingham Central High School's valedictorian in 1969. (Courtesy Charles W. White Sr.)

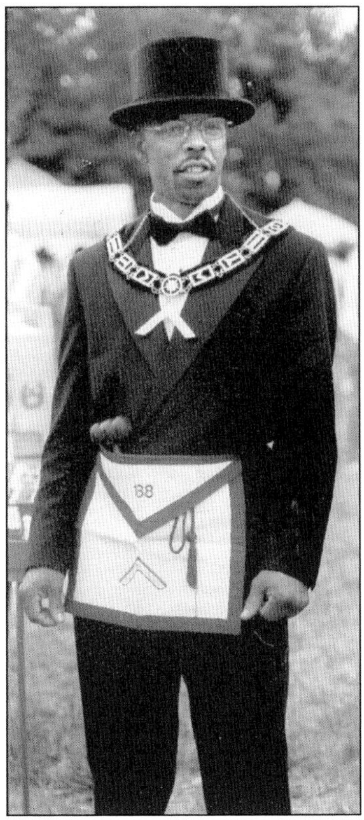

Pictured here is Larry Haskins, who is the worshipful master of the Keystone Lodge Number 188. The Keystone Lodge Number 188 is a fraternal organization that provides scholarships to high school graduates in Buckingham County among its charitable contributions to the community. (Courtesy Larry Haskins.)

Seven

20TH-CENTURY LIFE IN OUR COUNTY

All labor that uplifts humanity has dignity and importance and should be undertaken with painstaking excellence.

—Martin Luther King Jr. (1929–1968)

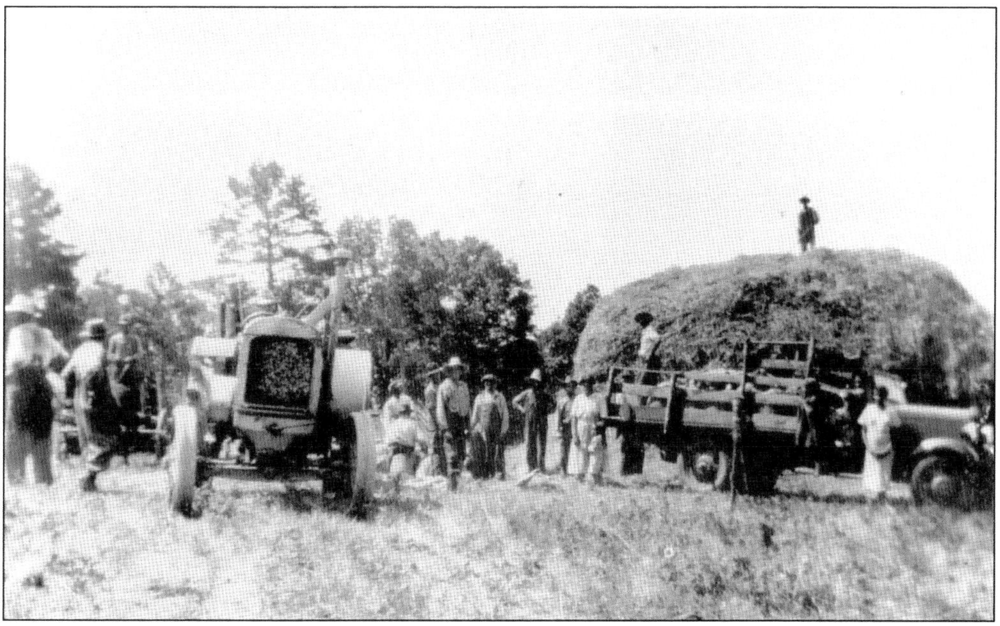

Here men thrash wheat in Buckingham County. Historically, the economy was principally supported by agriculture. For several generations, agriculture had been the mainstay for many African Americans in the county. During the mid- to late 1950s, following the national trend, the agricultural industry began to decline. (Courtesy Janie M. Osborne.)

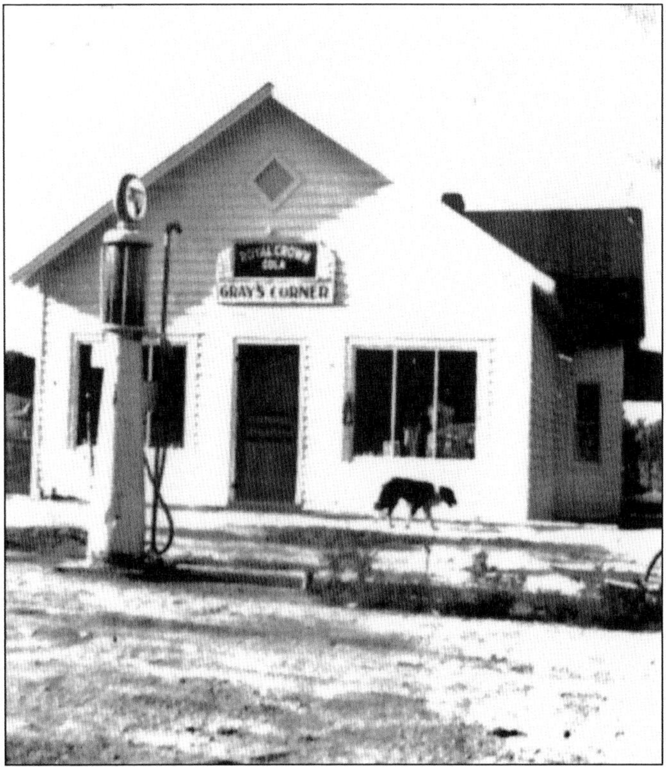

Gray's Corner Store and Gas Station was established in 1949 and located in the James River District in Buckingham County. (Courtesy Harvey W. Shelton.)

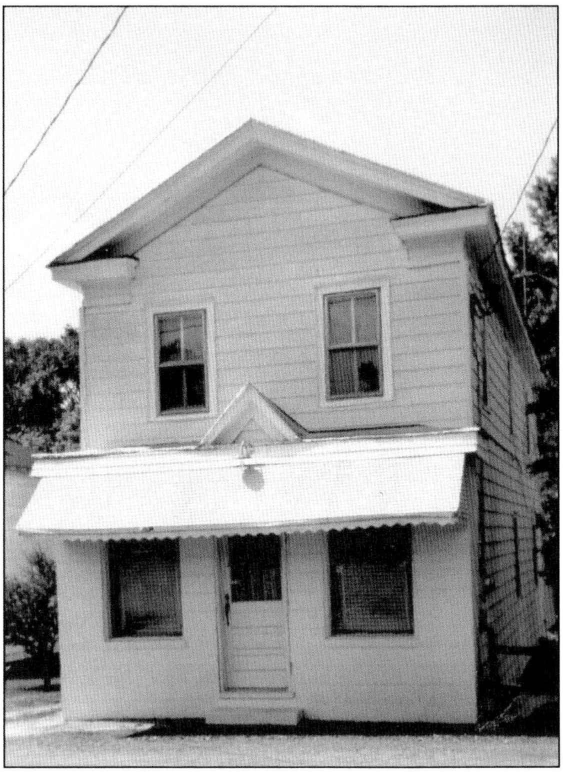

Walker's Restaurant was established in the mid-1930s and was in operation until 1958. This restaurant was noted for serving several educators in the community. The second floor served as a recreation center for African American youth in Buckingham County. (Courtesy of Charles W. White Sr.)

William Logan is posing on a farm tractor in this 1959 photograph. (Courtesy Irene Cottrell Collection.)

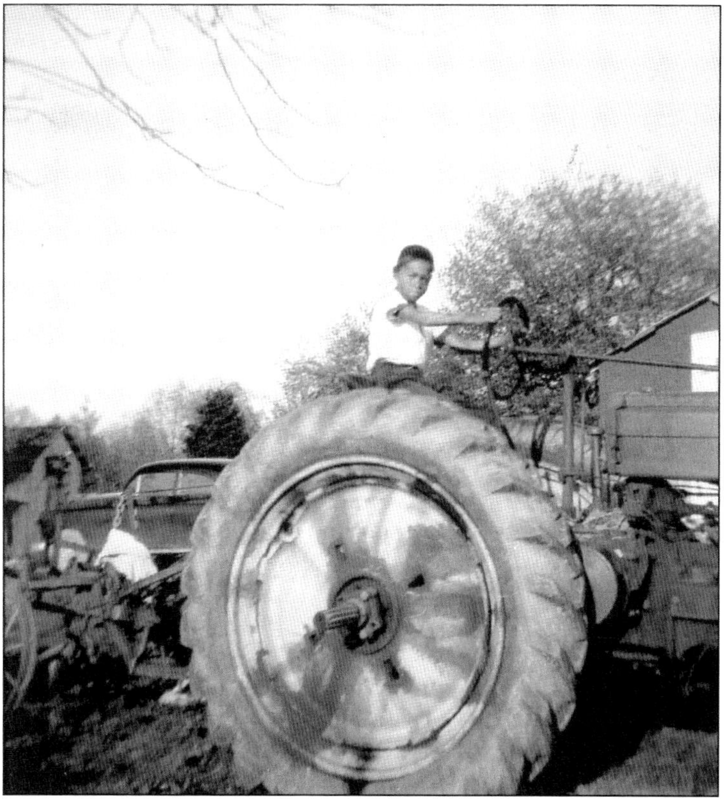

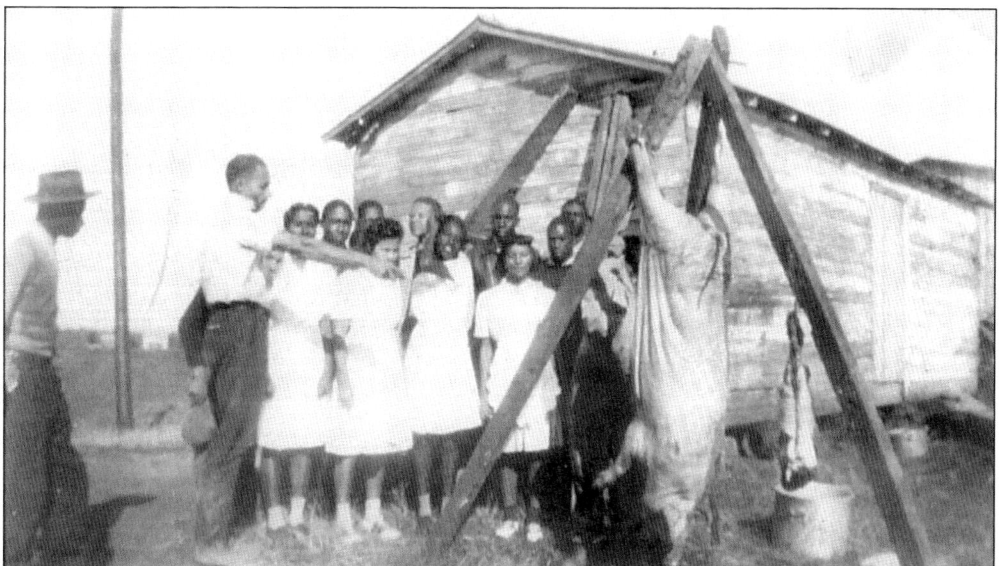

County extension agent Ulysses S. Washington of Buckingham County explains the process of hog butchering to a group of students. (Courtesy Otto K. Washington.)

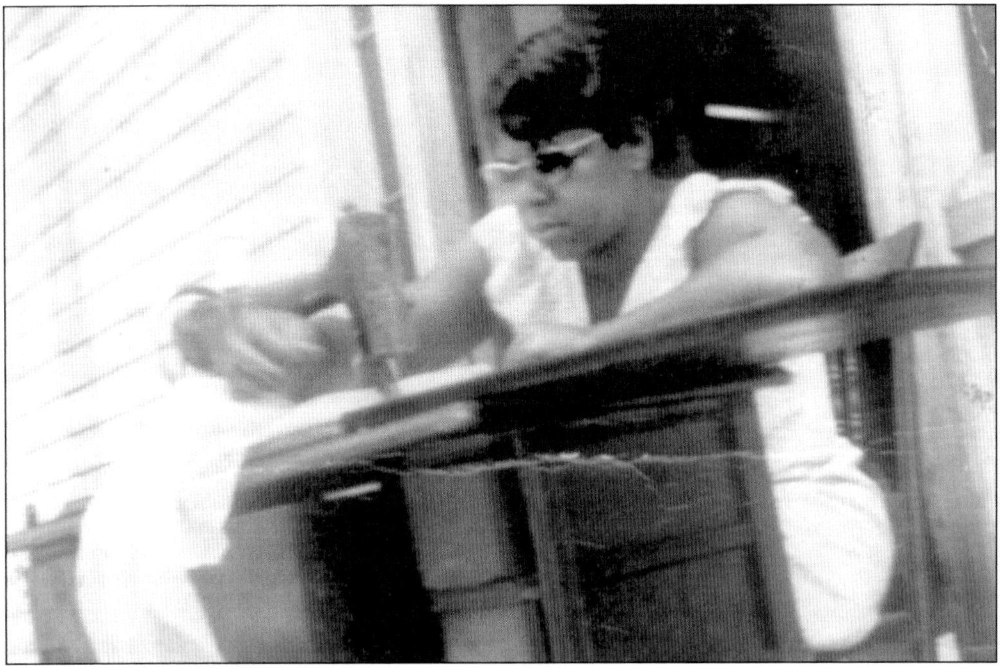

Belinda Patterson Robinson is making a garment. Sewing and quilting were important in the daily lives of county residents. Many quilting and sewing circles were established and engaged in fund-raising for various charitable projects in the community. (Courtesy Janie M. Osborne.)

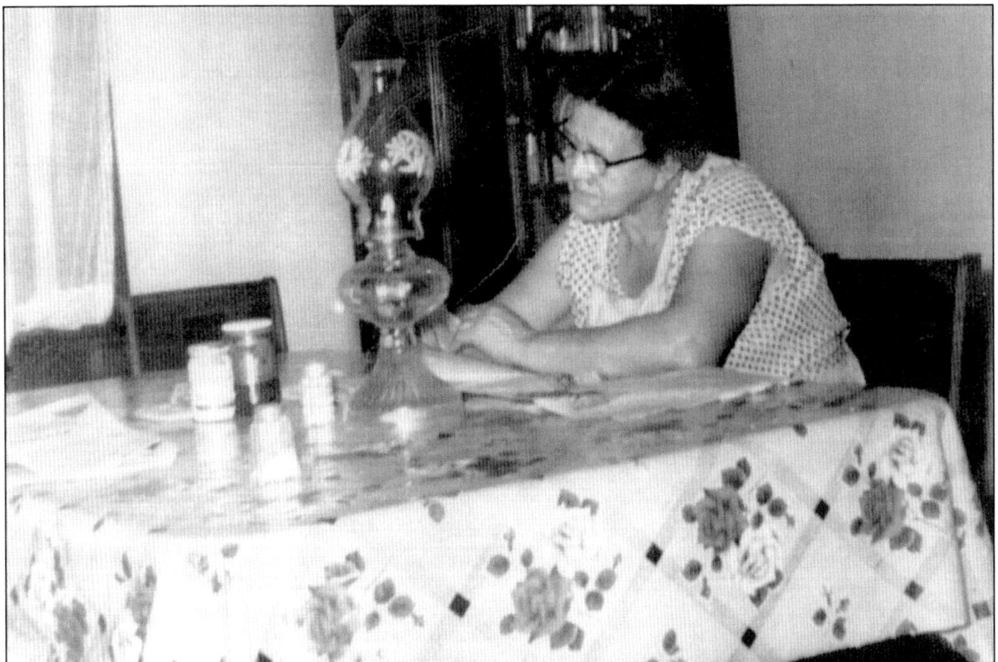

Freda Osborne is pictured here reading her Bible by oil lamp. (Courtesy Janie M. Osborne.)

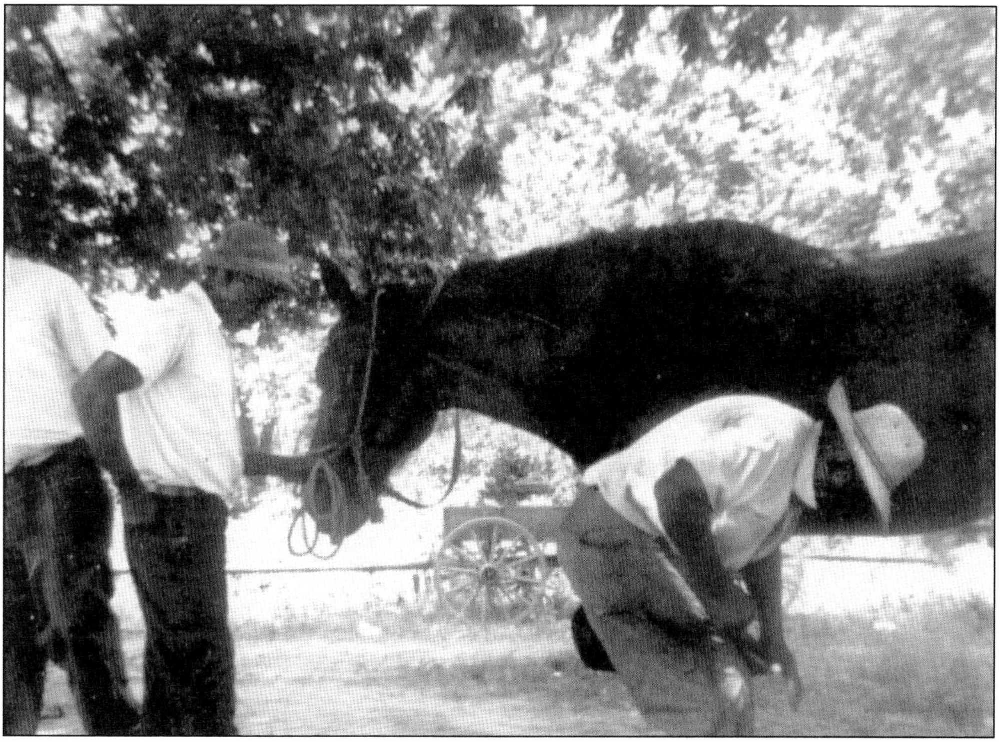

Robert Patterson is shown here shoeing his horse. Note the wagon in the background. (Courtesy Janie M. Osborne.)

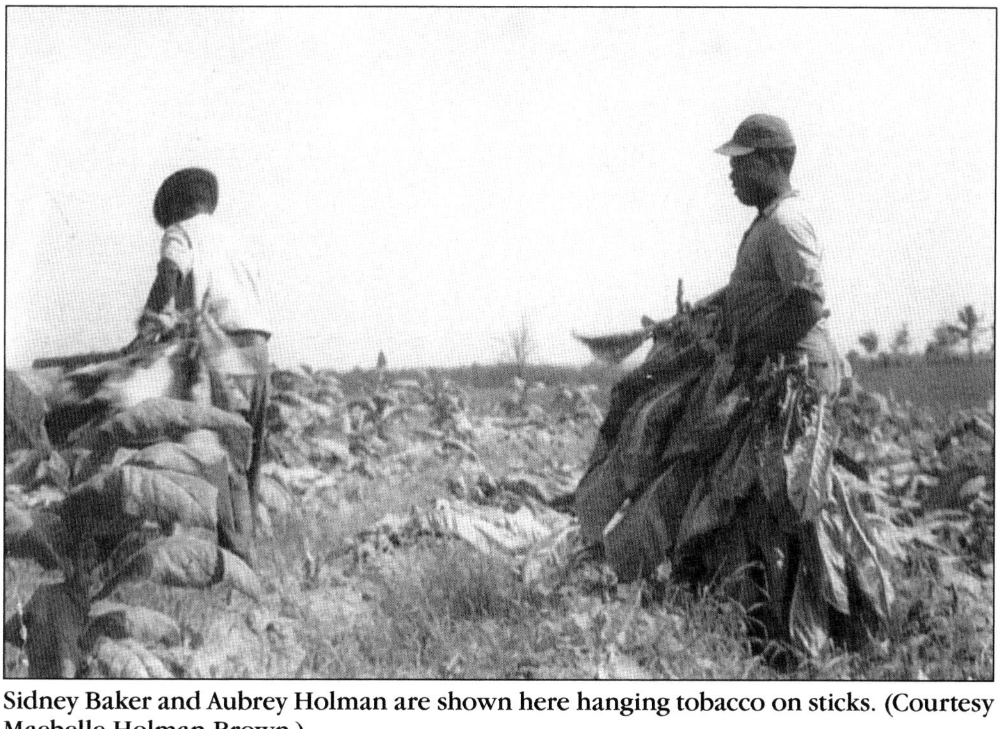

Sidney Baker and Aubrey Holman are shown here hanging tobacco on sticks. (Courtesy Maebelle Holman Brown.)

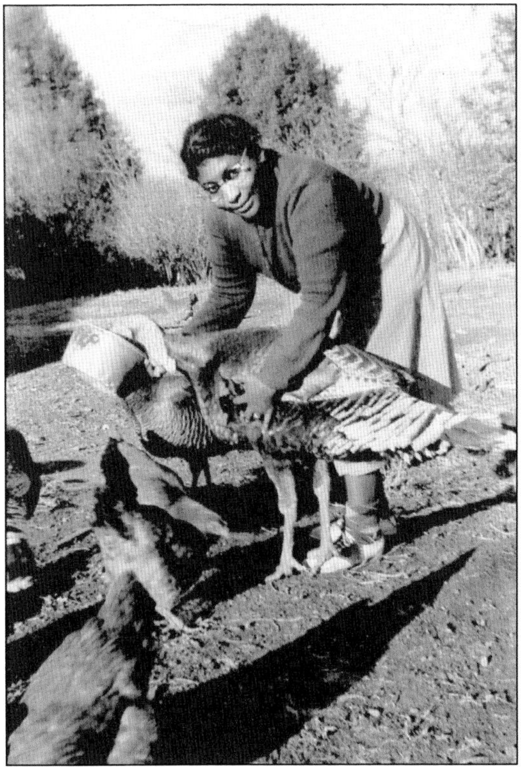

Pictured here is Lucy Chambers with her pet turkey in 1963. (Courtesy Irene Cottrell Collection.)

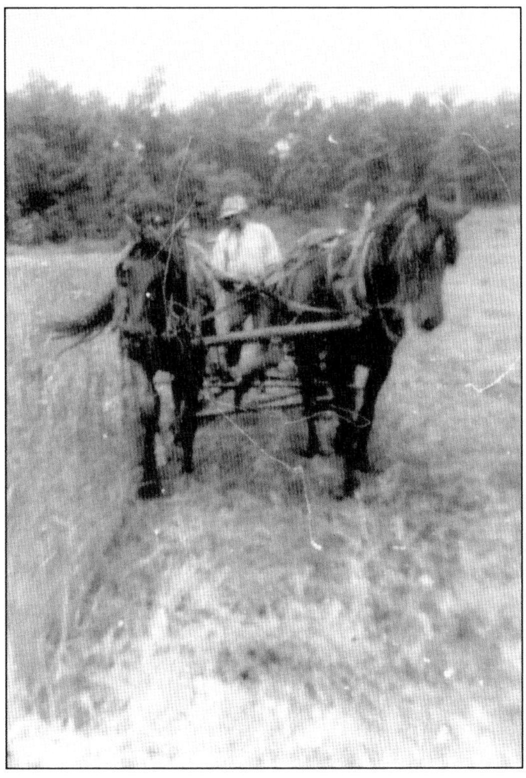

George Patterson cuts hay on his horse-drawn mower, *c.* 1945. (Courtesy Cora L. Perkins.)

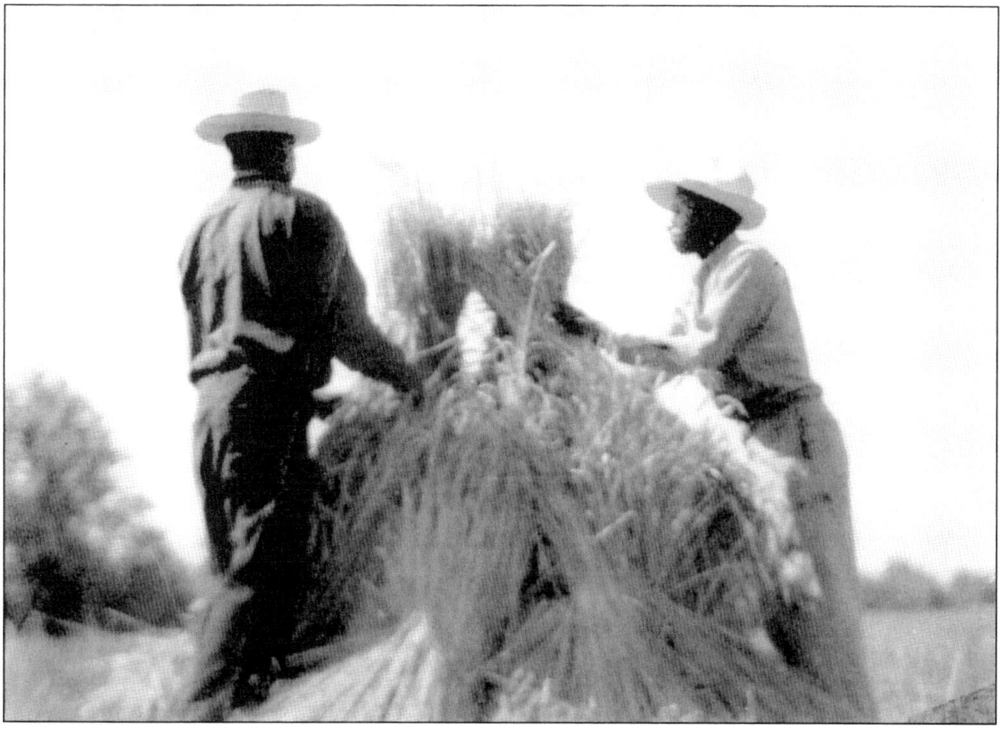

John Holman and Lou Braxton are shown here stacking wheat. (Courtesy Maebelle Holman Brown.)

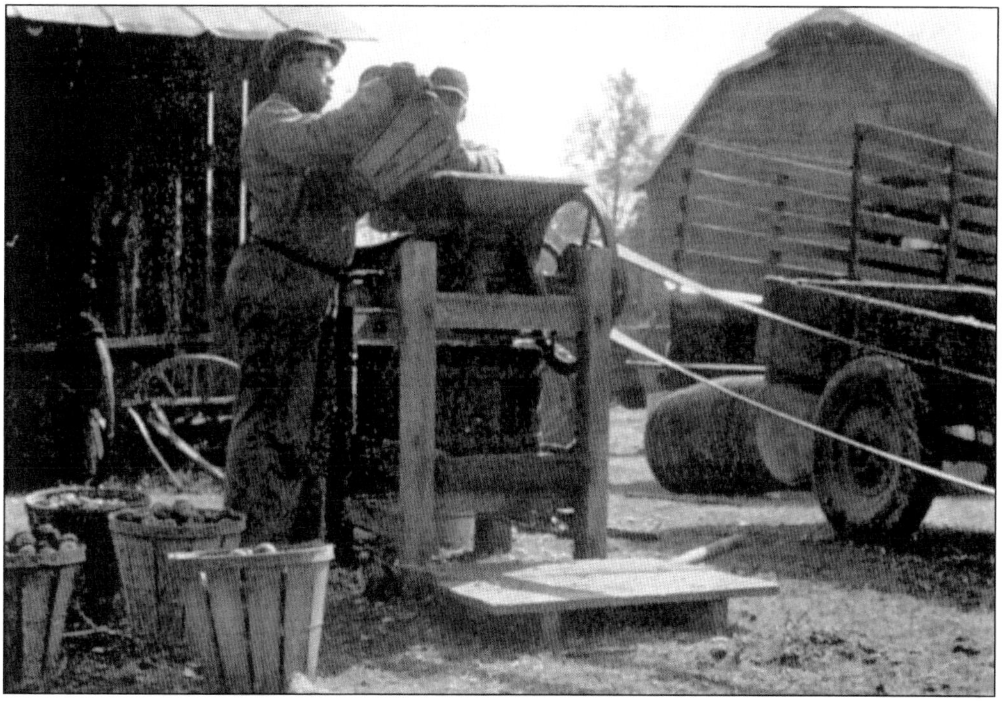

Pictured here are Sidney Baker and Allen Ross making homemade cider. (Courtesy Maebelle Holman Brown.)

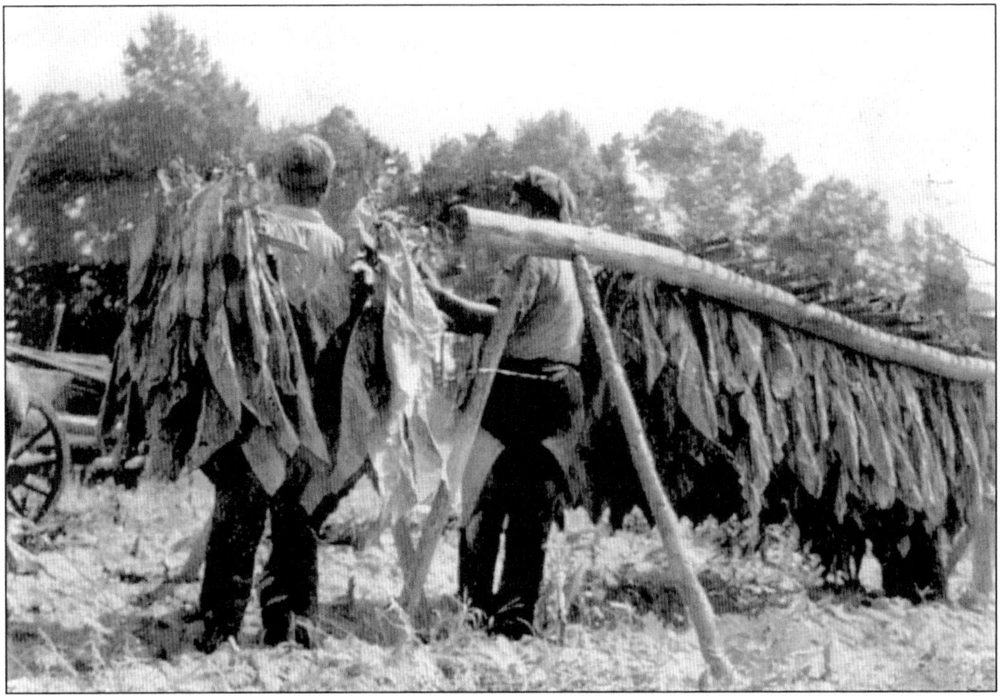

Buck Holman and Sidney Baker are hanging tobacco on a scaffold. As part of the tobacco harvesting process, scaffolds were used for field wilting. (Courtesy Maebelle Holman Brown.)

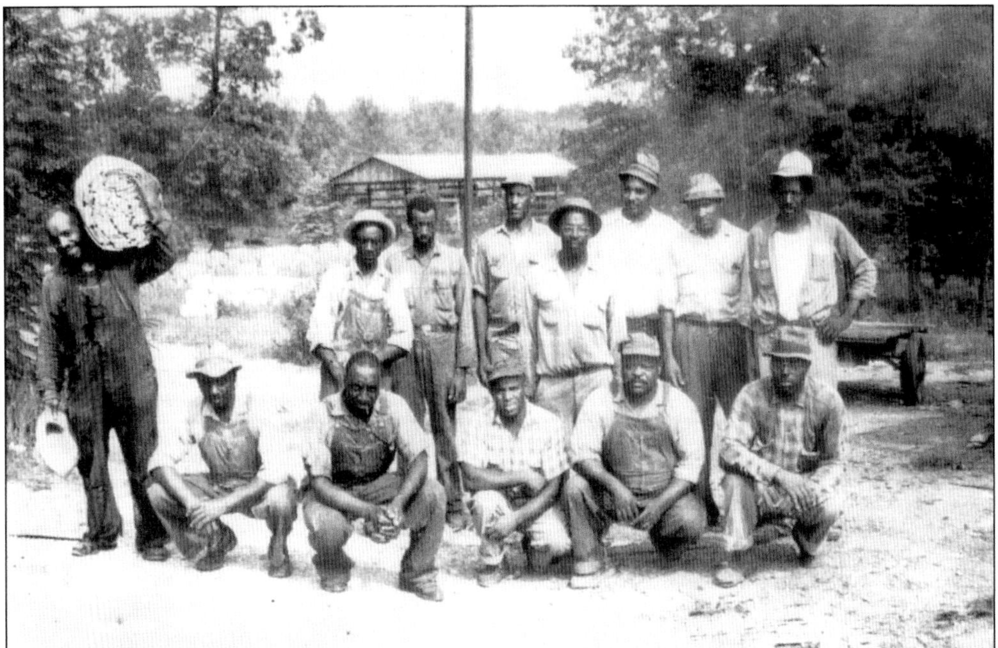

Stave mill workers in Buckingham County are pictured here, *c.* 1950. The man standing on the left is carrying staves. Typically, staves are stacked and taken to a kiln for drying. (Courtesy Charles W. White Sr.)

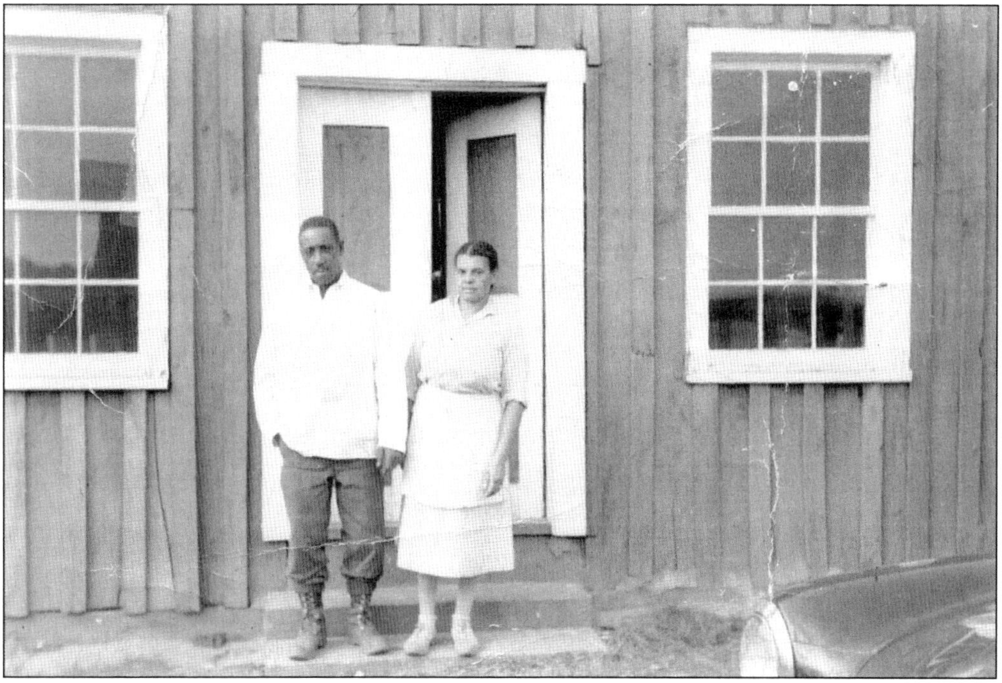

Pictured here are Susie and Charlie Claiborne in front of their place of work at the Sam Goodloe Hunt Club, which was located in Buckingham County. (Courtesy Claiborne family.)

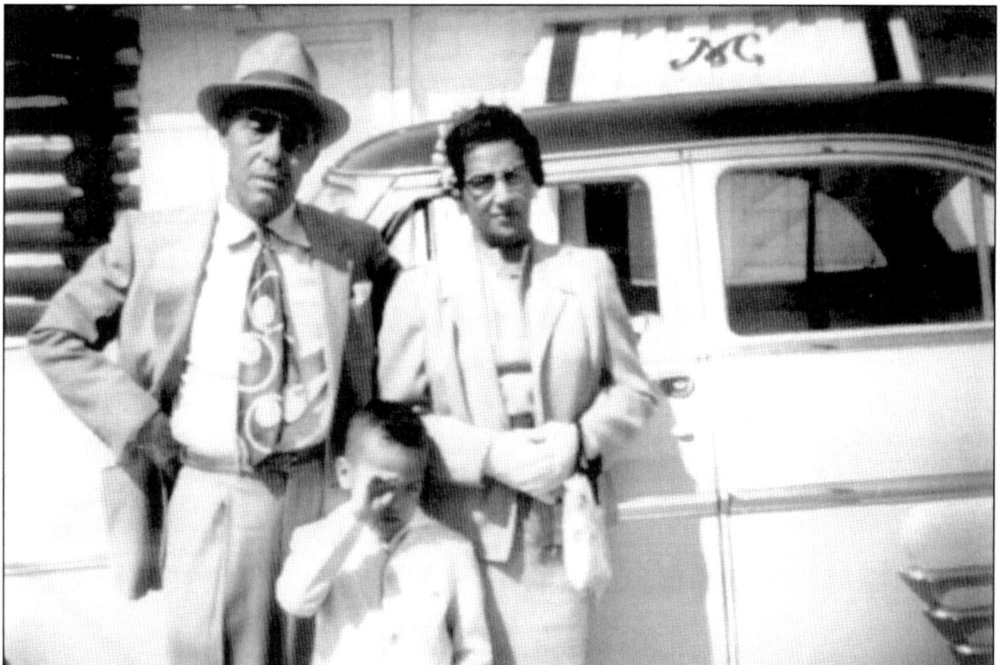

Willie and Lucille Mays, owners of May's Café, pose here with their grandson, Bruce. May's Café, which opened *c.* 1950, was in operation for 48 years in Buckingham County. (Courtesy Maxine M. McHaffey.)

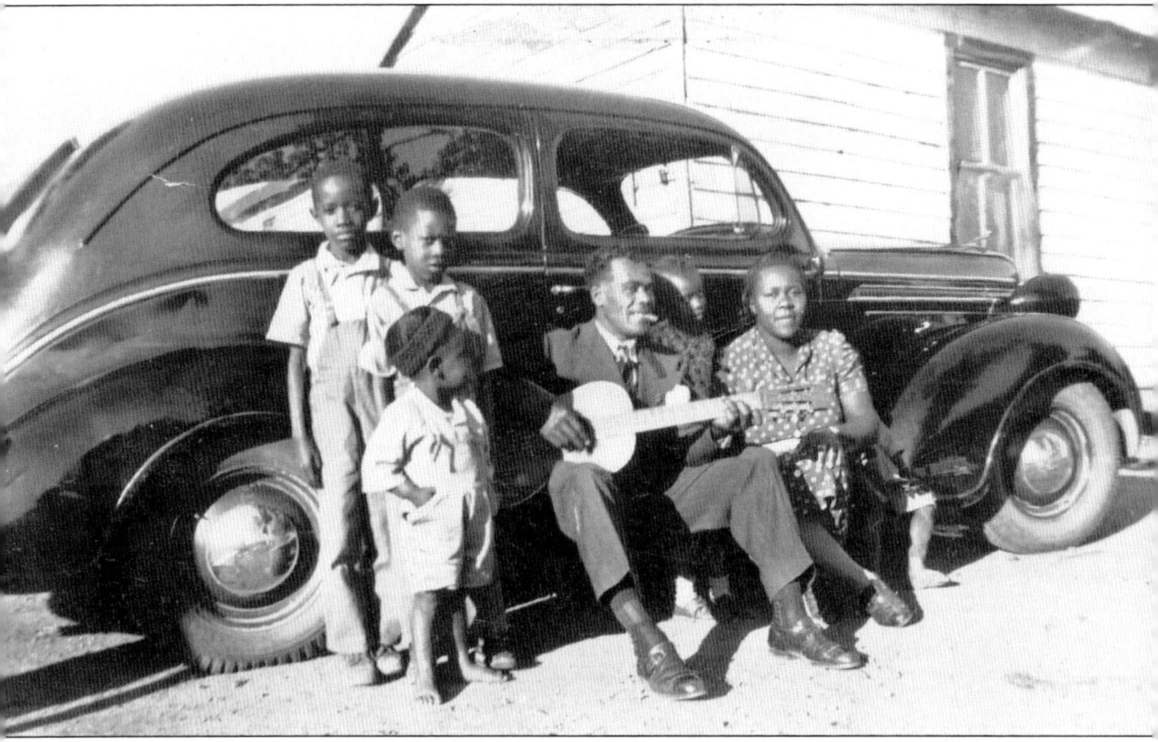

Percy Nance plays his guitar and entertains the children in the 1950s. (Courtesy Janie M. Osborne.)

Eight

Our Arts and Entertainment

Any form of art is a form of power; it has impact, it can affect change—it cannot only move us, it makes us move.

—Ossie Davis (1917–2005)

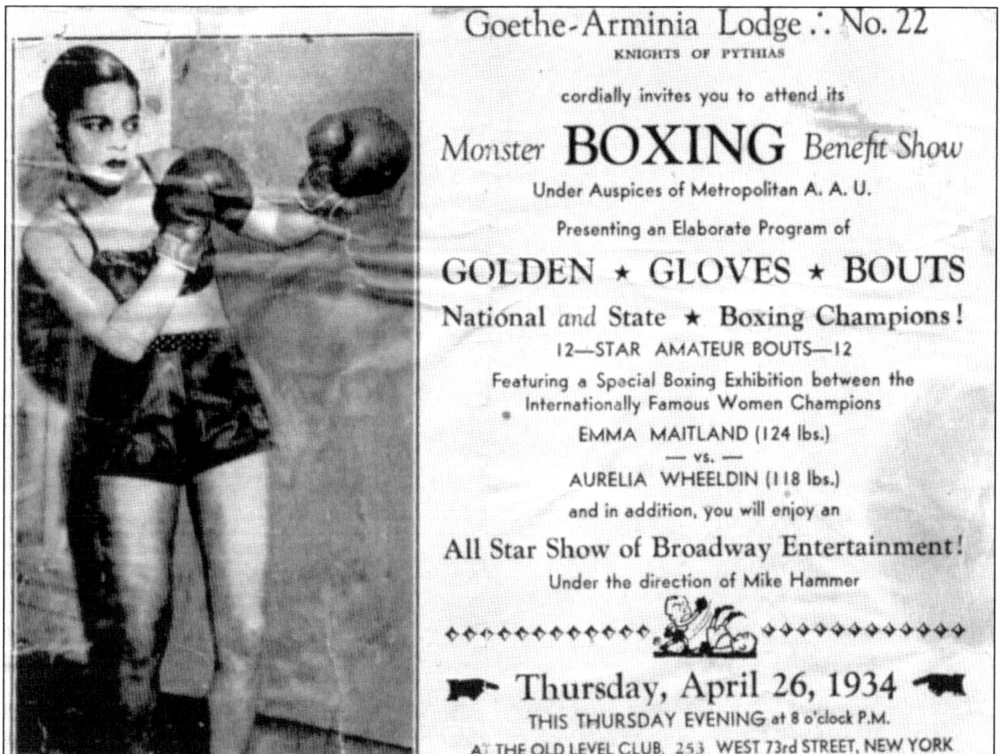

Emma Chambers Maitland, born in January 1893 in the James River District of Buckingham County to Wyatt and Cora Chambers, became an international champion pugilist in the 1920s and 1930s. In addition to boxing, Maitland was a stage actress and performed in Europe in the Broadway hit *Blackbirds*. (Courtesy John C. Jones family.)

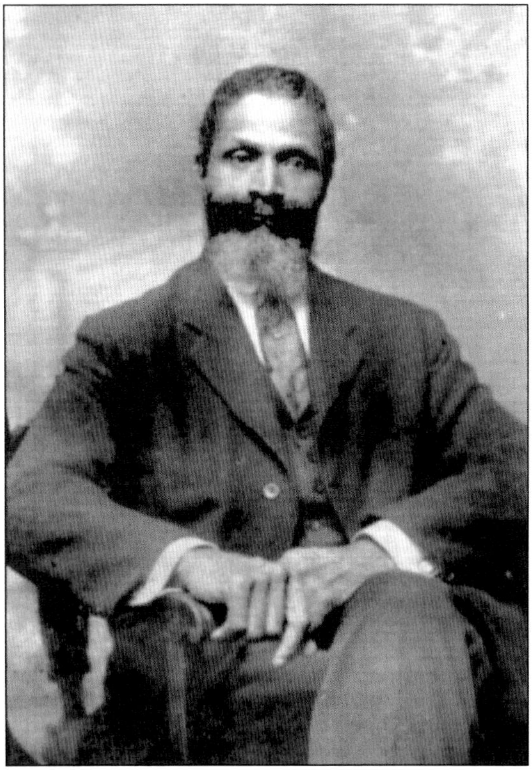

William Shedrick Miller, born into slavery in 1852 in Buckingham County, became a member of Chestnut Grove Baptist Church in 1870 and served as a deacon. In 1879, Deacon Miller organized a Sunday school known as Union Branch. He was also an author and wrote *History of the Straightway That Leads to Heaven.* (Courtesy Eugene T. Miller Jr.)

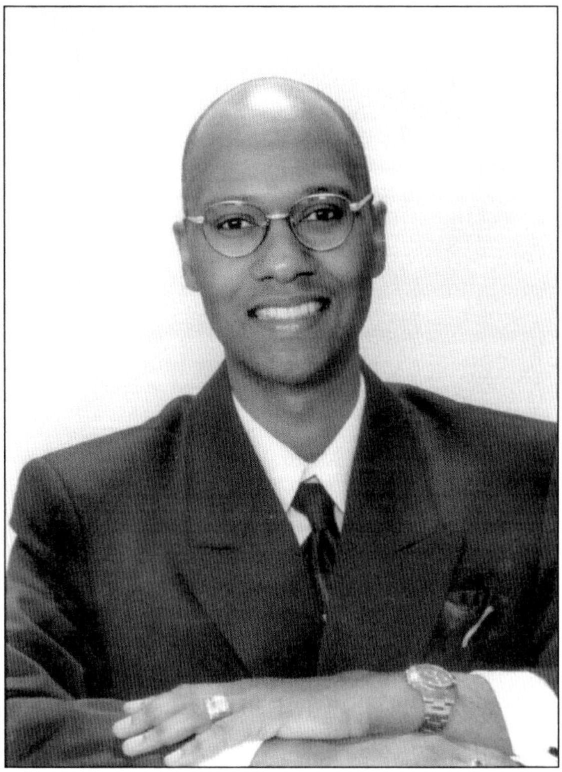

Thomas Lightfoot M. Garrett, son of Thomas and Jean Garrett of New Canton, in the Marshall District, is the author of *Letters from a Known Woman: Joan Fontaine*. In addition, he is a publicist for ICON Public Relations and a weekly columnist for *Canyon News* in Los Angeles, California. (Courtesy Thomas Garrett.)

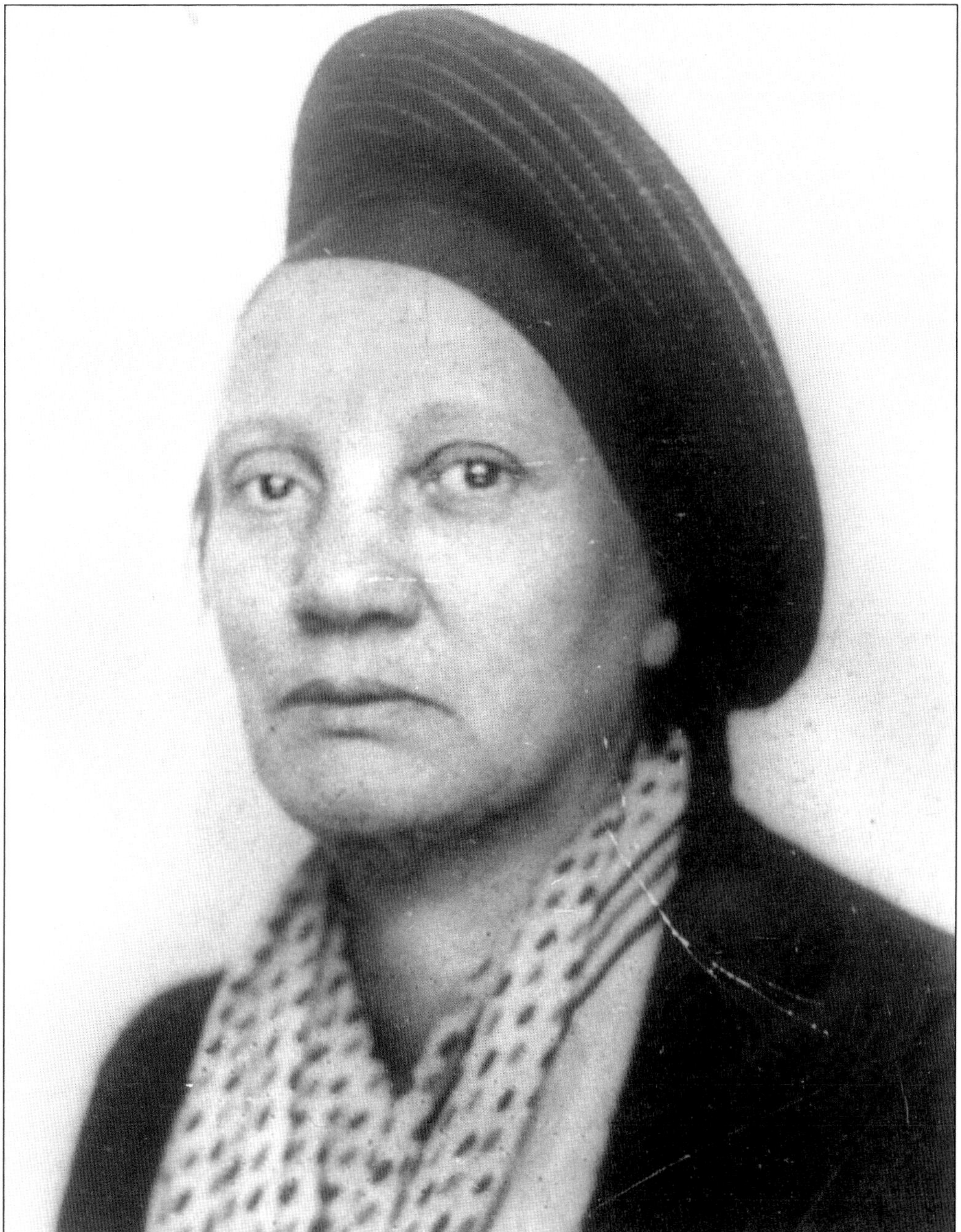

Poet Bessie Woodson Yancey, daughter of James Henry and Anne Eliza (Riddle) Woodson and younger sister of Carter G. Woodson, was born in 1882 in Buckingham County. She started her career as a teacher in the mining camp school near Montgomery, West Virginia, and later, Guyandotte, which was a part of Huntington, West Virginia. Her poetry in *Echoes from the Hills* acknowledges the disturbing social condition of black children in Huntington, West Virginia, during the 1930s. It was published in 1939 by the Associated Publishers, Inc., which her brother Carter G. Woodson founded in Washington, D.C. (Courtesy Belva Clark Collection.)

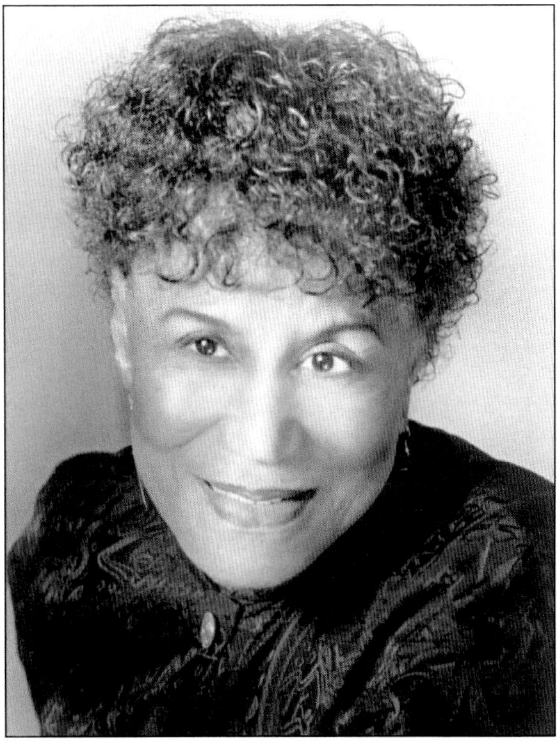

Actress, producer, and writer Clarice Taylor was born Claris T. Gibson on September 21, 1917, in Gold Hill, in the Marshall District of Buckingham County. The daughter of Leona (Booker) Gibson and Charles Gibson, she has produced, written, and starred as Jackie "Moms" Mabley off-Broadway and performed *Moms* throughout the country and internationally. She has received numerous awards including the 1987 OBIE for Outstanding Achievement in off-Broadway and off-off Broadway theatre (for her distinguished performance as Moms) and the 1993 Living Legend Award from the National Black Theatre. She has appeared in many films, including *Five on the Black Hand Side*, *Play Misty for Me*, *Smoke*, and *Sommersby*. (Courtesy Clarice Taylor.)

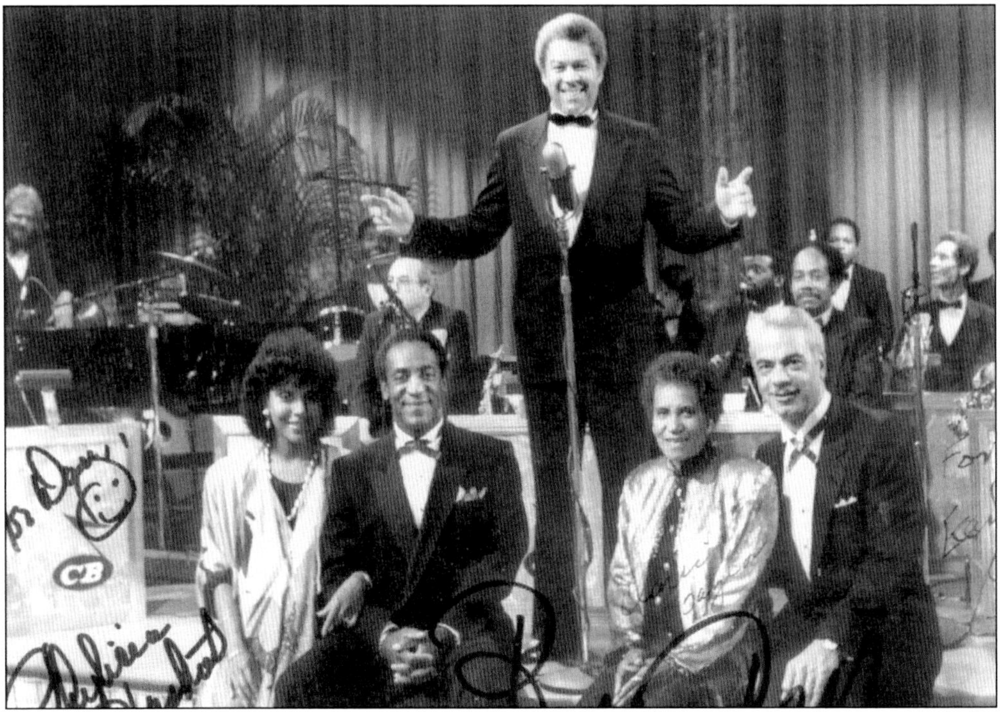

Clarice Taylor is widely known for her television role on *The Cosby Show* as Grandmother Anna Huxtable. Pictured here from left to right are Phylicia Rashad, Bill Cosby, Clarice Taylor, and Earle Hyman. (Courtesy Clarice Taylor.)

This is a photograph of Clarice Taylor as "Addaperle" in the 1975 original Broadway production of *The Wiz*, which was produced by Ken Harper. Geoffrey Holder was director and costume designer. Clarice Taylor was one of the original members of the Negro Ensemble Company, founded in 1967, and received the Beverly Hills/ Hollywood NAACP theatre award, the Trailblazer Award—Negro Ensemble Company, in February 2005. (Courtesy Clarice Taylor.)

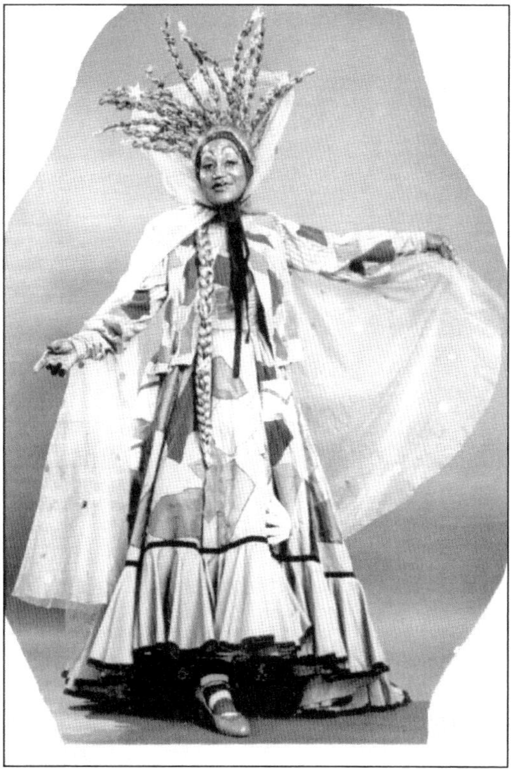

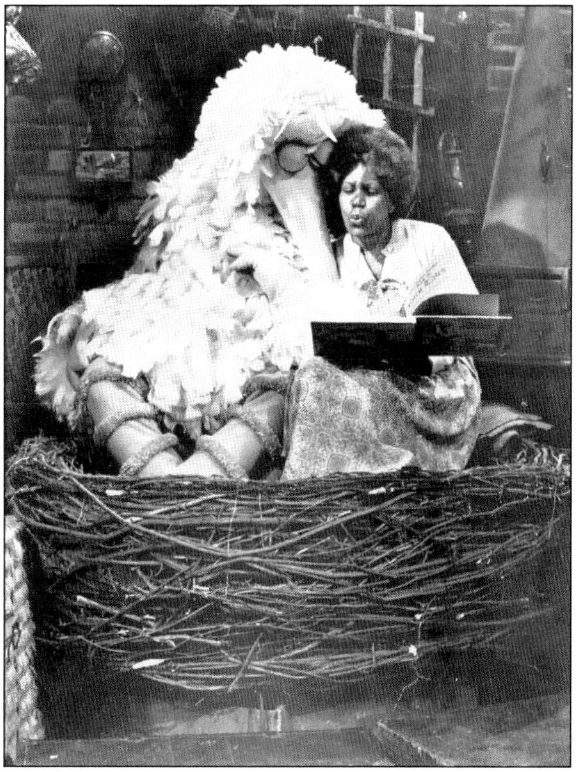

Clarice Taylor portrayed "Harriet," David's grandmother on *Sesame Street* from 1976 to 1990. *Sesame Street* is an educational television program designed for young children and is recognized as a pioneer of the present-day standard on combining education and entertainment in televised shows. (Courtesy Clarice Taylor.)

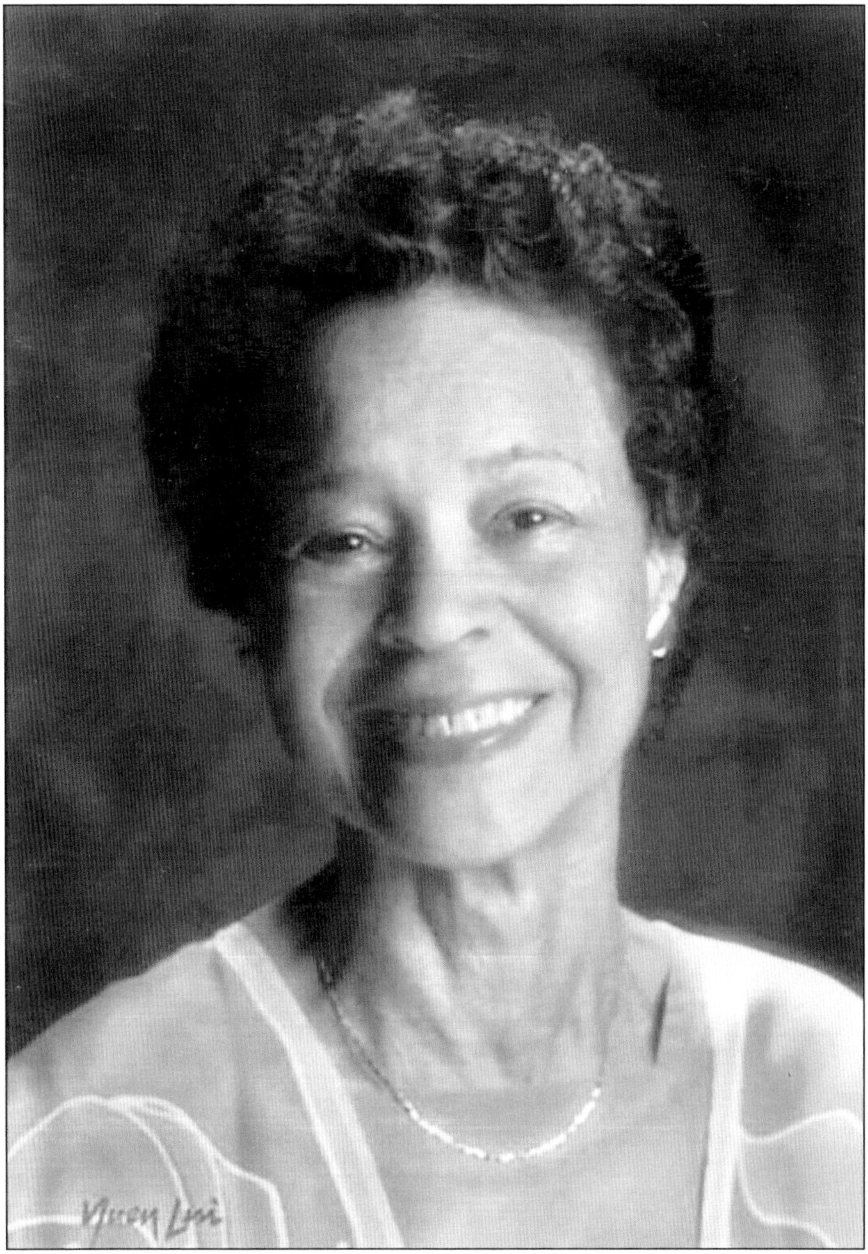

Edith M. Stanton Ingram, born August 4, 1921, in Penlan, in the Marshall District of Buckingham County, is the daughter of Znada (Fleming) and Sidney Trent Stanton Jr. and an accomplished painter and poet. Her work is in private collections throughout the United States and in the permanent collection at the Museum of the National Center of Afro-American Artists in Boston, Massachusetts. She has received several awards for her work and is noted in the publications *Afro-American Artists: A Bio-bibliographical Dictionary* and *Who Was Who in American Art 1564–1975: 400 Years of Artists in America*. She has recently written a historical novel entitled *A Walk Among Blue Slate Markers* as a tribute to her great-grandmother, Nancy Stanton, who was a free property-holder in Buckingham County in the early 1850s. (Courtesy Edith M. Stanton Ingram.)

Nine

Buckingham Today

We must go beyond textbooks, go out into the bypaths and untrodden depths of the wilderness and travel and explore and tell the world the glories of our journey.

—John Hope Franklin (born 1915)

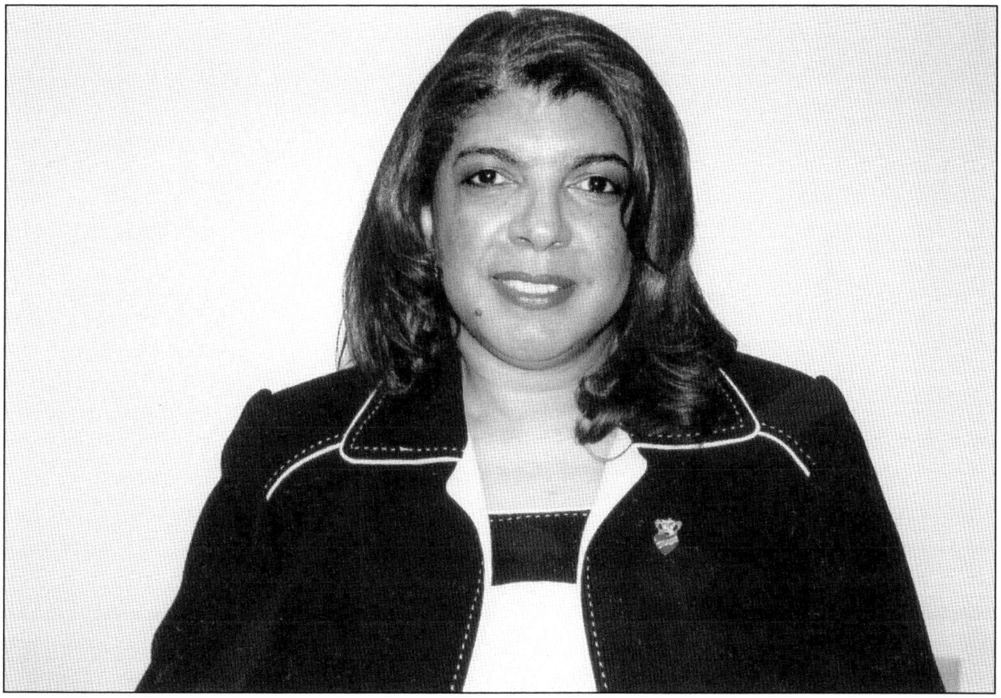

Jessie M. Woodson-Johnson, born October 22, 1955, is the daughter of Alexander and Rebecca Woodson of Gold Hill, in the Marshall District of Buckingham County. Woodson-Johnson was first elected in 1995 to the county's board of supervisors from Gold Hill and is currently serving her third term. She is also associate minister of the Petersville Baptist Church. (Courtesy Jessie M. Woodson-Johnson.)

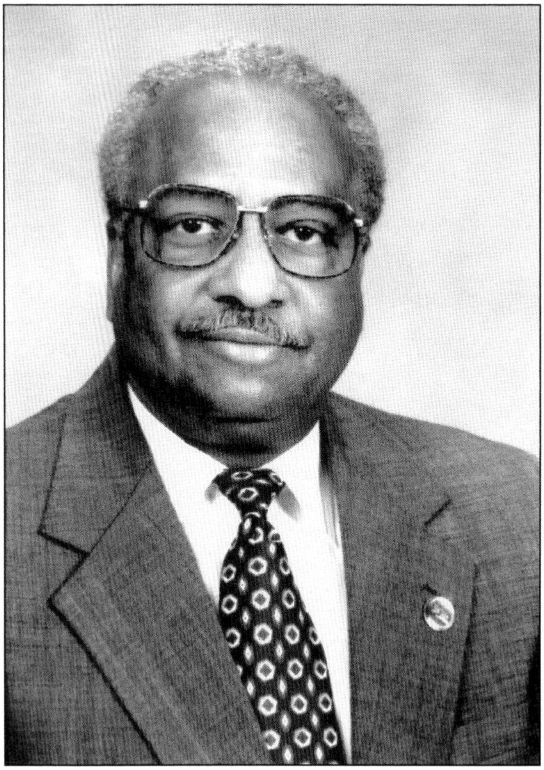

Otto K. Washington is first African American justice of the peace in Buckingham County and the first African American to be elected to public office in the county since 1888. Washington was elected in 1972. (Courtesy of Otto K. Washington.)

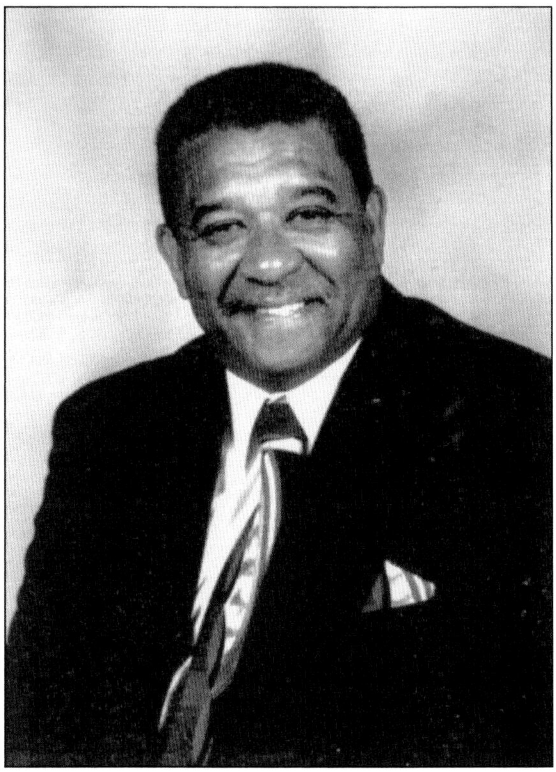

Rev. Joe Nathan Chambers is chairman of the Buckingham County Board of Supervisors and was first elected to this position in 2003. In 1990, Reverend Chambers was elected to the Buckingham County Board of Supervisors. (Courtesy Charles W. White Sr.)

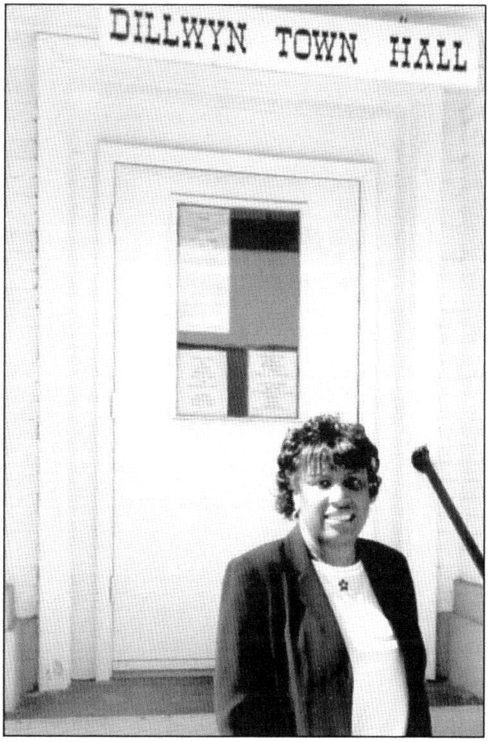

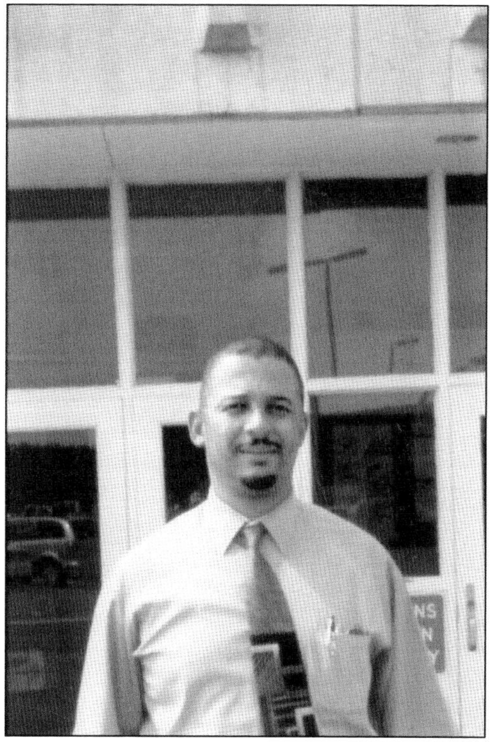

Above left: This is a photograph of Diane Holman James, Dillwyn Town Council member, who was appointed to this position in 2005. She is retired from the U.S. Government Accounting Office after serving 28 years. (Courtesy Charles W. White Sr.)
Above right: This is a photograph of Gerald K. Washington, who is senior warden at the Buckingham Correctional Center. He has served with the Virginia Department of Corrections since 1974. (Courtesy Charles W. White Sr.)

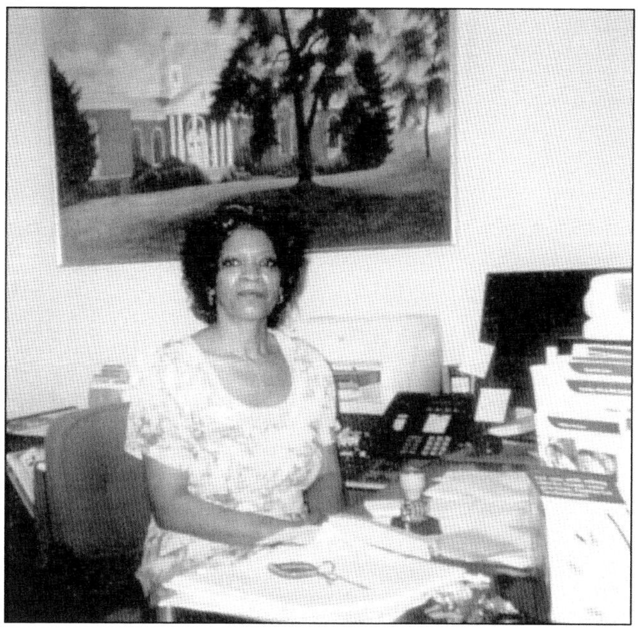

Thelma Holman Ross, manager of the BB&T Bank in Buckingham County, is the first African American in Buckingham County to hold a bank supervisory position. (Courtesy Thelma Holman Ross.)

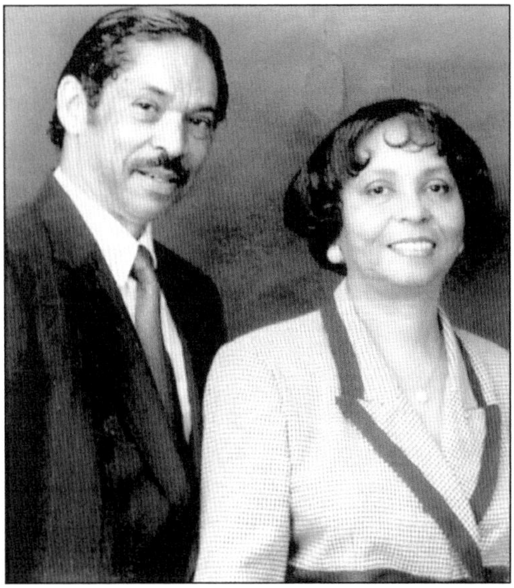

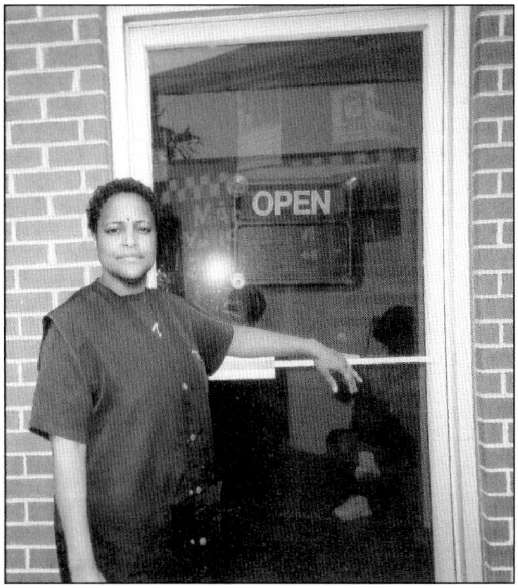

Above left: Bob and Lular Parson are the proprietors of Parson TV and Satellite. Parson TV and Satellite has been in operation since 1963. (Courtesy Lular Moore Parson.)

Above right: Pictured here is Cheryl D. White, the proprietor of Cheryl's Beauty and Barber Shop, which has been in operation since 1980. (Courtesy Charles W. White Sr.)

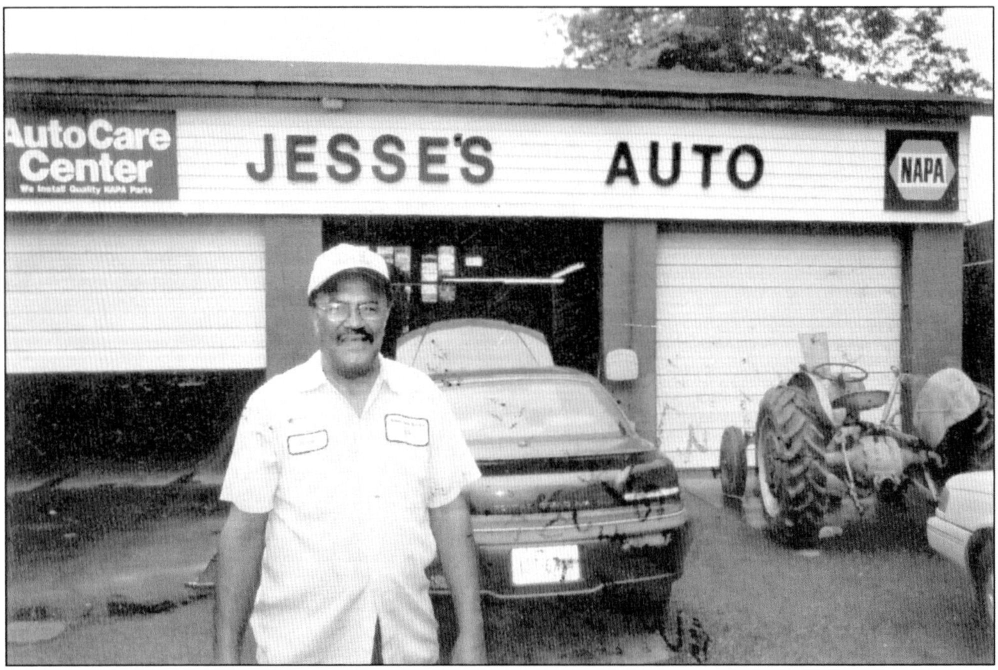

Jesse Davis, shown above, is the proprietor of Jesse's Auto Service. Jesse's Auto Service was established in 1989. (Courtesy Charles W. White Sr.)

Ten

Our Place in History

We black folk, our history, our present being, are a mirror of all the manifold experiences of America.

—Richard Wright (1908–1960)

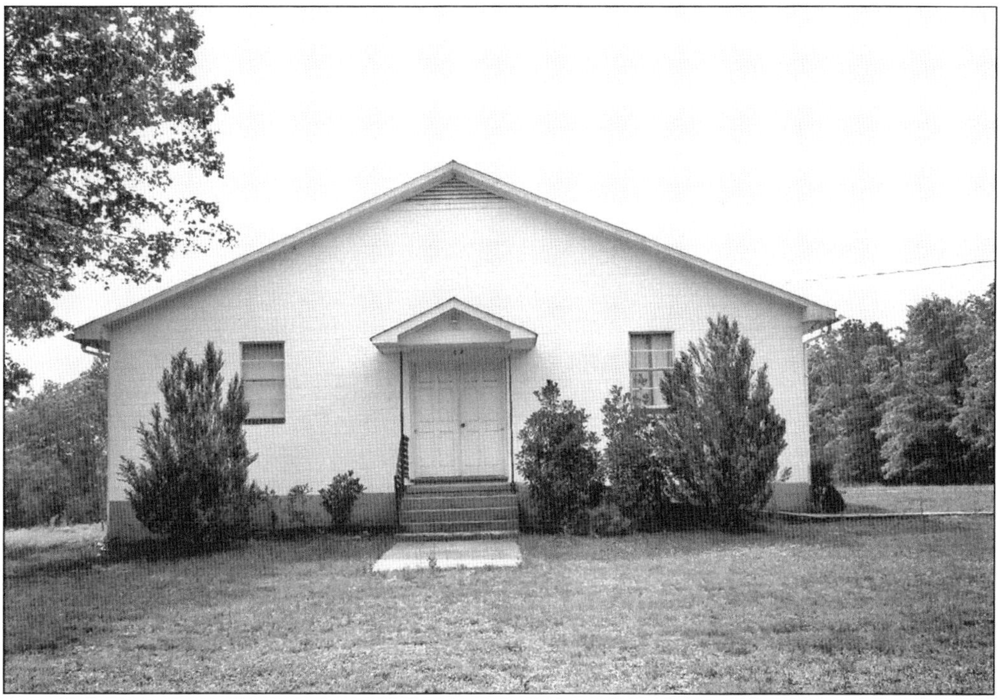

The Frances Redwood Educational Center is named in honor of educator Mary Frances Redwood, daughter of Mary E. and Lucian W. Redwood. Redwood was a graduate of Virginia Seminary and College in Lynchburg, Virginia, and taught in the Buckingham County public schools for several years. (Courtesy E. Renée Ingram.)

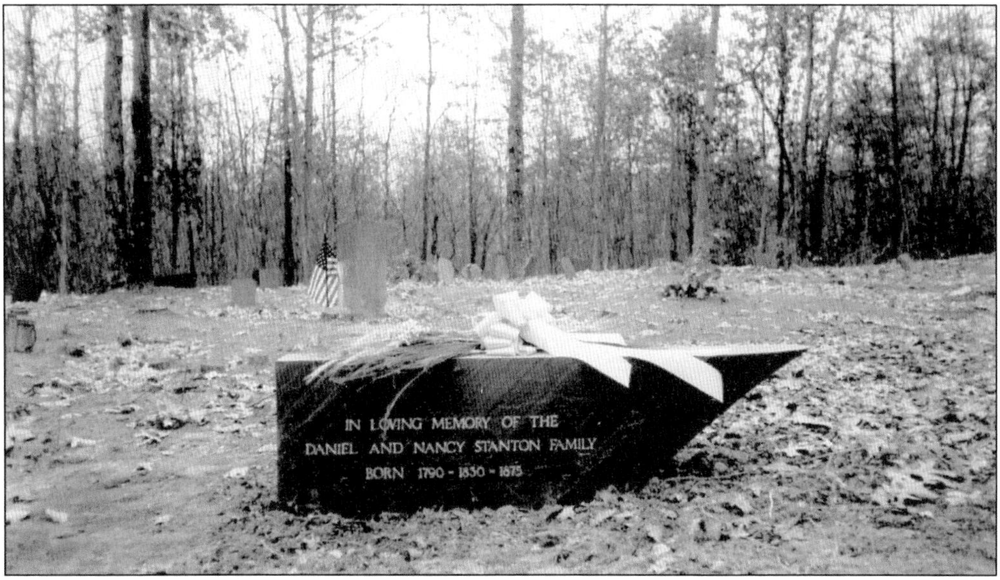

In 1853, the Stanton family of Buckingham County, Virginia, headed by Nancy and Daniel Stanton, purchased 46.5 acres of land, becoming one of the few free black landholders in the region. Nancy Stanton, who purchased the original holdings on which the cemetery is located, became the first known individual interred in the Stanton Family Cemetery when she died on October 6, 1853. The cemetery is a rare example of its kind. It was established not on a plantation, but by free blacks on their own land. The substantial size of the cemetery reflects the economic and social standing of the Stanton family in the county. It is a rare resource that reveals important information about rural burial practices, local cemetery design, and a significant cultural group about which little is known. The Stanton Family Cemetery symbolizes the notable contributions made by free African Americans in Buckingham County and the region. The cemetery was listed on the National Register of Historic Places and the Virginia Landmarks Register in 1993. (Courtesy E. Renée Ingram.)

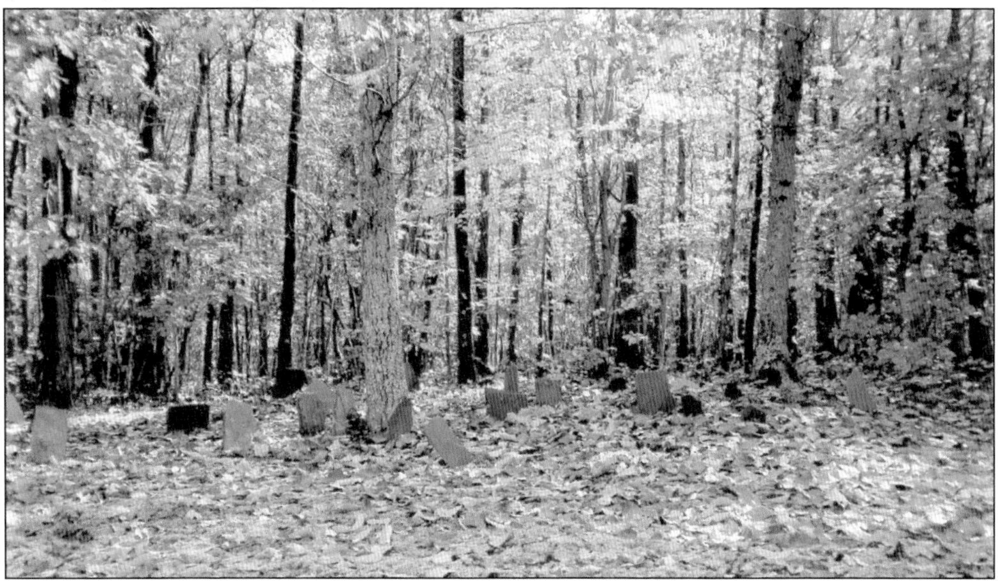

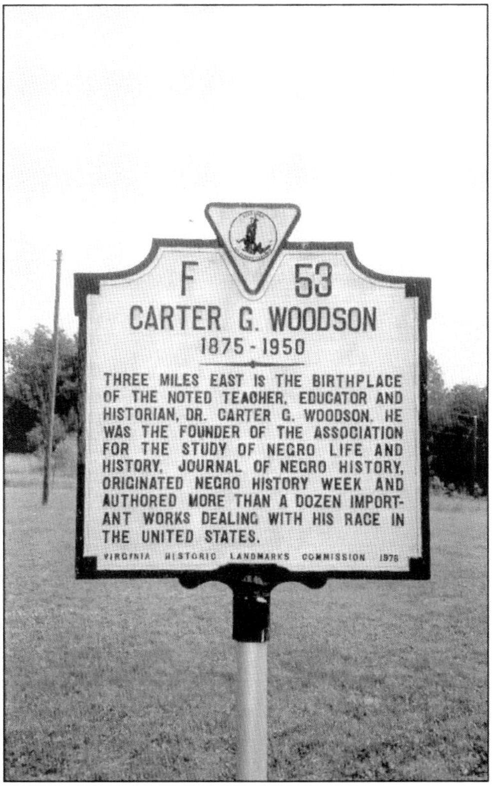

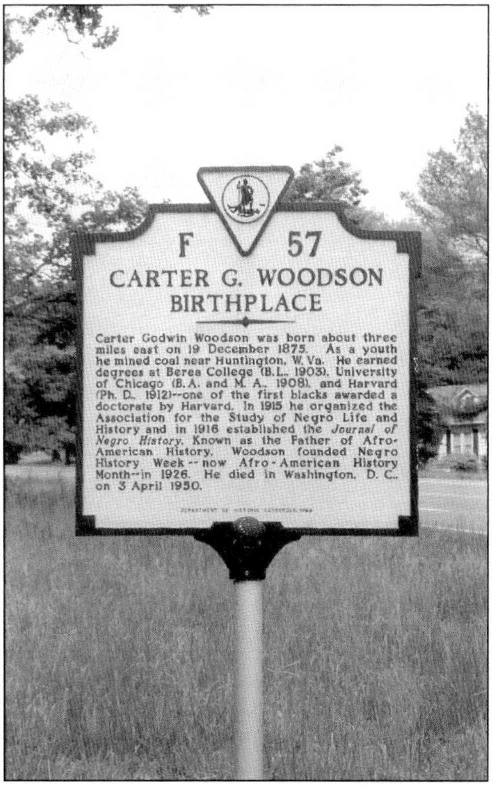

Above left: The Carter G. Woodson (1875–1950) (F-53) Virginia State Historic Highway Marker was erected in 1976 on U.S. Highway 15 north of Dillwyn in the Marshall District. Dr. Woodson's birthplace is located three miles east of this marker. (Courtesy of E. Renée Ingram.)

Above right: The Carter G. Woodson Birthplace Virginia State Historic Highway Marker (F-57) is located on U.S. Highway 15, one mile south of the James River near the county line in the Marshall District. This marker was erected in 1993. (Courtesy E. Renée Ingram.)

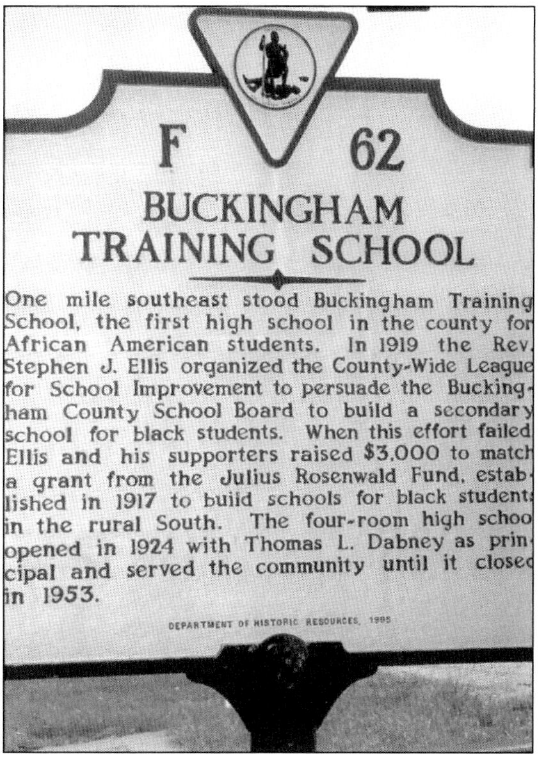

Right: The Buckingham County Training School Virginia State Historic Highway Marker (F-62), which was approved by the Virginia Department of Historic Resources in 1995, sits at the intersection of U.S. Highway 15 and Virginia Route 20. This historic Rosenwald-funded school was located one mile southeast of the marker. (Courtesy of E. Renée Ingram.)

About the Authors

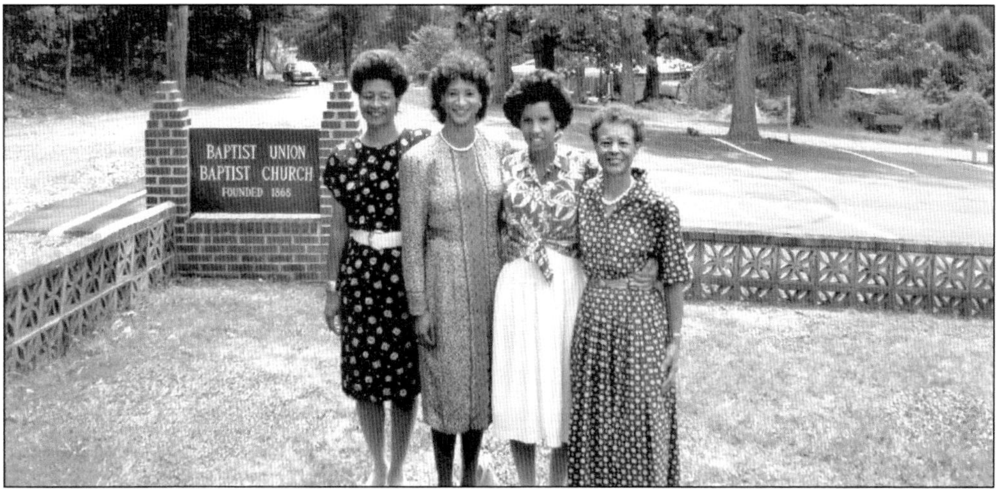

E. Renée Ingram and her family are pictured here at a Baptist Union Baptist Church homecoming in August 1990. From left to right are Joyce L. (Ingram) McGlaston, E. Renée Ingram, Michelle L. McGlaston, and Edith M. (Stanton) Ingram. E. Renée Ingram's great-great-grandfather, Thomas Trent, a shoemaker and free property holder during the antebellum period, donated the land to build Baptist Union Baptist Church. (Courtesy E. Renée Ingram.)

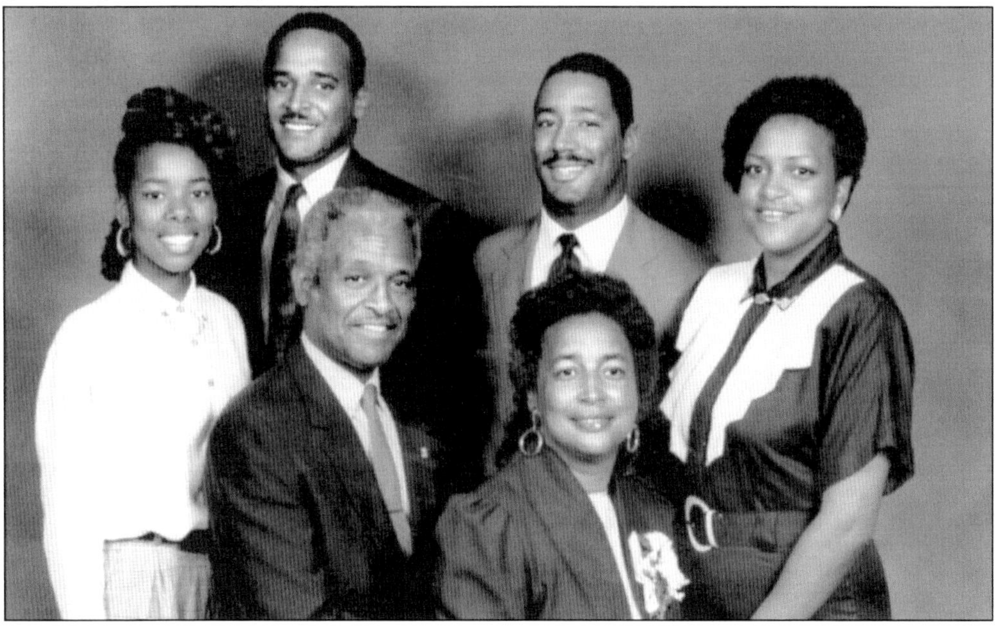

Charles W. White Sr. and his family are shown here. From left to right are (seated) Charles W. White Sr. and Margaret C. (Booker) White; (standing) their children, Christy, Craig, Charles Jr., and Cheryl. (Courtesy Charles W. White Jr.)